WHATEVER IT TAKES

Washington Journal: The Events of 1973–74

American Journal: The Events of 1976

Senator

Portrait of an Election: The 1980 Presidential Campaign

Politics and Money: The New Road to Corruption

Campaign Journal: The Political Events of 1983–1984

Election Journal: The Political Events of 1987–1988

On the Edge: The Clinton Presidency

Showdown: The Struggle Between the Gingrich Congress
    and the Clinton White House

WHATEVER

ELIZABETH DREW

IT TAKES

The Real Struggle
for Political Power
in America

VIKING

VIKING
Published by the Penguin Group
Penguin Books USA Inc., 375 Hudson Street,
New York, New York 10014, U.S.A.
Penguin Books Ltd, 27 Wrights Lane, London W8 5TZ, England
Penguin Books Australia Ltd, Ringwood, Victoria, Australia
Penguin Books Canada Ltd, 10 Alcorn Avenue,
Toronto, Ontario, Canada M4V 3B2
Penguin Books (N.Z.) Ltd, 182-190 Wairau Road,
Auckland 10, New Zealand

Penguin Books Ltd, Registered Offices:
Harmondsworth, Middlesex, England

First published in 1997 by Viking Penguin,
a division of Penguin Books USA Inc.

1 2 3 4 5 6 7 8 9 10

Copyright © Elizabeth Drew, 1997
All rights reserved

CIP data available.

This book is printed on acid-free paper.

 ∞

Printed in the United States of America
Set in New Caledonia

For David

CONTENTS

INTRODUCTION

THE REAL STRUGGLE for political power in America is much broader than the Presidential contest. The real struggle, in 1996, and afterward, was and is over the long-term alignment of power—over who will have hegemony in our politics for the next ten to fifteen years. For many groups, this was a far more important question in 1996 than which political party would win the Presidency. Moreover, the planning and scheming over this issue began well before the election year. Its outcome would have an impact on people's everyday lives.

The most dedicated contenders for the realignment were a set of groups on the right. Their number-one goal was to retain Republican control over the House of Representatives, which was where, as will be shown, the realignment would be decided. From control of the House would come means of further expanding their power. They saw things on levels and at distances that few people here do. Their task was complicated by the fact that House Speaker Newt Gingrich was now the most unpopular politician in America, and his most dedicated followers subject to the charge that they had joined him in "extremism" in the 104th Congress, and also by the fact that the Republicans had nominated a weak Presidential candidate. This set of circumstances required some hidden but brutal decisions along the way.

The struggle for long-term political power was total, and it was waged with new instruments of warfare. The campaign finance laws were put to new uses, or abuses. In following this story I came across heretofore undisclosed stretching—and perhaps violations—of the campaign finance laws. Various things were done, legal or illegal, that rendered these laws a sham.

Along the way, I also got to know some of the most interesting and colorful people that I have ever met in the political world—people not as famous as some of the leading elected officials—but, in some cases, equally powerful.

The Presidential campaign appears in this book only as a component of the larger struggle, where the one affected the other. I sought to understand what issues the country cared about and why—or why not—and also some new ways in which political practitioners tried to manipulate that opinion. I wanted to assess where the country came out in this larger confrontation—and get a sense of the next stage of the struggle. My search for the impact of the Clinton campaign finance scandals on the larger fight brought forth some surprising conclusions.

Elizabeth Drew
Washington, D.C.
February, 1997

WHATEVER IT TAKES

Chapter One

CONVENOR

As the representatives of some seventy activist conservative groups, centurions of the right, filed into the conference room of Grover Norquist's Americans for Tax Reform, near Dupont Circle, for their regular Wednesday morning meeting on February 21, 1996, the day after Patrick Buchanan won the New Hampshire primary, their consternation was clear. Gathered over the coffee, doughnuts, and bagels that Norquist provided before each meeting, they were stunned and worried. Though it might have seemed that the right would be pleased that as staunch a conservative as Buchanan might be blazing his way toward the Presidential nomination, in fact they saw him as an obstacle in the path of their most important goal: maintaining Republican control of the House of Representatives. To these groups, maintaining that control was far more important than who won the Presidential election.

Should the bombastic Buchanan get the Presidential nomination, the thinking went, he would probably fare so badly as to jeopardize their real goal. House Republicans themselves were in a state of panic over Buchanan's success. In Norquist's meeting and in phone calls around town that day, some Republicans were saying that they should get behind Steve Forbes, who had come in fourth in both Iowa and New Hampshire. Some thought they should join up with Lamar Alexander, who had come in third in both states, but was considered by many (including people in the White House) the potentially strongest candidate against Clinton. Though Alexander might have less in common with them ideologically, these groups were prepared to do whatever it takes to hold on to the House of Representatives. Bob Dole, who had come in second in New Hampshire, wasn't seen as either a particular ally or a strong candidate. (As for Colin Powell, Norquist was part of a group of conservatives who held a press conference in November, 1995, to make it clear to Powell that if he ran for the Republican nomination, they would oppose him. "Powell wasn't committed to our agenda," Norquist said later. "The point of the press conference was 'Don't run. We don't want to beat you up.'")

While most of the focus of the political coverage and commentary of 1996 was on the Presidential race, for virtually all of the powerful groups behind the Republican Party their overriding goal of keeping control of the House stemmed from their view that that was where the real political power—near- and long-term—lay. The House was where the political realignment of the country in favor of the Republicans would be nailed down or lost. If Republican domination of the House, gained in 1994 after forty years of Democratic rule, were to last only two years, it would be a grave setback. Control of the House mattered more to the Republicans than control of the Senate, or of the Presidency, because the minority has much more power in the Senate than in the House, mainly through use of the filibuster rule. Even if the Senate were in the opposition's hands, or if its Republicans were collectively of a more moderate temperament (as they were in the 104th Congress), the House could keep the Senate from doing things. In Grover Norquist's view, "Ultimately, the House sets the pace and limits on what a President can do. Even if you have fifty-one percent of the votes in the Senate you can't control it. You need sixty votes to stop a filibuster. You rarely have that."

The last two years, after the 1994 election, had seen a dramatic turnabout as House Speaker Newt Gingrich's triumphalism had turned sour, and his "revolution" ended with a whimper. He and Clinton underwent a reversal of fortunes. Now Gingrich and his fellow Republicans were in a difficult spot because Clinton had successfully painted the 104th Congress as "extremist."

The battles between the 104th Congress and the Clinton White House left a number of big issues unsettled: the role of government; the priorities within the context of a balanced budget, which Gingrich had forced Clinton to agree to; what to do about the big entitlement programs, including Medicare. The Gingrich Congress had shown the country what a difference who controls the House can make.

Though the real struggle for political power in America, much broader than the race for the Presidency, was consequential for far more than the Republican right, it was often unseen, but deadly. It subsumed the Presidential contest, but the two struggles were intermixed in surprising ways. The armies on both sides were large, and they threw all they could into the battle. Gingrich was later to call it—in this instance without exaggeration—"probably the most intense campaign for control of the House . . . in modern history."

Moreover, much of what happened in 1996, and in particular how the interest groups *on both sides* of the congressional battle waged their war, will show the extent to which the campaign finance laws are a sham.

When the conservative groups' strategy of giving priority to control of the House, irrespective of what would happen in the Presidential race, was already well set at the beginning of the year, it was no sure thing that Bill Clinton would be reelected. He had vulnerabilities, the economic outlook was uncertain, and neither the name nor the strength of whoever would become the Republican candidate were known.

From the time of the Second World War, through the Cold War, the Republicans, including those on the right, believed in the primacy of the Presidency. The conservatives' growing interest in controlling the House began during the Bush administration, when the Soviet bloc began to come apart, and also when new Republican congressional leaders, such as Whip Newt Gingrich, were beginning to drive domestic policy from Capitol Hill, challenging their own President.

The 1996 election was crucial to the contending forces on both sides of the ideological spectrum because Republicans felt that if they held the House for the second time in a row, they would have hegemony over it for ten to twenty years, using the powers of incumbency to protect their position and extend their power, just as the Democrats had for so long. Don Fierce, a consultant to the Republican National Committee and a major Party strategist, said in January, "If we can nail down a realignment it would be now, and if we can it would last a decade." The time scales varied in different strategists' minds, but the point was the same.

To retake the House, the Democrats had to pick up a net total of nineteen seats. The Republicans' controlling margin was smaller in the House in the 104th Congress than any since the mid-fifties. And congressional districts were becoming increasingly competitive, especially since the beginning of the 1990s. Incumbency wasn't as safe a perch as it used to be. An ever-larger number of seats was being won by narrow margins. Forty-seven of the seventy-three Republican freshmen had been elected in 1994 with fifty-five percent of the vote or less. At the beginning of 1996, nearly a third of the 435 House seats were in contest. This made the battle a daunting one for both sides.

Grover Norquist said in a conversation early in 1996, "This is not going to be a Presidential race—it's going to be a race for the House, the Senate, governorships, the state legislatures—and some butthead who wants to be President."

Though unknown nationally, Norquist, a stocky thirty-nine-year-old with a moon-round face, mischievous blue eyes behind horn-rimmed glasses, and a short reddish-brown beard, was one of the most influential figures in Washington, and—through the coalition of largely grassroots organizations he had put together—the nation. While the Democrats in recent years had largely depended on political action committees (PACs)—through which the various interests made limited contributions—Republicans had since the late seventies been backed by a growing number of grassroots organizations: groups that could locate, persuade, and motivate and get their people to the polls. Since the Republicans took the House in 1994, PACs quickly and predictably began to find them more worthy of support. If the Republicans kept control of the House, the PACs were also likely to increasingly favor them over the Democrats. (The Republicans had been none too subtle about suggesting that they switch allegiance.) "Holding the House is the way to controlling K Street," Norquist said, referring to lobbyists' row in Washington.

Norquist calls the coalition that he had put together the "Leave Us Alone" coalition, made up as it is of groups that wanted lower taxes and less government in almost every sense. Norquist described it as "a collection of groups who share something in common—they want the government to let them alone." It included landowner groups, largely from the West, who want their property protected against government seizure for preserving wetlands, protecting endangered species, and the like. This property rights movement is the descendent of, and more effective than, the "Sagebrush Rebellion" (of which Reagan Interior Secretary James Watt was a star) of the early eighties. These groups had backed legislation against "takings"—government seizure of land for environmental purposes without compensation—in the House in 1995 as part of the "Contract with America"; the measure died in the Senate. It also included the fast-growing "home schoolers" movement—parents who wanted to teach their children at home, often for religious reasons or because they felt the public school system had collapsed. Other members were three conservative seniors groups—intended to offset the powerful pro-Medicare American Association of Retired Persons: Sixty-Plus, Seniors Coalition, and United Seniors of America, who are for abolishing the inheritance tax and for medical savings accounts, a market-based reform of Medicare.

Other groups whose representatives regularly attended Norquist's meetings were the National Rifle Association, the Gun Owners of America, the U.S. Chamber of Commerce, the American Farm Bureau, the Small Business Survival Committee (which wants to eliminate the Small Business Administration, because it costs money and which conservatives see as a form of political bribery), the Christian Coalition, the National Right to Life Committee, and also Republicans for Choice. There's also a representative from GOPAC, Gingrich's PAC for electing state legislators—many of whom had gone on to the House of Representatives—as well as candidates for the House. Norquist says there is no list of the member groups, because there's no official membership—and this leaves him free to uninvite a group if it becomes "coalition-unfriendly."

Norquist also invited to his meetings individuals from conservative think tanks and activist groups. Norquist's insight in putting these groups together was that they had more in common than their differences—that he and pro-choice Ann Stone, of Republicans for Choice, and pro-life leaders from the Christian Coalition and Phyllis Schlafly's Eagle Forum agreed on virtually everything but abortion, and that the collective power of the group was substantial. Norquist said, "If everyone in the room can agree—the gun owners agree not to throw condoms at Christian kids, and the Christian groups agree not to steal anybody else's guns, and the small business groups, who are interested in regulations, taxes, and property rights, agree not to raise anybody else's taxes, and the tax groups agree not to take other people's property—as long as everybody agrees not to screw with anybody else—everyone's happy. And everybody can leave and spend the rest of the day crushing the left. It's a low-maintenance coalition."

Norquist was less hypocritical than those in conservative Republican circles who were against government activity with the exception of subsidies for the interests they represented (or owned). He was a bit elusive when it came to the government subsidies for the mining and grazing businesses. He argued that they weren't "corporate subsidies" but that he did feel that miners and grazers should pay "full price"—except that the prices "shouldn't be determined by a bureaucrat in Washington." He supported the Republican legislation, passed by the 104th Congress, to phase out agriculture subsidies while at the same time allowing farmers to plant as much as they want—a good deal for the big farmers.

Norquist has a worldview, with its own logic, that both explained and fueled his crusade. He sees the Democratic Party as a "takings coalition," which includes a "dependency lobby"—who want the government to do more, and thus create a large group of dependents and managers of dependency. He placed in this "takings coalition" labor unions, trial lawyers, big city machines, government workers, teachers unions, and recipients of government grants and contracts. Norquist said, "The reason why budget cuts are important to the Republicans and a threat to the Democrats is that budget cuts defund the takings coalition."

Conservative Republicans hold the view that the voters see their Representatives as dealing in constituency services, and Senators in loftier terms. As long as the public sees the government as the provider of largesse, the theory goes, the more likely it is to vote Democratic. Therefore, if the House becomes Republican, that is a more significant ideological shift than generally realized.

Norquist, who grew up just outside Boston—his father was an engineer for Polaroid—and graduated from Harvard in 1978, began his anti-tax crusade at an early age. He claims that when he was fourteen he started asking, Why doesn't one of the parties become the party that won't raise your taxes—because that's the way to win. He came to Washington right after college and quickly became executive director of the National Taxpayers Union. After then getting a degree from the Harvard Business School in 1981, he helped a friend get elected chairman of the College Republicans and returned to Washington to become executive director of that group, an official organ of the Republican National Committee which organizes chapters on college campuses, to provide shock troops to get out the vote, attend rallies, distribute literature, and groom budding politicians. (The Democrats have an equivalent group.) One of Norquist's assistants at the College Republicans was Ralph Reed, now the executive director of the Christian Coalition and a close ally of Norquist's. (Reed's first job was to run a project called the "Poland Will Be Free" campaign. Norquist says, "While the left wanted to talk about Nicaragua and El Salvador, we worked to get attention to how the Soviet Union was treating the countries it dominated.")

After stints at Americans for the Reagan Agenda, a grassroots effort that never really got going, and the U.S. Chamber of Commerce (as speechwriter and economist), Norquist worked for Citizens for America, another grassroots group backing the Reagan agenda, this one funded by Reagan's wealthy friends in his Kitchen Cabinet. Through Citizens for America, headed by Lew Lehrman, whose fortune came from the Rite-Aid drugstore chain and who had spent $11 million running unsuccessfully for governor of New York in 1982, Norquist got involved in supporting the "Reagan doctrine": to damage the Soviet Union by supporting guerrilla movements in client states—Nicaragua, Afghanistan, Angola, Cambodia, Mozambique. Norquist himself worked in Afghanistan and Mozambique, but was mostly active in Angola, to which he traveled ten times over the years, becoming a supporter of Jonas Savimbi, the conservatives' pet rebel against the leftist Angolan regime. Then some Reagan people asked him to form Americans for Tax Reform, to support Reagan's tax reform program, which passed as part of a bipartisan bill in 1986. Norquist then used A.T.R. as a coalition-builder and base of power. Along the way, he became close to Newt Gingrich, who provided the introduction for Norquist's book *Rock the House*, about the "Republican Revolution" of 1994–95.

Norquist's own particular passion for lower taxes was rooted in his strong desire for less government—as a way of diminishing the power of the opposition. To this end, he asked all candidates for Congress, and, later, candidates for state legislatures as well, to "take the pledge" to oppose any income tax increases, and worked with state groups to get an initiative on the ballot that would require a two-thirds vote in the legislature to raise taxes. Through 1996, he had helped get it on the ballot in eight states, all of which passed it. He has established, through the Republican congressional leaders, that there will be a vote in the House of Representatives on this proposal every April 15th. (Norquist brokered this deal between the leadership and the freshmen.)

But Norquist's and his allies' reach into the states was about more than just taxes: it was about the very nature of American politics. Norquist says, "The more guys you have who are good on taxes, the more guys you have who are Republicans and the more likely to be good on redistricting"—drawing congressional districts to favor the Republicans. He argues that "the most important shift in 1994 was the Republican victory in state legislative races. We picked up a net of over four hundred and eighty state legislators, giving us almost half of the state legislative seats all over the country."

Thus the Republicans' struggle for hegemony in American politics worked at several levels, and with a view toward the long term. In Norquist's opinion, the fact that Republicans held sixty percent of the governorships in states that included about seventy-two percent of the population, "will do the Democrats the most damage in the long run." He added, "The governors are our big-city mayors." He recounted, state by state, how many jobs each Republican governor could dispense, and said that in the 1994 election, the Republicans had won some fifty- to seventy thousand patronage jobs. "Those are political activists," Norquist said.

Norquist's Wednesday morning meetings had various guest appearances—a candidate for the House, a pusher of a certain cause—and sometimes ranged into recherché subjects, such as the politics of science fiction. Norquist explained his interest in this subject by pointing out that there are free-market, libertarian science fiction writers, such as Robert Heinlein, and those, like Isaac Asimov, whom he considered as favoring big government. The issue was whether people believed that technology would make them free, or would be a means of more government control over people's lives. In the early summer of 1996 two writers of *Star Trek* attended a Wednesday morning meeting, and told the group that the "politically correct censorship" promoting big government they had experienced under the program's previous producer had lessened. Norquist said, "Science fiction is like pornography: it's big for teenage boys and it's important to get them early."

Americans for Tax Reform gets its funding through direct mail, and from individuals and conservative foundations, and from a semiannual series of six dinners, at which Norquist's big-time political friends—Newt Gingrich, Trent Lott—speak. A company contributes $10,000 to attend the series. Norquist said A.T.R. didn't receive more than ten percent of its funds from any one company or industry, and that it had sixty thousand individual members through its direct mail. After the Republicans took over the House, Norquist also went into business as a paid lobbyist and consultant. One of his clients, Microsoft, opposed, as Norquist did, government regulation of encryption (which would allow law enforcement agencies to intercept communications and to know what was on a person's computer). Other clients are the Seychelles, which he had "helped resist their Socialist dictatorship," and Savimbi. The ideological crusader thus joined the legions in Washington whose access fuels their resources and whose resources fuel their access. But there was no question that Norquist's access and influence were lucrative: he earned over $200,000 from his clients. (He made additional money from speaking and writing.)

Norquist often traveled about, praising certain candidates for office as having the right attitude about taxes, since they had "taken the pledge," which he insisted didn't constitute endorsements. In 1996, however, to avoid accusations that his nonprofit, supposedly nonpartisan group might in its political activities appear to be violating the tax laws, Norquist formed his own PAC, called the Anti-Tax PAC (ATPAC), for which he held a fundraiser at his home in September.

A number of other projects are run out of Norquist's suite of offices, and he is personally involved in several of them: the Small Business Survival Committee; a monthly organizing meeting for backing the building of a Victims of Communism Museum (an analogue to the Holocaust Museum, approved by Congress and signed into law by President Clinton), of which Norquist is on the board of directors; a task force on privatizing Social Security; and a number of front groups (some of them run by his staff) such as the Association of Concerned Taxpayers, Students for a Free Society, and the Virginia Taxpayers Coalition. He's also involved in outside projects, such as establishing an Islamic think tank to promote the idea that the Koran and Islam are not inconsistent with a free society—and providing a venue where Muslims and conservatives can talk about areas of agreement.

Norquist's parties at his Capitol Hill townhouse, where Chinese food was the standard offering, were well-known in Washington. The parties might be fundraisers for a political candidate, book launchings, or efforts to bring together Republican congressional staff members who didn't know each other—all for the purpose of furthering the right's agenda. In early March, on the night of a number of primaries, Norquist gave a party for New England state societies, made up of Members of Congress and other political figures and lobbyists. Norquist and other conservatives had started Republican state societies, to compete with the long-standing bipartisan state societies, which, Norquist said, "have been ways for Southern Democrats [in a mixed delegation] to appear to be part of the team, or to give Democratic lobbyists an opportunity to meet Republican Members of Congress." He added, "Besides, Republicans need to socialize more—to build the movement."

Norquist and most of his allies had deep policy differences with Pat Buchanan, which made him a threat to their agenda, as well as to their ambition of holding the House—and which reflected schisms within the Republican Party. The two strongest differences were over immigration and trade. Unlike Buchanan, Norquist opposed reducing the current limits on immigration. He felt that the party that was less restrictive toward immigrants was more likely to get their—and their descendants'—votes; he wanted Hispanics to join the Republicans in a large bloc, just as Asian immigrants were doing. (While George Bush was losing, Asians gave him fifty percent of their vote.) Norquist said, "Immigrant-bashing is very bad for the Republican Party in the long run. The Democrats won the majority of Catholic immigrants in the eighteen hundreds, and held that vote for a century." (Norquist favored a strategy of uniting congressional Republicans and the conservative coalition in opposition to welfare for legal as well as illegal immigrants. That dealt with both the welfare issue and the immigration issue. Norquist points out that he's against welfare for people born in this country, too—"immigration, yes; welfare, no.") The National Rifle Association could agree with others in Norquist's coalition in opposing Buchanan's approach to immigration, Norquist said, "because to make immigration restrictions work you have to know where everyone is, and then the government might get their kids or take their guns."

Norquist and his various allies also opposed Buchanan's protectionism—Norquist argued that increased duties were the equivalent of a tax hike. Norquist told everyone he could—the *Wall Street Journal* editorial board, conservative journalists—that Buchanan was a protectionist and therefore a "tax-increaser." Norquist said later that Buchanan hadn't realized when, campaigning in South Carolina, he defended the flying of the Confederate flag over the state capitol, that the Civil War had been fought over the South's demand for free trade and lower tariffs as well as slavery.

Norquist also urged, through Dole advisers, that Dole stop calling Buchanan an "extremist." Norquist said later, "When Dole called Pat an extremist, Republicans said, 'That's what they called Reagan.' So calling Pat an extremist only strengthened him." He also urged that attacks on Buchanan not appear to be attacks on his followers—so as to keep them in the Republican Party. The right assaulted Buchanan as not a true descendant of Reagan. "We beat Buchanan when we went after him for not being Reagan," Norquist said. He himself argued publicly, "He's trying to be Ronald Reagan but he's got 'Dick Gephardt' stapled to his forehead." Norquist argued that Buchanan's protectionism, and his class warfare and calls for, in effect, a new industrial policy (through corporate reform)— which were winning him support from blue-collar workers—were more in tune with the Democratic leader than with conservative Republicans.

Norquist told me later, "The strongest argument used against Pat within the Party was 'He'll lose us House and Senate seats.' That cut, not the argument that he was 'extreme.' "

Chapter Two

BEER

IN JANUARY OF 1996, I asked Bill Paxon, a forty-one-year-old Republican congressman from Buffalo, New York, who headed the National Republican Congressional Committee for electing Republicans to the House, to list the most important people or groups behind the Republicans' effort to maintain control of the House. He replied: Grover Norquist, the Christian Coalition, the National Federation of Independent Business, the National Rifle Association, and the National Beer Wholesalers Association.

The beer wholesalers?

David Rehr, the vice president for public affairs of the National Beer Wholesalers Association, a tall, slim, enthusiastic thirty-six year-old, with a flattish face and blunt, straight-up hair, explained the origins of his group's power and influence. "There are over eighteen hundred beer distributors," Rehr said. "We're in virtually every congressional district." This, he said, gives the organization both grassroots strength and the wherewithal, in terms of members, to raise money for candidates.

Rehr is a close ally of Grover Norquist, attending or sending a representative to his Wednesday morning meetings and going to many of his parties, and he also works closely with the Christian Coalition, the N.R.A., and the National Federation of Independent Business. Rehr sees the alliance as "the center-right coalition that is realigning America."

Like Norquist, Rehr believed that maintaining Republican control of the House was more important than the 1996 Presidential race, or control of the Senate. The House, where Rehr had access and success, was also the best investment. Rehr explained, "In a House race, two thousand to five thousand votes can make the difference, and you can have so much more impact on these guys. You meet the Senate guys—they love you for your money and your contacts, but they don't remember who you are." Explaining why the outcome in the House was the most important to his and like-minded groups, Rehr said, "It's like an inverse pyramid. The House is like a microcosm of America. It is the pulse of the country. While the Presidency denotes leadership by a single individual and party, it means less day-to-day. The Senate is somewhere in between. Senators have to run every six years, but House members have to run every two years, so House members live and die by their day-to-day decisions."

The beer industry, Rehr explained, used to concentrate on state governments, which when Prohibition was repealed were given the responsibility for regulating alcohol. But it turned its attention more to the federal government when the Reagan administration, through Transportation Secretary Elizabeth Dole, raised the drinking age from eighteen to twenty-one in order to reduce traffic fatalities.

Then, in 1990, something worse happened: George Bush and the Democratic Congress raised taxes on beer by one hundred percent. "That cost thirty-eight thousand jobs in the beer economy," Rehr said, "mostly wholesale, as opposed to retail." (For credibility, the beer wholesalers organization uses figures half the size of those put out by Anheuser-Busch, but all such industry claims are suspect.) As a result of the tax, Rehr said, people bought less beer, and of that, less premium beer, on which wholesalers make more money. The beer wholesalers opposed the Clintons' health care plan, because it would have imposed coverage for workers in small businesses.

Rehr, the son of a postman, grew up near Chicago and once

worked for former Minnesota Representative Vin Weber, still an influential Republican, and then for the N.F.I.B. He was brought into the beer wholesalers organization in 1992, he said, to "make sure the tax wasn't raised again, and to be sure that anti-beer legislation didn't pass the Congress and get signed into law." Another goal was to reorient the wholesalers organization more to the Republican Party, which was more likely to protect its interests, and to strengthen his group's political influence. He explained, "Before I got there, they were disproportionately Democratic-oriented. And the beer and alcohol industry used to think that if we had a few people there [in the Congress] and we had access, nothing bad would happen. My philosophy is you should elect people who will be your allies. Members of Congress are risk averse."

In January, 1993, Rehr instructed his organization's members to jam the White House telephone lines with calls opposing inclusion of a tax increase on beer in President Clinton's upcoming economic program to reduce the deficit. (Then–Treasury Secretary Lloyd Bentsen had floated the idea of an alcohol-tax increase.) The wholesalers association also then acquired a "blast fax" capacity, enabling it to send out quickly more than three thousand faxes to its members, asking them to call the White House; faxes were also sent to Members of Congress. No administration proposal to raise taxes on alcohol was made. Rehr called this "the fax firepower network." (In 1994, Rehr's organization won an award from the American Society of Association Executives—a trade association of lobby groups.) Like other lobby groups, Rehr's summons up an adverse development, no matter how likely, in order to stir concern, and activism, among the members. The issue of taxes on beer, Rehr said, "is a rallying issue even if it isn't on the table."

Rehr, who has the demeanor of a big, friendly dog, says, "What I do can be summarized 'Don't screw around with the beer wholesalers. If you pick a fight with the beer wholesalers, (a) it'll be expensive and (b) it could cost you your political life. We'll go against you with candidates and we'll support opponents. And you'll probably end up by not winning in the end.' " Rehr continued, "My view is if you're pro–small business, we're with you, and if you're anti–beer wholesalers, anti–small business, we're your worst nightmare."

In 1994, the wholesalers, who have the fourth-largest trade association political action committee, contributed to forty candidates, seven of them for the House. (The three larger trade association PACs are two automobile dealer groups and the National Association of Home Builders.)

His members, the principal owners and operators of beer wholesalerships, earn anywhere from seventy-five thousand to more than a million dollars. "But we're politically united," Rehr said, "by being pro–beer consumption and small business." The beer wholesalers share some of the same antipathy as other small businesses toward certain government regulations—thus enhancing their political power. "Even if you have two hundred employees, when OSHA [the Occupational Safety and Health Administration] knocks on your door, you're a small business," Rehr says. In recent years, Rehr also helped stave off proposed legislation mandating that warnings about the effects of drinking beer be included in television and radio ads, or at the point of sale. His group supported the moratorium on new regulations passed by the House in 1995. (It died in the Senate.)

In 1994, Rehr worked closely with House Majority Whip Tom DeLay, a fierce opponent of government regulations—DeLay had owned a pest-control company before getting into politics and objected to regulations by the Environmental Protection Agency— in trying to fight off new OSHA regulations on ergonomics (repetitive stress injuries, in this instance from lifting cases of beer). Rehr, investing in a potentially valuable alliance, helped DeLay in his effort to become whip in 1995 by supporting his efforts to elect Republican candidates for the 104th Congress, especially new candidates—whose gratitude helped DeLay win his new role. Rehr said, "If you see a freshman and you say 'Tom DeLay' and 'David Rehr,' they'll say, 'Our guys.' " (As a congratulatory gift, Rehr gave

DeLay a large, framed whip, which hangs in his office.) After the 1994 election, Rehr helped several freshmen pay off their campaign debts—another time-honored way of winning legislative friends.

In 1996, Rehr's group was to give about eighty percent of its contributions to Republicans, with the emphasis on those who really needed the funds—thus incurring deeper gratitude—as opposed to those who have a safe district or a fat campaign treasury, or both. Rehr, like others, occasionally donated to candidates who didn't need the contribution, to ensure access. Democrats who have large breweries in their districts, such as Dick Gephardt, of St. Louis, where Anheuser-Busch is located, also received contributions from the wholesalers association, as did Vic Fazio, of California and as chairman of the House Democratic Caucus a man of some influence. "The beer industry is larger than the wine-making industry in California," Rehr said.

To enhance the power behind their efforts to keep the House in Republican hands, the interested groups stay in close touch. Rehr kept in regular contact with Bill Paxon and his staff, in particular the National Republican Congressional Committee's very smart executive director, Maria Cino; and with the Christian Coalition's top Washington officials, including a man named D.J. Gribbin, the head of the Coalition's Washington office, and a woman named Heidi Stirrup, who sometimes attends Grover Norquist's Wednesday morning meetings; and with Tanya Metaksa, executive director of the National Rifle Association's political arm. (Ralph Reed maintained his residence in Norfolk, Virginia, traveling to Washington frequently.)

The federal election law stipulates that interest groups aren't supposed to coordinate their efforts for or against a candidate, but what actually goes on appears to be a distinction without a difference. Rehr said, "The Federal Election Commission says you can't coordinate, but everybody talks to each other." He added, "We make a practice of not talking specific amounts with each other. We

talk about who's targeted, how somebody's doing, but not in terms of 'Why don't you throw in three thousand and we'll throw in five thousand.' " This is a very narrow interpretation of the law.

On occasion, the alliance split over a candidate. "Sometimes Heidi and I disagree and fight with each other; usually we find an accommodation," Rehr said. The Christian Coalition and the N.R.A. parted with the beer wholesalers in refusing to support Tom Campbell, a moderate, pro-choice, pro–gun control Republican in a special election for a California House seat in 1995—in which both parties had a high stake. (Campbell won.) There's also some tension with the Christian Coalition because of its faction that opposes the drinking of alcohol. Since there are fewer and fewer Republicans— at least those who run for the House—who are economic conservatives but social liberals, the alliance doesn't split often, but sometimes a group's support will be less open and aggressive.

Rehr tells me that although the beer wholesalers group takes no formal position on gun control, it doesn't want the government to ban guns, because it sees that as amounting to taking things from people, and next there might be a prohibition on beer. There have been some tensions between the Christian Coalition and the N.R.A., because of a stream of the religious right that sees controlling guns as a moral issue. But all of these groups fit under Grover Norquist's "Leave Us Alone" umbrella.

Like the House members running for reelection themselves, in the early months of 1996 Rehr and his allies concentrated on getting as much money as possible to favored candidates by March 31st, the Federal Election Commission's first filing deadline of the year, so that when the F.E.C. issued its report on April 15th, those candidates would look formidable. "It's used as a mark," Rehr said when we talked in early March. "If the incumbent shows he or she has raised four hundred thousand dollars and has two hundred and fifty thousand or three hundred thousand dollars in cash on hand, it gives a potential opponent pause." (Bill Paxon, chairman of the House Republican campaign committee, said in early March, "We've been

pounding on members to raise more money by the filing deadline; if they show a good balance, that could ward off opponents.")

This game of chicken was especially important at that point, when both parties were still recruiting candidates. The January report on contributions up to December 31, 1995, did scare off some potential opponents to Republican incumbents. Few thought then that the Democrats could retake the House, which also made the Democrats' recruiting difficult.

By early March, the beer wholesalers group had, in Rehr's words, "gone through all the freshmen and looked at who might have a difficult race, or might be targeted [by Democratic-oriented interest groups] and we've maxed out on all of them." In contributing parlance, "maxed out" means one has given the full amount allowed under the election laws—for a PAC, five thousand dollars in a primary and five thousand in the general election.

The Spanish Civil War of the 1996 elections was fought in January 1996 over filling the Senate seat of Bob Packwood, the Oregon Republican who had resigned in disgrace in September, 1995. The Christian Coalition, the N.F.I.B., the beer wholesalers, the N.R.A., and the Chamber of Commerce went into the state for the Republican candidate, Gordon Smith; labor and environmental groups provided people to help Smith's opponent, then-Representative Ron Wyden (the AFL-CIO contributed twelve people, plus twenty-five from its affiliates). Wyden won by a little over one percentage point. Rehr said, "The fact that Smith lost sent a wake-up call to Republicans in the House and the business community that they would see the same pattern used in seventy-five congressional districts across the country, and we couldn't sit back and let that happen."

Rehr sometimes escorted a Republican candidate who came to Washington to make the rounds of the Republican-oriented PAC groups. (The same exercise took place on the Democratic side.) So intense was the race for money that by early 1996, on any given night three or four incumbent members held fundraisers—usually

on Tuesday through Thursday, the nights Members of Congress were most likely to be in Washington. Members want a lot of their colleagues to be there, to show off their strength, and to attract PAC representatives on the ground that they can meet a number of members in one shot. Rehr said, "Your five hundred dollars is a lot cheaper when you can talk to other members as well." Members of Congress race back and forth between the House floor and the Republican Capitol Hill Club, or the National Democratic Club—where most of the fundraisers were held—collecting checks and casting votes. (In 1995, John Boehner of Ohio, a member of the House leadership, was caught handing out checks from the tobacco lobby on the very floor of the House. Democrats protested, and even Republicans decided that that was over the line.)

The arms race for money being what it is, fundraising starts shortly after someone is elected to Congress. There isn't even a decent interval. In 1995, Roger Wicker of Mississippi, the president of the freshman class, which had come to Washington "to change things," couldn't meet with a reporter for weeks, his staff said, because he was "working on his fundraiser."

There was another point to a would-be member meeting incumbents: they might campaign for him or her, or even make a contribution. Members who have a safe race or a substantial amount of cash on hand can donate two thousand dollars from their own campaign funds to another candidate. Members of the leadership and other powerful congressional figures also have their own PACs for helping members and would-be members—by giving up to ten thousand dollars—and enhancing their own power.

Rehr had big ideas for 1996: in 1995, he had created a special account, amounting to $400,000, to use over the last nine weeks of the 1996 campaign. (In 1994, he had contributed $1.3 million.) His goal for 1996—which he met—was another million or so, for a total of a little over $1.5 million. To meet his stepped-up goal, Rehr not only relied on owners, as he had in the past, but also asked employees to contribute. The upcoming fight was that important.

Chapter Three

CHRISTIAN POL

"I'M NOT ALL THAT WORKED UP over who wins the Presidential race," Ralph Reed, the executive director of the Christian Coalition, said one late-January afternoon as he dug into a hot fudge sundae at the American Cafe on Capitol Hill, his hangout when he came to Washington. (The Coalition had offices nearby, but Reed often received calls and messages and conducted business at this sandwich and snack shop.) While we were talking, Pat Robertson, the founder and president of the Coalition, called Reed at the cafe—the manager, who gave Reed the message, treated this as a routine event—and Reed returned the call on his cell phone. As rock music and a blaring television set provided background cacophony, Reed resumed our conversation: "Our movement has made the mistake in the past in focusing almost exclusively on the Presidential race, to the detriment of our other interests. The long-term interests of the movement do not reside at 1600 Pennsylvania Avenue." Reed added, "A realignment on the Hill will affect U.S. policy for the next ten to twenty years."

He continued, "The wisdom was that we had to overturn *Roe* v. *Wade* [the 1973 Supreme Court decision that sanctioned abortion in the first trimester] and the school prayer decisions which banned prayer in public schools. We tried that strategy for twelve years under two administrations and when it was over we had five Supreme Court appointments, and *Roe* v. *Wade* and the school prayer decisions were upheld. The strategy was a failure.

"The way you crack the Court is to create a new political environment that makes it move right or left. That's what Roosevelt tried to do when he failed in packing the Court." Reed believed that at least a couple of Supreme Court decisions in 1995—striking down the University of Virginia's refusal to give funds to a campus Christian magazine, on the grounds that this was a violation of free speech, and allowing the Ku Klux Klan to put up a large cross in front of the Ohio state capitol—came about because the Republicans were in power in both houses of Congress. "If you don't have Congressional majorities, if you don't have state houses, the courts can't move things," Reed said. He had in fact concluded that "we do better not having the White House and having Congress than we do not having Congress and having the Presidency."

Reed was particularly pleased that with the cooperation of the Republican Congress his forces were able to "reframe the abortion debate," by making an issue of "partial birth abortions" (a form of abortion in the late stages of pregnancy). Representatives and senators were made to go on record about this emotional subject, and the Congress passed legislation outlawing such abortions, forcing Clinton to veto the bill lest he alienate his pro-choice constituency. (White House phone lines were jammed with calls demanding that Clinton sign the bill.) Talking before Clinton vetoed the bill, Reed said, "We made them defend the killing of a child that was coming down the birth canal and was out of the mother's womb. Clinton will veto it and our voter guides will say, 'Clinton vetoes bill to bar late-term abortions.' " And he laughed. Reed has a big laugh.

At that point, Reed was in fact quietly helping Bob Dole, who he had concluded would be the nominee. Reed, too, didn't want to see Pat Buchanan at the top of the ticket, for fear of the effect this would have on races for the House, but he wasn't overly concerned because he didn't think that Buchanan, despite his early strong showing, could win the nomination. (Reed's support for Dole would turn out to be crucial in South Carolina, where Dole dutifully attended a rally laid on by Reed, and wrapped up the nomination.)

His support would presumably put Reed in a powerful position once Dole won the nomination, and even more so if he were elected President—but it also carried risks. In siding with Dole—and putting himself on the inside, as opposed to his rival Gary Bauer, the president of the Family Research Council—and trying to help Dole by creating some space for him on the abortion issue, Reed made himself vulnerable to charges that he was selling out the movement. (Reed's first effort to give Dole leeway on abortion was in his book *Active Faith*, published in May of 1996, in which he suggested that he would accept changes in the Republican Party platform on abortion. But then, after a furor broke out and Bauer, among others, criticized him, Reed backed off.)

The youthful-looking thirty-four-year-old operative with the famous choirboy face and super-sincere mien actually came out of a political rather than a religious background. No flaming televangelist he. In fact, Reed had never headed a congregation or taught a Sunday School class. He earned his Ph.D.—his office staff refers to him as "Dr. Reed"—in history (of evangelical education). He was planning to teach history when a chance encounter with Robertson at George Bush's Inauguration led to his role in the Christian Coalition.

From 1982 to 1984, Reed had worked for the Republican National Committee. Eddie Gillespie, the director of communications and congressional affairs for the Republican National Committee, said, "When you're dealing with Ralph Reed it's important to remember that he's a political operative that became a born-again Christian, not a born-again Christian who became a political operative. He became a born-again Christian after he left the R.N.C." Gillespie added, "Ralph learned his political tactics from Grover Norquist." In their work together in the College Republicans, Norquist and Reed studied the organizing tactics of the left and tried to imitate or build on them in starting or strengthening grassroots movements on the right. (Reed sometimes tells audiences that Norquist taught him what he knows about politics.) In his book, Reed wrote, "The religious conservative movement was the only hope to build a Republican Party in the South."

CHRISTIAN POL • 25

Norquist said, "Ralph teaches his people to talk in terms so that people understand what you mean—not to say Leviticus says so. Ralph thinks that the debate on abortion should be in terms of, Is the fetus a person?"

Reed played a large role in the Republicans' effort to recapture control of the House in 1994, delivering a large turnout of evangelical Christians for Republican candidates.

It was a sign of the acumen of Pat Robertson—who ran a weak race for the Republican nomination in 1988—that he put Reed out front as the Coalition's spokesman. Reed didn't frighten people as Robertson did—he wasn't a preacher, and he didn't speak in tongues, and had no anti-Semitic statements in his background. But Robertson was the chief of the Coalition, built out of the ruins of Jerry Falwell's Moral Majority, which had collapsed from its own extremism and gone out of business in 1989.

"We're different from other groups, such as the labor unions, that engage in highly selective targets," Reed said on that January afternoon. "We'll put a hundred thousand voter guides in every district; we don't care whose district." The voter guides, handed out in churches or placed on the car windows of worshipers at churches on the Sunday before the election, state how the candidates for President, the House, the Senate, and governor, and the candidates in about two-thirds of the state legislative races, stand on issues of importance to the Coalition—such as abortion, school prayer, and the like. The five-hundred-dollar family tax credit in the House Republicans' Contract with America, which the Coalition strongly backed (it also opposed any income limit below $200,000) was also in the voter guides. Though essentially a middle-class movement, the Christian Coalition has a number of members who earn $100,000 to $200,000, and they do a lot of the work for the Coalition and the Republican Party: knock on doors, turn up at state political caucuses, attend the national convention.

But even of the races the Christian Coalition got involved in, some races got more attention than others. Of the 416 congressional races in 1996 (19 were uncontested), about 150 were considered truly competitive. (Though the House has 435 members, in some districts there is no challenge to the incumbent.) Reed makes a big thing about the fact that the Coalition doesn't endorse specific candidates. As a corporation, under the election law it may not spend its funds "for the purpose of influencing any election for federal office." The "non-endorsement" policy also protects candidates from being labeled as creatures of the Christian Coalition, and it frees the Coalition from having to endorse candidates who supported its position on several issues, but differed on big ones. Reed said, "Some groups, in order to keep their friends on the Hill, promise to endorse them if they vote for their issues. We're free of that."

But the idea that the Coalition didn't prefer particular candidates was a fiction. It had a clear preference in most of the competitive races; the voter guides left no doubt as to the preferred candidate. The guides have been found to vary from district to district or state to state in the issues they raised, enabling preferred candidates to get high scores. It helps some preferred candidates in other ways. Reed said, "We may do enhanced phone banks in fifty to a hundred districts. We call not only our own members, but other voters as well." In the districts where the Christian Coalition is making an extra effort it not only distributes the voter guides but also, about three days before the election, sends neon-colored postcards giving the same information. The bright coloring "is very important," Reed said. "People don't open their mail." The Coalition also sends out "scorecards," which show how all House and Senate members voted on issues of interest to it.

"We can really bump turnout in a primary," Reed said. So many of its allies had been successful in 1994 that the Coalition was involved in fewer primaries in 1996 than it was then. In districts where neither candidate was pleasing to the Coalition, it sent fewer voter guides. Also, there was the matter of having a receptive audience. "There aren't as many evangelical churches in the Upper West Side of Manhattan as there are in a blue-collar district in Pennsylvania," Reed said. But some voter guides go to Manhattan.

The Coalition made one of the largest single efforts in its history in the special Oregon election. Reed said, "We thought it would set the tone, the parameters, and in a relatively liberal state Smith would have been a pro-life and the first conservative Oregon senator since the 1950s."

Reed's goal is to build the Christian Coalition into a great force in American politics. "Our objective is a little bit different from other organizations," he said. "Their object is to defeat their opponents and elect their allies. Our mission is to take the sleeping giant of conservative evangelical Protestants, pro-family Catholics, Greek Orthodox and observant Jewish allies—identify them, make sure they're registered, and get them to the polls in record numbers." Reed added, "In the end it's a *Field of Dreams* strategy—build it and they will come. If we create the constituency and turn it out to the polls, the candidates and the policies will follow."

The Christian Coalition has grown quickly. By 1996 it had nearly two million members and nearly two thousand local chapters, and controlled between fifteen and twenty state Republican Parties. Reed said that it was "the dominant structure" in many states and congressional districts. But Reed had more than the outcome of any particular election in mind. He told me, "If twenty-five to thirty-five percent of the electorate consists of evangelical Christians, and other religious conservatives get involved, the more the electorate will come our way. We're trying to shift the political culture as well as win an election. I'd like to do both, but in the end it's more important to change the political culture."

Sometimes Reed takes a clever tangent to produce support for his policies. Vic Fazio, the House Democratic leader from California, had long been a Coalition target, not because Reed thinks Fazio could be defeated but because, he said, "If Fazio sees our voter guides and people turn up with our scorecards with his and his opponent's voting record, it has an impact—not on Fazio's voting record, that's not what we're looking for. I want him to go into the cloakroom and complain about how active we are in his district, and others will hear this and it might affect *their* behavior."

Reed said, "Our goal is turnout." The bigger the turnout, the more impressive his forces. So, Reed planned to make a big effort in the 1996 race between Jesse Helms, Republican of North Carolina, and his Democratic opponent, Harvey Gantt. (Helms won their previous confrontation, in 1990, using ads playing up the fact that Gantt was black.) Reed believed that Helms would win this time, too, "but we will work it hard because we want a huge turnout."

One day a few months later, just before we met, Reed had noticed in *The Hotline*, a daily compendium of political doings and developments, a poll showing a close race between Andrea Seastrand, a freshman Republican from California, and her Democratic opponent. "We'll be in there heavy," Reed said.

Reed acknowledged that cooperation goes on between his group and its allies—but said that most of it takes place at a lower level. "There is no formal, structured cooperation," Reed said, adding, "The big question is, Are the N.R.A., the N.F.I.B., and the Christian Coalition in the same districts? If they are, there's a synergism that's very powerful."

Chapter Four

POLLINATOR

MARC NUTTLE, forty-seven, lives in Norman, Oklahoma, but travels to Washington once a week and buzzes about town, picking up and depositing information. As the national political consultant of the National Federation of Independent Business, one of the groups Bill Paxon had said was critical to the Republicans' cause of holding the House, Nuttle was a major participant in this effort.

Addressing the question of the Republicans' priorities in 1996, Nuttle said in a conversation in June, "There are great conflicting pressures within the Republican Party. There's a group within the Republicans who think that protecting the Republican House is more important than winning the Presidency. This is a new concept for the Republican Party. It's almost a trauma for people in the Party. It's an earthquake."

Nuttle explained that two types of Republicans were more interested in the House: the social conservatives and the economic conservatives whose priority is a balanced budget. Both groups thought that their agenda was safer in a Republican House than in the hands of a President Dole. Nuttle said, "If Republicans maintain control of the House, and Bill Clinton wins the Presidency, he's in a second term, and things never work as proposed in second terms, and the next off-year election, in 1998, could be disastrous for the Democrats.

"If we maintain control of the House," Nuttle said, "where all the taxes are raised, where regulatory policies and mandatory programs are usually initiated, that's more important than holding the Senate." Echoing Ralph Reed and Grover Norquist, he said, "Having a Democratic President and a Republican Congress is more important than having a Republican President and a Democratic Congress." He continued, "If Republicans lose the House, what comes up for debate, for votes, what ends up on the President's desk, is changed."

The importance of small business to the Republican Party was a clear sign of the degree to which the Party was changing, from the party of big business and the rich to a more populist party. (Big business, to the dismay of many Republicans, was continuing to hedge its bets.) Haley Barbour, the chairman of the Republican National Committee, liked to say, "We're the party of Main Street, not Wall Street, the party of bass boats, not yachts." To some extent this was propaganda, a deliberate attempt to change the Party's image. Polling by the R.N.C. following the 1992 defeat of George Bush found that people thought of the Republican Party as the party of the rich, and out of touch. At the same time, the small business and evangelical groups were creating their own party-within-the-Republican Party, and becoming an increasingly powerful force.

The N.F.I.B., with a claimed 600,000 members, had long been a strong lobbying presence in Washington because of the size of its membership. Nuttle says that forty-two percent of households have members employed by small business. In 1994, Nuttle, then a high official of the group in Washington, set out to turn the N.F.I.B. into a national political force, and it was one of the major forces behind the Republicans' gaining control of the House.

Nuttle, a slight, dark-haired man, with a soft drawl, had a long history of political activity, having at one point been held on retainer by all three national Republican political committees: the R.N.C., the National Republican Senatorial Committee, and the National Republican Congressional Committee. Nuttle says he recognized the potential of the Christian right movement as a political bloc and, beginning in 1978, he helped organize it; he helped build Jerry Falwell's Moral Majority and in 1988 he ran Pat Robertson's Presidential campaign.

Under Nuttle's direction, the political staff of the N.F.I.B. was increased eightfold in 1994 and the organization's PAC was used far more aggressively than before. Jeff Butzke, the organization's political director (who was installed by Nuttle), said, "The decision about '94 was that the most direct way to assure that small business was effective was to elect more candidates."

The catalyst for building the N.F.I.B. into a national political force, Nuttle has written, was the Clintons' 1994 health care plan. Small businesses argued that the plan's "employer mandate," which required businesses with fifty or more employees to offer them health insurance, was an undue burden on them, and, along with the health insurance industry, they organized an effective grassroots effort against it. The N.F.I.B.'s agenda already included taxes and regulations that affect small business. Nuttle also says that small business is one of the two most respected voices in politics (the other is farmers), because people listen to their grocer, their dry cleaner, their small store owner.

The N.F.I.B. was quickly transformed into a national political operation, with directors in all fifty states. In 1994, it was involved in 224 House and Senate races, and claims that between 180 and 190 of its candidates won. Candidates endorsed by the N.F.I.B. were the beneficiaries of its mailings in the district, research on the opponent, advice on how to "communicate" the fruits of such "opposition research," and several thousand dollars in contributions.

Nuttle claimed that more than half the voters in 1994 were small business owners, employees, or members of a small business household. He said, "We didn't know that small business owners went to the polls thinking of themselves as small business. Now we know they do." Several items in the Contract with America, the agenda for the House Republicans in the new Congress, were intended to help small business: regulatory reform, limiting damages, curbing the role of the Occupational Safety and Health Administration (OSHA), and "takings." More broadly, the N.F.I.B. also backed a balanced budget, and the line-item veto. This agenda met with only mixed success—much of it was watered down or died in the Senate.

Now the N.F.I.B.'s objective was to protect its 1994 gains, and enlarge on them. Its agenda included what one would expect from a small business lobby: deregulation, no price controls, no employer mandates—which most definitely included no minimum wage—no unfair subsidies to big business, no inheritance tax, and a flatter tax system as well as a cut in capital gains taxes.

Nuttle said that the N.F.I.B. would support Democrats who supported his organization's agenda, and who rated high on its "conservative index"—for "free enterprise and less government"—of people who voted for the N.F.I.B.'s issues. He added, "But they're hard to find." (Some conservative Democrats whom the N.F.I.B. backed were among the five who switched parties after the 1994 election.)

In 1996, the Federation's political activity continued to grow. In the 1993–94 election cycle, it contributed $370,000. It hoped to spend a million dollars in the 1996 election. The funds that would be left over once the limits on PAC contributions were met would be spent—like Christian Coalition money, like labor money, and a lot of other groups' money—on "communication" with its members (or "issue advocacy"), on which there is no spending limit. (At the same time, the National Republican Congressional Committee, which was now striving desperately to expand its money base, raised vast new sums from small business people through telemarketing.)

A self-described political consultant who did economic and political analysis, including state-by-state strategy advice, Nuttle had amassed a collection of clients, several of which could be useful to each other. Though he was no longer formally an official of the N.F.I.B., he was still its most visible and powerful representative. He also advised corporate clients on trade and international economics. At the same time, he advised a number of senators and House members on such matters as their personal finances, their businesses, problems with their families, or problems in their districts. He also gave them economic analysis of the impact on their districts of various legislative proposals.

On top of all that, he said that he "maintains a relationship" with about 35,000 interest groups at the state level. Nuttle said that as people became increasingly frustrated with national politics and political parties, they began to form their own grassroots organizations, and as the number of people who were registering as independents grew—who had no party, and therefore no conversation with each other—there was an opportunity for a political operator with national experience. Nuttle said, "If you wanted tax reform there was little you could do within your party, so you set up a group within your state. You'd find five thousand people who were so upset they'd each pay you ten dollars to figure it out—and you'd have a fifty-thousand-dollar operation." He added that some of the state groups are "a lot larger." In turn, he said, corporations, and Members of Congress—especially in an election year—paid him for access to his 35,000 groups. Nuttle acknowledged that the income from managing this agglomeration of interests was "not bad."

A representative of the N.F.I.B. regularly attended Norquist's weekly Wednesday meetings, and Nuttle and Norquist colluded to wield their combined power at the Republican Convention—especially on the platform. Both the N.F.I.B. and Norquist, of course, were most interested in the tax issue. "Dole won't be able to dictate to these groups," Nuttle said. The N.F.I.B. worked together with the beer wholesalers on a number of matters of importance to small business.

Though the N.F.I.B. has a coincidence of interests with the other groups in the coalition to keep the House Republican, Nuttle was not as personally close to them as Norquist and Ralph Reed and David Rehr were to each other. Nuttle, in the early months of

1996, sought to increase his own influence by persuading the Christian Coalition and the N.R.A.—both of which he termed "radioactive" (that is, they drive away some members of the coalition because of their stands on abortion and gun control)—to come in under the umbrella of the N.F.I.B. As Nuttle saw it, the majority of businesses in America were family owned, and therefore the Christian Coalition could get behind a family-business agenda, and gunshop owners were small business. Nuttle's concern was that it had been easier to unite these groups in 1994—against the liberal threat in the persons of Bill and Hillary Clinton. Now there wasn't the same galvanizing threat. At the same time, the Democrats were uniting against Newt Gingrich—a fight, Nuttle said, that Republicans had to make district by district. Republicans weren't about to wage a national campaign defending Gingrich. Nuttle said, "If we could hold the base—the Christian Coalition, the gun owners—on small business issues, which are positive issues, we can hold the Congress and win the Presidency." Nuttle hoped to have his new grand coalition in place by September. But Ralph Reed—who was familiar with Nuttle because of the Robertson campaign—wasn't interested in marching behind Nuttle's banner, and neither was the N.R.A.

Nuttle said that he and other N.F.I.B. officials talk to Bill Paxon and Maria Cino, the executive director of the National Republican Congressional Committee, about the status of House races, "but, quite frankly, we know as much about it as they do." He added, "The number-one stop in town for any conservative is the N.R.C.C., then it's the N.F.I.B.—sometimes it's the N.F.I.B. first."

But despite its influence, the N.F.I.B. wasn't powerful enough to stop the increase in the minimum wage that rolled through Congress in the summer of 1996, even when it worked in concert with the National Restaurant Association, the U.S. Chamber of Commerce, and others. The minimum wage bill was a highly contentious issue within the Republican Party. Gingrich knew that the minimum wage was popular (surveys said it was favored by at least eighty percent of respondents), and he had long been concerned about the reelection prospects of moderate Republicans from

Northeastern or other strong union states. He had been lobbied by about twenty-five of them, who said that they had the votes to combine with the Democrats to pass the measure.

After an angry internal debate with his fellow leaders—particularly the more ideological Dick Armey, the majority leader, who strongly opposed taking up the bill—Gingrich prevailed, and the bill was allowed to come up for a House vote in May. The N.F.I.B. was slightly assuaged by some small business tax breaks that were put in the bill. Similar breaks were put in the Senate bill, which passed overwhelmingly in early July—after Trent Lott, who had just taken over as majority leader in early June, broke with Bob Dole's strategy of trying to keep the issue from coming to a vote. In both chambers, crippling amendments, which would have exempted a large number of small businesses, were rejected. The Democrats and their allies, in particular the labor movement, had outpoliticked and outdefined the small business lobbies.

Nuttle was of course unhappy about this defeat and felt that Gingrich had made a political mistake by letting the House be stampeded into a vote. There should have been hearings, Nuttle believed, but he largely stayed out of the arguments over how to handle the issue, because it had caused a real rift between Gingrich and Armey, even though he felt that Armey understood the matter correctly. That an increase in the minimum wage was popular, Nuttle argued, showed that the country was "economically illiterate," and so was the Congress. His argument—one that had been debated endlessly—was that a raise in the minimum wage led to higher consumer prices, and unemployment, and was "one component of wage and price controls."

When I saw Nuttle in early July, he had been discussing the forthcoming Republican Convention with the Dole campaign. The idea, Nuttle said, was "if the social issues get out of control we'll have economic issues to fall back on." He also said that he had been asked by the Dole campaign to "bring my clients to the table"—the N.F.I.B., and the 35,000 state-based groups.

Though the House was his priority, Nuttle had been worried

that the Republicans might lose the Senate for some time. This could happen, he thought, despite the fact that a larger number of Democratic senators than of Republicans were up for reelection, and that because of Democratic retirements there were four open Senate seats in the South. Also, the Democrats in some cases had put up more moderate candidates than many had expected. (Bob Kerrey, the chairman of the Democratic Senatorial Campaign Committee, had made a deliberate effort to recruit moderate business-men as Democratic candidates. He was angry with Democratic consultants who had encouraged Harvey Gantt to run against Jesse Helms again, because he believed Gantt had little chance of winning.) In early July, Nuttle, who had access to the Republican Party's data, predicted that the Republicans would lose the Senate—"We're down by three"—but would hold the House, unless Dole lost by a wide margin. He did notice, though, one disturbing trend: that independents, who voted two-to-one for Republicans in 1994, were now telling pollsters, two-to-one, that they would vote Democratic.

Chapter Five

GUNS

TANYA METAKSA, the director of the federal affairs division of the National Rifle Association, decides which races the N.R.A. will go into and how much it will spend on them, and also which legislation to support or oppose. As a top official of an organization that has developed the reputation of representing the loony right, Metaksa seems an anomaly. A woman of medium build, a grandmother, with short-cropped steel-gray hair and a deep, authoritative voice, but not humorless, Metaksa seems quite normal. She has developed ways of making her case in what appears to be a most reasonable manner.

To take one example, the N.R.A.'s effort to repeal the ban on assault weapons passed by Congress in 1994—an effort that even some of its friends thought was hurting the N.R.A. Metaksa has a little show-and-tell in response to critics of the N.R.A.'s position. She holds up photographs of two weapons that appear identical, until it is pointed out that one of them has a bayonet lug (a small removable piece of metal to which a bayonet can be attached). That's a banned assault weapon, she says; the other is an accepted rifle. "Nobody has been killed by a bayonet lug," Metaksa argues. (However, on closer inspection of the matter, it turns out that the assault weapon has additional characteristics that put it on the banned list.)

"The ban has nothing to do with functionality," Metaksa asserts. "All it has to do with is cosmetics. There is absolutely no difference in the functionality of the assault weapon and the politically correct rifle." Therefore, Metaksa says, when President Clinton says he's got assault weapons off the street, "It's not so. They can shoot the same number of bullets."

Bill Paxon said of Metaksa, "She is way, way to the right. She's very, very tough. She leads the jihad there. Others may be more out-front, but she runs the show."

Metaksa says that she regularly hunts deer, quail, pheasant, duck, and geese. She adds, "I got married to an N.R.A. life member thirty-seven years ago." (Metaksa's husband is an engineer. They have three daughters and three grandchildren. Her father had fled Russia in 1917; her husband's parents were also Russian immigrants.) As a housewife, Metaksa, who had gone to Smith College, took up shooting in order, she says, to get to spend time with her husband, and she evolved into a grassroots N.R.A. activist in Connecticut in the late 1960s. In the seventies she was hired to run the opposition to a Massachusetts referendum limiting the possession of guns, and after that succeeded she moved to Washington in 1978 to work for the N.R.A. (In the 1980s there were stints with the Reagan-Bush campaign and with Al D'Amato.)

Metaksa's problem in appearing reasonable is the "camel's nose" factor—the view that once the camel's nose is in the tent, the rest will inevitably follow—which makes the N.R.A. come off as absolutist and therefore unreasonable. Its solicitation mailing in April, 1995, signed by executive vice president Wayne LaPierre—accused by N.R.A. hard-liners as too moderate—after the bombing in Oklahoma City and after sieges at Ruby Ridge, Idaho, and Waco, Texas, calling the Bureau of Alcohol, Tobacco and Firearms "jack-booted government thugs," made the organization seem off the deep end, and even caused George Bush to tear up his membership card. Metaksa herself stirred controversy when news accounts said that she had met with leaders of the Michigan militia in early 1995. (There was also an erroneous report that she met with them after the Oklahoma City bombing.) Metaksa says that she was appearing in a debate in Hillsdale, Michigan, near Lansing, and had met with two Michigan militia leaders, at their invitation, in a hotel lobby bar in Lansing. (The militia members said that she had requested the meeting.) Metaksa says simply that they asked for the N.R.A.'s help in supporting their movement, and that she declined, and that was the end of it.

A high proportion of the N.R.A.'s roughly three million members becomes worked up over any sign that the federal government wants to regulate arms, and it is the business of the N.R.A. to get them worked up over any such possible move, so as to keep its raison d'être. And, it would say, protect their "right to keep and bear arms." Therefore a circular process goes on. The headquarters tells the members that the federal government is trying to encroach on its Second Amendment right "to keep and bear arms"—a highly questionable interpretation, since the amendment begins, "A well-regulated militia, being necessary to the security of a free State," and federal courts have uniformly held that there is no constitutional right for an individual to own a gun. Like other lobby groups, the N.R.A. deals in threats—real and hypothetical—to its members.

Any proposed legislation is seen as the "camel's nose," a move toward denying gun owners their right to own even lawful hunting rifles, or any handgun for self-protection. Therefore, the assault weapons ban was seen as a camel's nose. So was an administration proposal, after the Oklahoma City bombing in the spring of 1995, to include taggants, colored markers about the size of a poppy seed, in explosives and gunpowder, to help in identifying, say, a terrorist who has used a bomb. There had in fact been conflicting studies on whether taggants were a danger to those who use firearms for recreation and self-protection because they might explode. (The N.R.A. says that taggants when combined with the powders are a particular danger to people who make their own ammunition or use muzzle-loading, Civil War–era, guns.) Given this, the N.R.A. sought, and won, another study, thus holding off the automatic regulations that the administration supported. In her public presentations, Metaksa emphasized safety problems with taggants, not mentioning, because she couldn't, that this was another camel's nose issue. But in a later conversation she conceded that it was. Still, the camel's nose of taggants was real enough to Metaksa. "I really believe that those people who are out to deny law-abiding citizens their firearms are going to use everything they can to make it more difficult, more cumbersome, and more dangerous," she said.

As the sudden attention to militia movements after Oklahoma City brought out, there is a true lunatic fringe that believes such things as that the U.N. is trying to take over the world—and that training for this was taking place through the use of unmarked black helicopters which had allegedly been sighted. But politically, there is a continuum from the perfectly normal hunter, to the somewhat paranoid gun owner, to the truly crazed, and as far as the N.R.A.'s political interests are concerned, it doesn't much matter where worried or angry gun owners are on the continuum.

Metaksa says, "I have been involved in this movement since the late sixties. The questions remain the same: Why are they doing this to me?"

To Grover Norquist and other groups on the right, gun control is a form of federal control, a means toward requiring citizen identity cards and other barriers on individual freedom. So the N.R.A. is a natural part of Norquist's coalition. Joe Phillips, the N.R.A.'s director of federal affairs, who reports to Metaksa, regularly attends Norquist's meetings and remains in close touch with him. He, or other N.R.A. officials, are part of the circle which includes David Rehr and Christian Coalition officials that shares political gossip and information.

Metaksa or her colleagues also kept in close touch with Bill Paxon or Maria Cino, of the National Republican Congressional Committee. Smiling, fully aware of the import of what she was transmitting, Metaksa said to me, "People in the political process want you to support certain candidates. They're willing to share polling and other information."

The N.R.A. was highly active in 1994. Early in 1996, Paxon told me, "The N.R.A. and the Christian Coalition are our two most important allies, bar none." According to Metaksa, in 1994 the N.R.A. was involved in 10,000 federal, state, and local races, and she claimed an eighty-two percent success rate. It took part in over two hundred House races. "That was probably our all-time high involvement," Metaksa says.

The problem with success claims, whether made by the N.R.A., the Christian Coalition, or the AFL-CIO, is that victory in any close race—and many of the 1994 races were very close—can be attributed to the efforts of any group that took part, but might not have been due to its efforts. It might have taken combined efforts—this is, after all, the basis on which these groups work. It may be due to issues other than those that the individual group raises. Maybe even the quality of the candidates has something to do with it.

Metaksa explains that in 1994, "We backed many more Republicans than Democrats, mainly because in the 103rd Congress we had two major legislative efforts backed by the Clinton White House and supported by the maximum number of Democrats." She was referring to the Brady bill, named in honor of Ronald Reagan's press secretary who was grievously wounded in the assassination attempt on Reagan in 1981. It required a five-day waiting period before a handgun could be purchased. Then the crime bill, passed at the end of the session in 1994, included the ban on assault weapons, and also limited people's ability to own guns if they had been accused of a crime. The N.R.A. says it prefers an instant check of criminal records of anyone applying for a gun, rather than the Brady bill's five-day wait; its position is, in effect, that it doesn't mind if the government keeps a list of criminals and insane people, but it does object to its keeping a list of gun owners. Besides, the N.R.A. couldn't say it was against any restraints at all. Gun control advocates argue that many states' records won't be computerized by the time the Brady law expires, in 1998, and is to be supplanted by an instant check, and that the waiting period provides a "cooling off" for people about to commit an impulsive act. Neither the Brady law nor the assault weapons ban would prevent law-abiding citizens, including hunters, from obtaining a gun. They would simply be inconvenienced. But both laws were camel's noses.

"Our F.E.C. report shows us one of the top contributors in 1994 to Republican candidates for the House and Senate," Metaksa said, referring to the required reports to the Federal Election Commission. "We worked very closely" with the Republican Senatorial and House campaign committees. In 1994, the N.R.A. ran ads, starring Charlton Heston, in several Senate races. But its most spectacular achievement in 1994 was in contributing heavily to the defeat of House Speaker Thomas Foley. Foley lost by only two percentage points, or roughly 4,000 out of 200,000 votes cast, and therefore various groups and issues could be said to have contributed to his defeat. But the N.R.A.'s special effort—this was the only House race in which it ran an ad (starring Heston)—definitely was a factor. Foley had over the years come under attack from liberal groups and editorial pages for his opposition to gun control. Then he changed his position, and lost his House seat. The N.R.A. wasn't the sole factor, but it was a big one. "He'd been good until 1994," Metaksa said. Foley had committed the sin, in the N.R.A.'s eyes, of not only supporting the crime bill but also, in a rare act for a Speaker, advocating it from the well of the House.

Metaksa said that the ads were "independent expenditures"—in effect, contributions over and above the limits on direct financial contributions to the candidates by PACs—but given the interlocking relationships and the communications among like-minded groups, there is reason to question how independent such "independent expenditures" are. Metaksa argued that they were independent because the N.R.A. did the spending without communicating with the campaigns it was trying to help. She did acknowledge that "Maria"—Cino, the executive director of the N.R.C.C.—"will talk to anyone who will listen about her top-priority races." And Cino is of course in touch with the campaigns. Metaksa said, "We decided we were interested in trying to move the Democratic Senate to Republican." (This did happen in 1994, though most of the attention was on the more dramatic Republican takeover of the House.) "We went out and made the commercials and bought the time. We just did it," Metaksa said.

Now Metaksa and the N.R.A. were gearing up for 1996. It had already forced a House vote in March, 1996, on repealing the assault weapons ban. The proposition carried the House, 239–173. The N.R.A. had accepted postponements imposed in 1995, first by the House leaders' giving the Contract priority and then by the feeling, which the N.R.A. shared, that following Oklahoma City the atmosphere wasn't right. Bill Paxon was among those pushing for a vote on the assault weapons ban in early 1996, on the theory that this would help many of his members. Metaksa had been pushing for the vote with Paxon and the House leadership. (Eddie Gillespie, then on Majority Leader Dick Armey's staff, argued to Paxon that it would hurt some members from urban or suburban districts who had been elected by narrow margins and that it would "confer legitimacy on the 'extremist' label the Democrats are trying to stick us with.") The N.R.A.'s push for a vote in the Senate later in the year was to lead to a major crisis within the Republican Party. Metaksa insisted to me that the three million gun owners "needed the vote," so that they could carry on their work in the congressional districts. She often describes the N.R.A. as the passive vessel of its members' desires. "These people look to the N.R.A. to help save their Second Amendment rights," Metaksa said.

By June, 1996, the N.R.A. was still formulating its election-year plans. "At the moment, we don't know exactly what we're going to do." Metaksa said. "We didn't in June, 1994, either." But it had already contributed directly to some candidates. Metaksa was planning to "puddle jump" to appear with certain candidates.

When I asked her if she wanted to keep the House in Republican control, she smiled and said, "I like the current leadership of the House and Senate."

Chapter Six

LANDSCAPE

THE LANDSCAPE AGAINST WHICH the battle for political preeminence was fought in 1996 was a nation with a continuing modest economic recovery despite a wave of layoffs and continuing stagnation of median wages; and a President who, if not overwhelmingly popular—his average approval rating was in the mid-forties and the polls were reflecting deep ambivalence about him—had regained his equilibrium and his confidence following the voters' rebuff of him and his wife in 1994. His successful effort in 1993 to cut the deficit was yielding low interest rates and steady economic expansion.

In reality, Bill Clinton's victory in the battle against the Republicans, in particular House Speaker Newt Gingrich, over the budget in 1995 and early 1996 masked a major substantive achievement by Gingrich. He had maneuvered Clinton into moving from a budget that didn't have balance in sight to one that was to be balanced in seven years. But the Republicans got caught up in the narrow issues of "scoring" (counting), and didn't know how to declare victory.

And Clinton succeeded in painting the Republicans as "extremist" because of their proposals for budget cuts for programs that helped the middle class as well as the poor (school lunches, Medicare), and their efforts to roll back environmental regulations, and by making sure that they got the blame for two government shutdowns during the impasse. Clinton and the Democrats got the better of the Republicans in the argument over whether the Republicans were, as they maintained, increasing spending on these programs but slowing their rate of growth, or whether, as Clinton and the Democrats insisted, the Republicans were "cutting" the programs. The argument started with the school lunch program and reached its greatest intensity over Medicare. Because the Republicans were voting to increase the funds spent on these and other programs, but not keeping up with inflation and growth in the number of eligible recipients, Democrats argued that what the Republicans were doing amounted to a cut in benefits to the recipients. Technically, both sides were right, but the Democrats—with Clinton having the largest megaphone—won the argument. Republicans insisted that Clinton and other Democrats were being demagogic because he, too, had proposed to slow the rate of growth of Medicare, and they had a point.

By early 1996, Gingrich was the most unpopular national politician. (He had only a thirty percent approval rating.) He had helped Clinton restore his political fortunes. The showdown between Clinton and Gingrich was the predicate for the 1996 congressional as well as Presidential elections.

Both major political parties were seeking a new definition of themselves. The Republicans had gotten a lesson in 1992 and the Democrats in 1994—and then the Republicans got another one in 1995.

The Democrats' problem was that the New Deal model—which carried through the Johnson and even the Nixon administrations—was out of fashion, and they had yet to find anything to replace it. Clinton was groping for an answer. The American people's confidence in government was low—in part deservedly but also in part because of demagoguery about it on the part of politicians and distortion by some of the media. The flaws of politicians—their self-dealing, the shouters, the oddballs, the angry scenes—were the preferred television fare, not the good guys or the quiet business of getting things done. Those didn't make good stories (or good television). That civility in our politics, and on Capitol Hill in particular, was on the decline was indisputable—Pennsylvania's freshman

Senator Rick Santorum's daily calls in 1995 (while waiting for Clinton's budget plan) on the Senate floor of "Where's Bill?" was a new low. But the discord and the dysfunction of government weren't the only things going on. Successful government programs (and there were several) made for less interesting news stories than those that failed, or than stories about bloated contracts.

Other things were wrong, of course. Politicians were too dependent on, and indebted to, their financial supporters. The monied interests had more political power than those without the cash to contribute, or the strength-in-numbers of the middle class. The workhorses in the Congress were increasingly replaced by show horses. But neither the good nor the bad was the whole story.

There was a shrinking middle in both parties, leading to greater partisanship. (By now, of course, the Republicans had virtually no left left.) Politicians were dropping out at an increasing rate: some because they themselves were put off by the incivility and breakdown of comity on both sides of Capitol Hill, some because they were frustrated at their inability to influence decisions (moderate Republicans). New ethics rules, barring most earned outside income, including honoraria for speeches, while necessary, put more of a financial squeeze on Members of Congress, many of whom maintained homes in two cities. "It's not as good a job as it used to be," one former member says. Many of the recent dropouts were Democrats who didn't see any possibility of regaining their majority status—and power—anytime soon. This same sense made it more difficult for Democratic Congressional Campaign Committee Chairman Martin Frost, of Texas, and House Minority Leader Dick Gephardt, who was aching to become Speaker, to recruit promising Democratic challengers for the 1996 election. As 1996 began, there was an unusually large number of open seats in both the House and the Senate.

Still lacking definition, deliberately, Bill Clinton continued to redesign himself as he asked the voters to extend his Presidency for another term. His advisers were divided over some big questions, and, as was his wont, he listened to both sides and picked his way along, often adopting the advice of both. There was no grand vision, though Clinton in the past had had a vision—largely unnoticed because he talked about so many things and tacked so often. The vision, which he had stated well when he stated it at all—more frequently in his first two years than later—was of growth and opportunity: people should have a lifelong opportunity to learn and acquire new skills as the economy changed and grew. Clinton hadn't completely dropped these subjects, but they had become virtually lost in the thicket of his many thoughts and in his maneuvers toward the political center. Once Clinton donned the balanced budget flak-jacket, he stopped trying to expand job training programs, as he had done in the first two years. His school-to-work program, which provided apprenticeship training for high school students not going to college, was only half-funded.

The exigencies now for Clinton were to establish himself as a man looking to the future (as opposed to the Republicans), as one concerned with the problems of the middle class but not bent on big government programs, and as sufficiently safe on the social issues, such as crime, with which Republicans used to wallop Democrats. He had to campaign and govern within the confines of a balanced budget and a public that was increasingly skeptical about big government.

The fact that the Republican Congress had overreached, leading to a backlash among the public, was not in itself an answer. The anti-government sentiments that fed the 1994 Republican takeover hadn't completely died out.

Clinton was beginning to invent a replacement for the New Deal to meet the public's lowered desires and expectations of government—and also to ease the concerns of middle-class families—with calls for such things as school uniforms, support of the television V-chip, curfews for teenagers, and small programs such as a two-billion-dollar effort to get computers into every public school classroom by the year 2000. But this approach took a certain nerve and ideological flexibility, and also cynicism, and it wasn't at all clear that other Democrats could pull it off—or agreed with this approach. (Mrs. Clinton had championed the school uniforms, and Clinton came close to saying, when he introduced the idea in a speech in Long Beach, California, in February, that she had "nagged" him on it.) Clinton was also trying to redefine the social agenda—away from such issues as abortion and school prayer and toward other "family values" issues, for which he now had proposals.

This new approach came about largely because, acting mainly on the advice of Dick Morris, the cross-dressing political consultant to whom Clinton (actually, the Clintons) had turned after the 1994 debacle, the President had been trying to shake his image as a liberal who believed in big government and to coopt the center. In 1995, Morris had Clinton give a series of speeches on "common ground," to show that Clinton and the Republicans could agree on many things. This was a variation on Morris's theory of "triangulation"—that Clinton should hold himself apart from both parties. Clinton's opening line in his 1996 State of the Union address—"The era of big government is over," which originated in a draft by Morris that didn't include the word "big"—set the stage for the latest Clinton.

A holy war had broken out among Clinton's advisers over what had caused his comeback in the polls. The centrists—who included Morris; Bill Curry, who also joined the White House after the 1994 election and was a close ally of Morris; communications director Don Baer; Jack Quinn, formerly Vice President Al Gore's chief of staff and then White House counsel; Robert Squier, the President's new media adviser and longtime Gore ally; and the President's new chief pollster, Mark Penn, of Penn & Schoen, whom Morris had brought in—argued that it was Clinton's adoption in June, 1995, of a balanced budget, over the howls of his liberal advisers and the liberal Democratic congressional leadership, and other moves to the center that had brought him back. They cited Penn's polls as proof. His more liberal advisers, who included Chief of Staff Leon

Panetta, senior adviser George Stephanopoulos, and Deputy Chief of Staff Harold Ickes, argued that it was Clinton's standing up for (appearing to stand up for was closer to the truth, since Clinton was readier to compromise than his liberal advisers and the Democratic congressional leaders) traditional liberal programs, such as education, Medicare, and Medicaid, as well as his attacks during the budget fight on the Republican onslaught against environmental protection, that had caused Clinton's resurrection. They cited as proof the work of Stan Greenberg, formerly the President's chief pollster, who still polled for the Democratic National Committee and whose product regularly reached Stephanopoulos and Ickes. Greenberg's compilation of public polls showed that Clinton's support level was high after Oklahoma City, when he had acted as national pastor, then dropped over the summer of 1995—during which period he was making the speeches on "common ground," talking about such things as school prayer, and had his famous meeting with Gingrich in Claremont, New Hampshire—and then began to rise as the budget battle took shape, shooting up when the battle reached its apogee at the end of the year.

The Morris claque saw themselves in a long twilight struggle with the "liberals" on the President's staff. They held a secret conference call at 10:00 A.M. each day, in between official staff meetings. (The last such conference call was made on the Wednesday of the Democratic Convention, the day Morris departed the campaign.)

The White House was riddled with suspicion and plotting. Morris thought that Ickes and Stephanopoulos were trying to undermine him, which wasn't far from the truth; and Ickes and Stephanopoulos, and of course Panetta, worried about what Morris was whispering in the President's ear. The weekly Wednesday night political meetings in the family quarters of the White House were ostensibly chaired by Panetta but were dominated by Morris.

Even some of Morris's opponents said that he was a source of energy at the White House, empowering certain White House aides by pushing their ideas, or extricating ideas from the Cabinet departments. But Morris was indiscriminate. This led to a lot of Presidential appearances in which he proposed one small initiative or another, that one official termed "boutique events" which he thought unpresidential. But Morris had a considered purpose: to show Clinton governing—being President—by signing executive orders and bills, and proposing things to help middle-class families deal with violence and drugs in schools, and violence on television.

The one thing that worried Morris most was the across-the-board tax cut that Bob Dole was expected to propose. So Morris pushed for a steep cut in the capital gains tax, and backed various "targeted" tax cuts aimed at the middle class—to provide everyone with an opportunity to attend a community college for two years, to make it easier for first-time home buyers to purchase their homes. Sometimes Morris had to push these things over the objections of other Clinton advisers, including Chief of Staff Panetta and national economic adviser Laura Tyson. They warned against getting into a "bidding war" with Dole over taxes, and undermining Clinton's newfound credentials as fiscally prudent, and insisted that ways be found to pay for each of these cuts. (They were, albeit sometimes shaky or redundant ones.) In fact, Morris wanted the President to offer to everyone two free years of community college. Panetta argued that the American people don't think anything is free, that Clinton had been saying that government should be disciplined, and that, in any event, "we can't afford it, and we couldn't deliver and we'd be seen as lying to the American people." He got the program paid for—sort of.

The division among Clinton's advisers over how far he should go to get a budget agreement, with Morris arguing he should reach a compromise with the Republicans, and his more liberal advisers—plus Vice President Al Gore and Senate Minority Leader Tom Daschle and Gephardt—restraining Clinton, continued well into 1996. (Morris had been right in pushing Clinton to adopt the concept of a balanced budget, because it kept Clinton in the argument and provided him political protection for the fight.) Clinton remained interested in getting a deal. Morris kept his back-channel relationship with Senate Majority Whip Trent Lott (a former client), and argued strenuously that a budget agreement was essential to Clinton's reelection. Stephanopoulos believed otherwise and remained on the prowl against any such deal. He and his allies believed—rightly—that such an agreement would rend the Democratic Party, and deprive Clinton of his best issues against the Republicans. But the Republicans and the White House were too far apart to reach an agreement anyway. And the Republicans' essential view was that they shouldn't do anything that would help Clinton—but this was to change.

The division among the President's advisers over budget tactics spilled over into other arguments that were important to the election effort, such as how the President should address the issue of the economy. This, too, was rooted in the dueling pollsters' assessments—in this instance of who were the swing voters in the election.

Greenberg argued that the blue-collar, lower-middle-class voters, who had turned the Democrats out of Congress in 1994, had to be won back, and therefore, the President must acknowledge that though the economy had improved not everyone was enjoying the benefits. Clinton was particularly vulnerable, it was argued, because in 1992 he had promised the middle class a tax cut and hadn't delivered. Therefore, Clinton must speak to the anger of the middle class, especially now that Patrick Buchanan's campaign had demonstrated widespread upset over the recent wave of corporate downsizing and gaping disparities between executives' and average employees' pay.

The more people thought the economy was in good shape the more likely they were to vote for Clinton, Greenberg agreed, but he pointed out that only half the electorate thought the economy was in good shape, and half of those who thought the economy was in good shape didn't think their own situation was good. Greenberg argued that Clinton's message should be about people's standard of living. Greenberg said, "If your economic argument is this is the best economy in thirty years, you're going to lose ground in important swing sectors in the electorate." (Clinton, in his State of the Union address, said, "Our economy is the healthiest it has been in three decades.") Greenberg continued, "An overwhelming majority doesn't believe it's the best economy in thirty years; they believe that there are more jobs around but living standards have not gone up." The worry, Greenberg said, was that Clinton could be "George Bushed—people think you don't understand reality."

In early March, the Democrats were ten points lower than the Republicans on the question of whom do you trust to handle the economy—despite the period of sustained recovery. (At least, they used to be twenty points down.)

Morris and Penn argued that the swing group, the target, was suburban voters who would be moved by "values" issues. They said that it was a bad idea for the President to talk negatively about the economy, which would suggest that he should have done more on the economic front, or that he favored greater government interference in the economy.

In December of 1995, Labor Secretary Robert Reich had begun addressing what he termed "economic anxiety" with a series of speeches calling for corporate reform—making companies more accountable to their workers. Reich saw his role as being the populist in the administration, to speak to the concerns of blue-collar workers. Among his ideas was one to grant tax breaks to corporations that offered certain benefits to their employees—job training, health coverage, pension plans. A nervous White House removed specific proposals from Reich's speeches. The idea of corporate reform enjoyed some fashion in early 1996. Senator Edward Kennedy and Gephardt urged such reforms as ending the tax deductibility of the costs of mergers and acquisitions, giving favorable tax treatment for new investments that create jobs, or for sharing profits with their workers, or providing health care coverage. Reich tried to convince the White House to move in this direction, and Kennedy buttonholed Clinton about it at an event where Clinton had spoken.

George Stephanopoulos and Harold Ickes were Reichians, but Stephanopoulos was worried about anything that suggested to people that Clinton might want to *raise* taxes on anyone—in this case miscreant corporations. James Carville, who though he had no official relationship with the Clinton White House was still a voice in its deliberations and enjoyed Clinton's favor, also urged that Clinton adopt Reich's approach. Treasury Secretary Robert Rubin, who commanded great respect within the Clinton administration, and whose constituency was Wall Street, was opposed, arguing that companies would feel that they were being criticized even when they were being responsible. Rubin hated the term "corporate responsibility." Rubin and Reich were friends, and this was a principled disagreement. Though the corporate responsibility movement began before Buchanan had begun to take hold in the primaries, Democratic advocates of corporate reform argued that unless they took the subject on, "Buchananism" was going to grow.

Laura Tyson, the head of the National Economic Council, though personally closer to Reich than to Rubin, was sufficiently concerned about the open fighting over corporate reform, especially when the President was about to go another major round with Congress on the budget, and about the implications of some of Reich's suggestions, that she went to the President. She thought that some of Reich's suggestions weren't thought through. (If you give a company a tax break because it is doing good things for its workers, do you, in hard times, take the tax deduction away because it can't finance such efforts?) Tyson warned the President of forthcoming news stories about the fight and urged him to decide what to do about the issue.

Clinton, typically, went back and forth, saying in an interview with the *Los Angeles Times* in early March that he had "encouraged" Reich. But he was actually working his way through the issue, in his speeches. Economic populism was a tricky matter—it had a dark side, which was apparent in Buchanan's campaign—and it wasn't suited to Clinton's style. He decided to talk in a modified way about "corporate citizenship," which still left Rubin unhappy. Vice President Gore, a continuing major influence in the Clinton White House and looking to his own political future, pushed for the President to talk about a "family-friendly workplace," and a more flexible family-leave policy, and to "jawbone" companies about their policies toward workers. The first part of Gore's strategy ultimately prevailed—for a while.

The argument over corporate reform was also an argument over whether the President should stress economic or social issues. A White House official, one of the centrists, told me in late February, "Buchanan, Reich, and Gephardt say we need a whole new agenda about workers being laid off and stagnant wages. It's floating out there that we're dissing the economic issues as opposed to the values issues, but we don't buy the Gephardt-Reich agenda right now." He argued that Clinton was getting at the economic issue by backing an increase in the minimum wage (as he hadn't in his first two years in office), an expansion of health care coverage (through the bill sponsored by Kennedy and Nancy Kassebaum, Republican of Kansas, to let workers keep their health coverage if they changed jobs and provide a limited amount of protection for those with pre-existing conditions), and an increase in college loans. It was an argument over how much emphasis should be given to shoring up the support of "the base" of the Party—liberals, labor, minorities—and how much to reaching out beyond the base to the suburban middle class, the "swing voters," over which this election would be fought. The centrist said, "No one would say we don't have to have our base. The question is how you hold the base and reach out for people beyond the base. It's a constant tension." As for Morris, his supposed ally said, "He doesn't believe shit. He looks at how you expand the base. It's not just being reelected; it's putting the President in the strongest possible position to get things done."

For a while, Clinton talked about corporate reform, and on May 16, 1996, he held a show-and-tell White House Conference on

"Corporate Citizenship." But he dropped the issue as the economy continued to improve and he chose to stress economic progress—noting also that things hadn't improved enough for some people.

Clinton was also struggling with how to talk about a balanced budget without, as Mike McCurry, the White House press secretary, put it in an interview, "sounding like an accountant." What emerged was talk out of the White House about balancing the budget "the right way." McCurry said, "A balanced budget is still an enormously popular idea." The approach Clinton was attempting, McCurry said, "to stick to fundamental principles but keep government within its means—a synthesis of the New Deal and Prop 13 [California's famous 1978 referendum limiting property taxes]—was the domestic equivalent of the end of the Cold War."

Clinton's faithfulness to fundamental principles was to be seriously questioned before the year was over.

Clinton was running on what one Democratic consultant called "a strategy of tactics." He bowed to pressures from congressional Republicans to roll back the increase in the gasoline tax enacted in 1993 as part of his successful effort to cut the deficit. George Stephanopoulos said in May, "Once it [the rollback] got traction, we weren't going to let them turn it into a tax debate."

One of Clinton's less noticed but most telling moves in his march to the center was to call for a Constitutional Amendment to protect victims' rights. Clinton had taken a principled stand against amending the Constitution for political or policy purposes, but that principle gave way to the exigencies, as he saw them, of getting reelected. The origin of the proposal was typical of the Morris era at the White House: it was imposed on the "substance people" by the "political people."

It wasn't new that campaigns determine policies—that politicians are ready to suspend their beliefs or policy positions in the name of electoral success. When belief collides with public opinion, belief often goes. Ronald Reagan allowed a bill requiring companies to give sixty days' notice before shutting down a plant to become law in 1988, something he never would have done but for George Bush's asking for help. Dole, an apostle of reducing the deficit, wouldn't have considered a large tax cut in 1996 but for his advisers' mistaken belief that it would be quite popular. But Clinton's readiness to shape policies for the sake of electoral success was of an unusual order.

Clinton enjoyed the spectacle as the Republicans fought among themselves for the Presidential nomination, and spent their federal campaign funds. While Bob Dole and the other Republican contestants were slugging it out in Iowa and New Hampshire, Clinton romped in both states, putting in appearances while having no opposition for the nomination. (Ickes, who had strong lines to the liberal community, had successfully discouraged would-be challengers.) Money was spent on ads for Clinton's reelection as early as the spring of 1995 (on crime); Clinton aides would argue to the end of time whether those ads—which were urged upon the President by Morris—made much difference. The ads were decided on in the Wednesday night meetings. (Some Clinton advisers were so rude as to point out that Morris and his colleagues earned fees from making the ads and buying time for them.)

Stephanopoulos said early in 1996, "It's an odd period. We're trying to preempt every possible issue." He continued, "We don't know whether Dole will ever get it together, but we say he might— that's the way the Clinton culture is. We fight every day. We don't take anything for granted."

Much was made in the press of the "rapid response team," headed by Stephanopoulos and Gene Sperling, an economic aide who would stay up all night to get the right numbers or policy arguments. The idea was to slam back at Dole, or at something critical said by a Dole surrogate, within the same news cycle. The atmosphere within the White House was wired, aides running around to each others' offices to decide on the next shot.

It was government by Nintendo.

And the White House staff—not to mention the President and his wife—were keenly aware that one very large matter, the independent counsel's proceedings on Whitewater, was out of their hands. They were much more worried than they let on in public. One sign was the White House's deliberate efforts to smear the independent counsel, Kenneth Starr. When Starr won convictions of James and Susan McDougal, partners of the Clintons in the Whitewater venture, and Jim Guy Tucker, the governor of Arkansas, on another matter involving McDougal's Madison Guaranty, in late May, the Clintons were more shaken than the public was told. They counted on one thing: that the closer the election got, the less likely Starr was to take some dramatic action before then.

Republicans spread rumors that Mrs. Clinton and others close to the President were about to be indicted—they named names and dates—but this turned out to be wishful thinking and mischievous disinformation.

Predictably, Clinton combined the strategies of his centrists and his liberals by both talking "values" and stressing the issues that came out of the budget fight—Medicare, Medicaid, education, and the environment. Clinton's election strategy, as described by one senior official, was: "Don't give them an opening on values, keep the recovery going, answer every attack, keep Clinton optimistic and looking to the future. Draw a comparison to Dole as mean and the past." He said that, as in the 1992 campaign, Clinton was running on "Change versus the status quo" (the first line in the famous war room dictum, taking precedence over "The economy, stupid")—and he added, "but we have to make Dole the status quo."

The House Republicans, too, were in a quandary. Having overinterpreted their 1994 mandate, they were on the defensive by 1996. They now had a new respect for Clinton's political skills, which they had laughed off only a year before. They knew that they didn't have the option of shutting down the government again. Their discipline wasn't what it had been in early 1995, principally but not only because moderate Republicans were increasingly going their own way.

The cohesion of the Republican Conference (the full caucus of

House Republicans) had broken down further after the second shutdown was ended in early January. The people back home were raising the matter of the shutdowns, saying that they "just didn't look right." Republican members had openly told Gingrich that he should be less visible and less talkative. He had embarrassed them too many times, and he hadn't worn at all well with the American people. One House Republican told me, "In discussions, people used the analogy of Hillary Clinton after the health care debate. I haven't heard anyone say that to Newt directly, but we talk about it privately." The "extremism" attributed to the Republican Congress was essentially laid at Gingrich's feet even though he was less ideological than his fellow Republican leaders. Gingrich himself came to understand that he had tried to do too much too quickly.

From the outset of 1996, there was also tension within the House Republican Conference between the goals of helping Dole, their presumed nominee, on the grounds that that might help the House Republicans, and of going their own way, on the grounds that that would help them more. But if they tried to help themselves by passing more pragmatic legislation that might be signed into law, that could help Clinton. Dole didn't seem a very promising candidate, and fear that he might pull them down with him developed early in the year. John Boehner, the Conference chairman, was a leader of the "throw Dole over the side" school.

Gingrich was caught in the middle of this argument. Despite their patchy relationship the year before—Dole broke openly with Gingrich on the government shutdowns—Gingrich supported Dole, not so much out of affection for him but because, a close associate said, "Newt's terrified of Forbes and Buchanan. He doesn't think they can unite the Party." This person added, "Newt doesn't care that much who's President; he's most concerned with holding the Party together in order to protect its congressional seats."

Gingrich had returned from the Christmas holiday break, after meetings in Tampa and Atlanta with gurus and staff advisers, with the idea that he should be less of a legislative tactician—leaving that to Majority Leader Armey—and more of a grand strategist for the election. This sat well with Gingrich's fellow congressional Republicans, who felt that legislative strategy wasn't his forte. But they believed—correctly as it turned out—that Gingrich wouldn't hand over the reins as much as he was vowing he would. (They had also concluded, from the budget talks, that Gingrich was a terrible negotiator—a pushover for Clinton.) A Gingrich aide said, "Our first priority is to retain control of the House. The second is to elect a Republican President so that we stop getting blocked in everything we do." In February, Republican leaders held two retreats at the Library of Congress, in which they discussed strategies but came to no agreement. Boehner said afterward, "Some members were concerned with how do you deal with the fact that Clinton is going to say we've done nothing."

The Republicans had a lot to worry about at that point. A key strategist said urgently in early March, "We're at our lowest ebb right now. Our messages are very confused. Our contenders for the nomination are sending totally different messages. Survey data we just got puts us ten points behind right now on the generic question of whom would you vote for today for the House of Representatives—a Democrat or a Republican." Richard Wirthlin, a Republican pollster, had just conducted a poll for the Republican National Committee that asked, Who has more common sense? The Democrats won by six points. Another Wirthlin poll measured the relative popularity of well-known figures: Gingrich ranked close to the bottom, just above Louis Farrakhan, Prince Charles, and Rush Limbaugh, and just below G. Gordon Liddy. Colin Powell was on top by far.

The Republicans' search for their identity was apparent in the primaries, where there was virtually no talk about the Contract with America. But no substitute had come along.

Though Dole didn't officially wrap up the nomination until late March, it was a foregone conclusion by late February, after the Arizona primary, which Forbes won, followed by Dole and then Buchanan. The Republicans' panic over Buchanan ceased after he came in third there, despite (or because of) his dressing up in black cowboy hat and boots, playing gunslinger at the O.K. Corral.

That Dole was a weak candidate should not have come as a surprise. He had run on the basis of primogeniture ("It's my turn"). His mind was a tactical one—the tactics of the parliamentarian—not that of a national leader. He didn't think big issues and he had trouble articulating what he did think.

People often asked why "the Republicans" didn't put up a stronger field, but there is no such thing as a Republican Party for the purpose of nominating a candidate (no Democratic Party, either). All the parties do is set the rules. The candidates are self-starters who join the race for various reasons: because they actually want to be President, to "test the waters," to get attention to their ideas, to get attention to themselves. Having the experience or the qualifications—temperamental, political, judgmental, moral—to be President has little to do with campaigning, and the public doesn't always demand these things. As was the case with the Democrats who thought that George Bush couldn't be defeated in 1992, several major Republicans sat out 1996. Some thought, whatever Clinton's problems, it was tough to beat an incumbent President. Others stayed out because they couldn't accept the rigors of fundraising or the loss of—and invasion of—their personal lives. The last time "the parties"—that is, powerful brokers—played a dominant role in choosing candidates was the Democrats' selection of Hubert Humphrey, in 1968, and the Democratic nominating system was then reformed to leave it up to the participants in primaries and caucuses. Self-selection became the norm. The Republican nominating system evolved similarly.

Our election system is more of a crapshoot than we like to think.

Though the concept of "coattails" is quite overdone, there was little question that how Clinton and Dole fared would affect the all-important struggle for realignment. For the Republicans, the heart of the matter was to produce the energy and motivation that would get enough people to the polls to hold on to the House. In 1994, a large part of the Democratic base—labor, women, and blacks—had stayed home because they were fed up with Clinton, felt he didn't stand for anything, and that the election wouldn't make any difference. The 104th Congress taught them otherwise.

But there was a question about Clinton's enthusiasm for the cause of the Democrats' winning back the House. In an interview early in the year, Stephanopoulos argued that "the best thing we can do for the House is to have the President win by a large margin." He cited an analysis by a Democratic elections expert that for every point over fifty-one percent the President won, the Democrats would pick up ten House seats. The House Democrats, for their part, were uncertain about Clinton's concern for them. He had, after all, gone the way of "triangulation." And in January, Clinton had told the *Washington Post*, "The American people don't think it's the President's business to tell them what ought to happen in the congressional elections." The remark caused a bit of a stir on Capitol Hill—"I'm getting used to this," a Democratic House member said wearily. But Clinton had a point that was little understood at the time. Focus-group polls were telling him—and every batting of an eye on Clinton's part, it seemed, was determined by polls—that the public didn't want the politicians to be "political," or "partisan."

Chapter Seven

ENDANGERED

RANDY TATE, a thirty-year-old freshman Republican from just south of Seattle, was considered by both Democrats and Republicans to be one of the most vulnerable House Republicans. When he came to Congress in 1995, Tate was the youngest of the freshmen, and was shortly brought into the inner circle by being made one of Newt Gingrich's freshman advisers and a deputy whip. Tate had been a supporter of Pat Robertson in 1988, and was strongly backed by the Christian Coalition in his 1994 campaign and had its backing again in 1996. He was quite aware that he was in for a tough fight for reelection.

Once in Washington, D.C., he was a leader of a freshman effort to require a three-fifths vote to raise taxes as part of a Constitutional Amendment requiring a balanced budget—but this went too far for Gingrich and others and was considered a sure route to defeat for the Amendment itself, so it failed. (But Grover Norquist worked out a compromise.) Tate led the march of the freshmen over to the Senate to bring pressure on that chamber to pass the Balanced Budget Amendment (which failed by one vote). Tate received some unwitting (according to him) fame shortly after he arrived in Washington, when Tom DeLay, eager to cash in on the Republicans' new majoritydom, wrote to the PACs that had contributed to Tate's opponent and strongly suggested that they now contribute to Tate. And though he had run against "the old ways" of doing business in Washington, Tate became the seventh-highest freshman recipient of PAC money in the first six months of 1995.

———

Tate was one of three House Republicans I chose to follow in 1996, to watch how they handled the Gingrich factor, to see how they tried to get reelected and what they were up against, and what the issues were in these congressional races. In a complete turnaround from the 1994 election and the Contract, the National Republican Congressional Committee had urged its candidates to run on local issues. All three of the candidates I followed—the others were Greg Ganske, a freshman from Des Moines, and Peter Torkildsen, a sophomore from the Massachusetts North Shore—were on the lists provided by the House Democratic and Republican campaign committees of the most endangered Republicans. The criteria used by both sides were the margin of victory in 1994, the political nature of the district, the strength of the probable opponent, and the incumbent's performance once elected—which included the degree of support for the "revolution," but went beyond their voting record. (A few turned out to be oddballs even by congressional standards.) Seventy of the original seventy-three freshmen were running for reelection. (One ran for the Senate, and two had to retire because of personal problems.) Since so many of the freshmen elected in 1994 came in on an anti-Clinton, anti–big government tide, and had won narrowly, and now that "the Gingrich Congress" was unpopular with the public, a large number of them were seen by the Democrats and their allied groups as ripe for the picking. But in all the attention to the freshmen, people overlooked the fact that several of the forty-eight Republican sophomores elected in 1992 had also won by narrow margins, and might also be vulnerable. The two parties' lists of the endangered were remarkably similar. Tate was high on both of them. I deliberately selected people from different parts of the country, who had sought different degrees of separation from Gingrich.

Tate, a slight, dark-haired but prematurely bald man with pale skin and large blue eyes and an earnest mien, was considered endangered because he had won narrowly (with 51.8 percent of the vote) in 1994, in a district almost evenly divided between Democrats and

Republicans, and because of his close association with Gingrich. He had been targeted by a coalition of groups that were trying to help the Democrats take back the House. The AFL-CIO, which in March, 1996, had announced a $35 million effort for the 1996 elections, targeting seventy-five House races, had begun to run ads against Tate the previous August, but when I saw him in March, Tate felt that the union effort had "made little dent" because it started so early. Environmental groups, in particular the Sierra Club, and the Association of Trial Lawyers of America were also trying to defeat Tate.

David Rehr, of the Beer Wholesalers, said, "Every group trying to take back the House for the Democrats is basically against Randy." Of course, Tate received substantial aid from the groups trying to help the Republicans hold onto the House. The N.R.A. had already "maxed out" in its contributions to Tate. The National Federation of Independent Business had put him on its list of ten Republicans for whom it would make an extra effort. Tate refused to take funds from the alcohol industry—but Rehr found other ways to help him. The National Republican Congressional Committee would give the full $60,000 allowed for a "coordinated campaign" plus the $5,000 for the primary and $5,000 in the general election allowed under the law. Tom DeLay had already been to Tate's district, had written letters to other members asking them to help him, was making calls to major donors. (DeLay, once again, was building up his own PAC, Americans for a Republican Majority, which, like other PACs, could give candidates $10,000.)

Even though he had already raised far more money than his Democratic opponent, a fellow former state legislator named Adam Smith, Tate was concerned about the "infrastructure" that labor could provide Smith—volunteers to talk him up and get people to the polls. Otherwise, he said, he was confident that he could beat Smith "hands down."

For all his assertions that the labor ads had begun too soon, Tate was agitating within the Republican Party for more ads. But Party chairman Haley Barbour had a plan to save most of the spending for ads until closer to the election. "We've tried to educate our fellow Republicans in the Conference. I've spoken to the leadership a couple of times—to make them aware of what's going on," Tate said. Gingrich got very agitated about the AFL-CIO announcement—even some Democrats thought it was less than wise to make such a big deal of it—and asked Bill Paxon, chairman of the N.R.C.C., to keep him abreast of what labor and the other Democratic-oriented groups were doing. The Republican leaders instantly embarked upon a campaign of attacking the "labor bosses."

To get the support of the conservative groups in Washington, Tate put together a presentation that he made to them, and he appeared before Grover Norquist's Wednesday morning group.

Tate believed that his close association with Gingrich would be an asset in his campaign. "Except for my opponent, who raises his name all the time," Tate said, "there is very little that comes up from my constituents."

Tate felt that he could hold on to his seat because the blue-collar workers at Boeing and elsewhere in his district liked his views on the social issues (he was against abortion and for "pro-family" policies) and on gun control (he was against). "For the Plumbers and Fitters, the right to keep and bear arms is their key issue," Tate said. He likes to point out that his father was a union member for twenty-two years. "Labor people won't walk in lockstep with the AFL-CIO. They're trying to create a groundswell that is not there."

Greg Ganske, a reconstructive and cosmetic surgeon, took his first shot at politics in 1994, running against a thirty-six-year Democratic incumbent, Neal Smith, by driving around in a 1958 (the year Smith had first come to Congress) DeSoto—Gingrich's idea, Ganske proudly told people. (Ganske's office in the Longworth Building is decorated with medical certificates.) A man of some means, Ganske spent over $600,000 of his own money for his 1994 campaign.

Sensing danger, in the fall of 1995 Ganske's staff started putting together a "Ganske Accomplishment Book," of which one theme was to be, according to a staff memo, "Not a Newtoid." Ganske was to run, the memo said, as an "independent voice for Iowa"—Iowans pride themselves on their independence, and expect it in their politicians. Ganske had in fact taken a few positions against Gingrich and the House leadership in 1995, leading a group of over a hundred Republicans who pressed—unsuccessfully—for a scaling back of the earnings level at which families would receive a proposed $500-a-child tax credit, and he and others who represented rural areas held out their vote for the Medicare bill until Gingrich offered a deal that changed the formula to provide such areas more help. (Ganske's district encompassed Des Moines and some rural areas.)

Ganske, forty-seven, a man of medium build and short, brown, wavy hair parted off center, seemed like an amateur at politics, which he was. But he had a determined streak, and a stubborn and also calculating nature that put him at the center of some key issues and allowed him to declare himself "Iowa independent." Not long on humor, Ganske seemed too tightly wound to be effective in the cloakrooms, but he did manage to establish himself as a force among the freshmen.

Targeted by the AFL-CIO, which ran ads against him starting in August, 1995, attacking him for wanting to cut Medicare and Medicaid and charging that he "went along with Newt Gingrich and shut down the government," Ganske replied early, in February, with ads he financed saying that he had voted to increase spending on Medicare. (This argument went on in virtually all of the races the AFL-CIO entered.) Ganske's ad also said that he voted to "solve the problem" of the shutdown. (He did vote against a plan to partially reopen the government, saying that it was "silly." This vote could be interpreted in two different ways.)

In July, 1995, Gingrich appeared in Iowa at a fundraiser for Ganske, but when I asked Ganske in March of 1996 whether he planned to invite Gingrich into his district again, he replied, obliquely, "I think we've had so much national politics in Iowa, what with the Presidential caucuses, that I'm not planning to have many national figures come in." But then he added, "If I could get George Bush to come to a fundraiser, that would be great."

Peter Torkildsen, thirty-eight and youthful-looking, chunky, with blue eyes and straight brown hair, was a mild-speaking moderate Republican who had set more distance from Gingrich than most others in his Party. Yet, as he put it with some frustration at lunch in the House Members Dining Room in late March, "I'm still being accused of being a rubber stamp for Gingrich." He was perturbed that the House leadership had decided to bring up the bill that afternoon repealing the assault weapons ban. He was planning to vote against repeal.

He had won his seat in 1992 by defeating a Democrat who had been indicted for tax evasion, influence peddling, and bribery. In 1994 the Democrats had targeted him, on the theory that his was essentially a Democratic district, but Torkildsen defeated his opponent, John Tierney, 51 percent to 47 percent (an independent got two percent), by talking of his own efforts for congressional reform and charging that Tierney was "way too liberal for his district." Now Tierney was taking him on again.

In the 104th Congress, Torkildsen had opposed a strict welfare bill and differed from the majority of Republicans on some environmental issues, but now he was being tagged as anti-environmental; he had opposed the Medicare bill but was being tagged as anti-Medicare because he supported the final budget bill that contained the Medicare proposal he had first opposed.

Asked how he was handling all this, Torkildsen replied, "Through emphasizing those issues I voted against the leadership on—issues that any rational person could see that I opposed it." As for the assault weapons ban, Torkildsen had once voted for it and once against it. At lunch he said that he thought his district was "overwhelmingly against repeal."

Labor had begun to run radio ads against Torkildsen in 1995 (the Boston television market was too expensive). The issues were the same as those used against other Republicans—Medicare, the government shutdowns. No quarter was given for having stood apart from Gingrich on some issues.

The difficulty of his position was increasingly apparent. "I've been very out front," he said. "I'm not saying this shows I'm voting against Gingrich. I'm letting the issue stand out there for people to see. It probably does help me politically, but it doesn't help the Party for me to be outspokenly against the leadership."

Torkildsen tried to deal with his problem by stressing his work on local issues—getting contracts and government grants for his district, helping museums in the historic towns of Salem and Peabody.

"Newt campaigned for me in the '94 election," Torkildsen said, "but now I think any money he could raise for me would be overshadowed by being associated with any position he took." A fundraising mailing sent out to registered Republicans in the fall on Torkildsen's behalf and signed by Gingrich actually lost money. "It was the worst prospecting piece I've ever done," Torkildsen said.

Along with other Republican moderates, Torkildsen complained to the leadership about "what seemed like an unending series of votes on abortion." (Torkildsen took a middling position—for *Roe* v. *Wade* but against public financing of abortions.) He was against the ban on partial birth abortions, on the grounds that "I don't think a Member of Congress is in a position to tell physicians what they should do."

Torkildsen was hoping that the leadership wouldn't bring any more environmental bills to the House floor. "You outsmart yourself by thinking that a compromise environmental bill would be any more welcomed by the environmentalists," Torkildsen said. He added, "It's too late, but I would hope they'd stay away from abortion."

Chapter Eight

THE OPPOSITION

ARRAYED AGAINST the rightward groups was a collection of equally determined Democratic-oriented groups intent on regaining Democratic control of the House. Like the groups on the right, these people all knew each other. They were liberal, and they were out to make 1994 an aberration. Theirs were the voters who, unhappy with Clinton and thinking it mattered little who controlled the Congress, hadn't turned out then. The 1994 election was an embarrassment for these groups, so they were also working to restore their own political strength as well as to elect a more sympathetic Congress. Like their counterparts, they understood that this was about more than 1996: that if the Republicans retained control of the House they would probably be dug in for some time and have a stranglehold on domestic policy. A realignment will have taken place. Making the same calculations as their counterparts, many of them believed also that who controlled the House was more important than who controlled the White House.

This was particularly true of organized labor, which was making an unprecedented effort to elect a more friendly Congress. Its own political strength had been on the decline for more than a decade. In undertaking its special effort to dislodge the Republicans, labor wasn't so much "throwing its weight around," as the Republicans heatedly charged, as it was trying to gain weight. (Much of its trouble stemmed from its opposition to the North American Free Trade agreement, or NAFTA, in 1993, which Clinton championed.

Not only was its opposition futile, but the battle caused many labor members to stay home or vote Republican in November, 1994.) Thus, at a special convention in Washington in late March, the AFL-CIO ratified the decision already taken by its leadership to spend $35 million on a special effort to dislodge the Republicans. In a fiery speech, the labor federation's new president, John Sweeney, elected the previous October as an insurgency candidate who vowed to reverse the decline in labor's political power, singled out Randy Tate and Greg Ganske, along with the House Republican leaders, as special targets of the effort.

When we talked a few days after his speech, Sweeney, a balding, white-haired, pink-complexioned man with blue, watery eyes and pronounced eyebrows, who was wearing red-and-blue suspenders, made it clear that the labor effort had a larger purpose than the immediate battle at hand. He said, "There's an opportunity for labor unions to organize to play a stronger and effective role in political battles." He added, "Our declining membership and less effective voice in politics—that was what my campaign was all about and our political activity is all about." He added, "We hope to be active in every single congressional district in the country, and we want to be more effective in politics for a long time to come."

When I asked him why he had singled out Tate and Ganske for mention in his speech, Sweeney replied, "Because they're among the most outspoken on anti-labor issues"—an observation that was debatable in Ganske's case. (He insisted that Ganske had supported a tax cut for the very wealthy. Ganske had tried to lower the income cap, but did vote for the final bill.) The more I spoke with union leaders, the clearer it became that, in their own version of Willy Sutton (who said he robbed banks because that's where the money was), they were choosing to fight in the districts with large numbers of union members. Both Tate and Ganske represented such districts.

Both Sweeney and Steve Rosenthal, the AFL-CIO's political director, were defensive about some points. They were at pains to say that the $35 million—or, Sweeney said, more if possible—they planned to spend on the fight for Congress amounted to only fifteen cents per member per month, and that money would come out of existing treasuries, not out of new dues assessments. Republicans argued, nonetheless, that labor was spending members' dues for a partisan campaign, which is illegal. Therefore, despite Sweeney's tip-off speech, and despite the obvious, union officials, including Sweeney, were at pains to say that they were simply engaged in an "educational" activity, or "issue advocacy." Because of the laws, they denied that they had "targeted" certain Republican candidates.

Corporations and labor unions can have PACs, which are restricted in their contributions—the AFL-CIO has its PAC, the Committee on Political Education (COPE), and the affiliates have their own PACs—but, under the law, they cannot use treasury money or union dues to make contributions or expenditures "in connection with" a federal election. In 1986, the Supreme Court defined "in connection with" as use of the words "vote for" or "vote against," "support" or "oppose." Thus, the Court ostensibly drew a line between candidate advocacy and issue discussion, but the line was a nonsense, as 1996 was to prove. Groups on both sides interpreted the decision as allowing them to do virtually anything as long as they didn't use those particular words. In June, 1996, the Supreme Court opened up another vast canyon by ruling that political parties could spend as much as they wanted on behalf of their candidates as long as they did this "independently" of the candidates' campaigns—an absurd distinction that added to the ways in which the campaign finance laws were rendered meaningless in 1996.

Labor ads against Tate and Ganske and others named their names, showed their pictures, and accused them of being on the wrong side of certain key issues, such as "cutting" Medicare or eviscerating the environmental laws or voting ("with Newt Gingrich") to shut down the government. (One ad particularly distorted the facts by implying that the Republican malefactors had voted for a pay raise for Members of Congress—which occurred before the freshmen were elected.)

Sitting in his office on the sixth floor of the AFL-CIO building on 16th Street, political director Steve Rosenthal said that labor, too, saw the House elections as the most important of 1996—more important than the contest for the Presidency.

Rosenthal, forty-three, had curly dark hair speckled with white, and large brown eyes, a thick beard, a barrel chest, a deep voice, and an easy manner. He looked more like a friendly revolutionary— with most of the revolution in his past—or a college professor than a stereotypical "labor boss." This former union organizer and political strategist, who most recently worked in the Labor Department under Robert Reich, was an amiable zealot. His mission was simple: take back the House for the Democrats. He had helped engineer Sweeney's successful race for president of the AFL-CIO, and since then he and Sweeney had been out to wreak vengeance on the 104th Congress.

But Rosenthal had to be careful. Not only were there the legal restrictions on unions' using dues in advocating the election or defeat of a candidate, but another legal prohibition was that if a group makes expenditures, like the union "issue advocacy" expenditures, or an "independent" expenditure, to help specific candidates, even if it doesn't use the forbidden words, but coordinates its efforts with the candidate, or a party committee, that amounts to a contribution to a candidate. Moreover, labor's own polls of its members showed that, by large margins, they didn't want to be told whom to vote for. Labor was also fighting its members' increasing cynicism that any elected official could get done what they wanted done.

With the legal restrictions in mind, the labor federation's officials tried (not always successfully) to avoid using the word "target" when speaking of its seventy-five targeted races—forty-five involving Republican incumbents and the rest Democrats it wanted to protect or open Democratic seats. Rosenthal also said that "there will be no list." Rosenthal insisted that labor's effort was "not candidate driven, it's issue driven." But labor didn't go after every candidate who voted a certain way on a given issue. The members'

voting records were part of the equation; the potential for success—
the base of union members in a district—was another. If a Republican had voted a hundred percent against labor, Rosenthal said, but
had few union members in his or her district, "we might run some
spots," but not make a full-scale effort. Republican moderates were
considered fair game, and thus Peter Torkildsen was also a target
(the unions' euphemisms notwithstanding). Rosenthal argued that
"even the most moderate members, under Newt" had, for them,
unusually low scores on labor issues.

Rosenthal added, "We talk about it in terms of electing people
who reflect these views. This is the first time there's been a con-
certed effort by labor unions." The AFL-CIO asked the affiliates to
lend staff to it, and trained the staff. This, too, had a long-term purpose. Rosenthal said, "They will help us rebuild the infrastructure—
union councils, coordinators in the workplace." He added, "We
want to sign up a hundred to a hundred and fifty activists in each of
these seventy-five districts and use them as filters of information,
down and up. . . . We want to build up a base of union activists who
will be injected into the local debate and the national debate. If you
have a hundred to a hundred and fifty activists in every congressional district, elected officials can't ignore that."

The charge against the 104th Congress, Rosenthal said, was
"We believe that this Congress has waged the worst assault on
working families in the last seventy-five years and they have tried to
dismantle every protection that workers have had for fifty years." He
listed attempts to reduce OSHA regulations to protect workers,
efforts to change the nature of collective bargaining.

To Republican charges that forty percent of union members
had voted for Republicans in 1994, Rosenthal's response was that
that was the point of the 1996 exercise.

When I saw Rosenthal a few weeks later (on the wall behind him
was the famous, unfortunate, photograph of Bob Dole lounging in
bathing trunks in Bal Harbour, talking on a telephone), he said he
thought that the Democrats had a thirty to forty percent chance to

retake the House. "If you said at this point that the Democrats will retake the House, people would say you're crazy." He predicted (accurately, as it turned out) that for all the ruckus stirred up by the Republicans over labor's announced $35 million effort, it would be greatly outspent by the forces on the other side. I asked him how he felt about being called a "labor boss." He smiled and replied, "I prefer that to being 'irrelevant.'"

The AFL-CIO worked more closely with other groups than in the past. One was EMILY's List, which backed pro-choice Democratic women. EMILY's List, in turn, announced it would work closely with the Democratic National Committee in a joint project to mobilize women voters in five states; this number later grew to six, but the collaboration was to be less extensive or munificent than the EMILY's List people had hoped, as the contributions it expected from the D.N.C. went instead to more media advertising for the Clinton-Gore ticket. EMILY's List itself ended up working with state parties in thirty-one states. (EMILY's List made a point of raising money early so as to be able to persuade women candidates to run; the name EMILY stands for Early Money Is Like Yeast. "We make the dough rise," says Ellen Malcolm, the president of the group.) Others the AFL-CIO worked with were environmental groups such as the Sierra Club and the League of Conservation Voters; the National Abortion Rights Action League (NARAL); and the National Education Association. The AFL-CIO's training centers, used primarily to train union activists for the elections, also trained activists from the other groups.

EMILY's List, using work by pollsters Stan Greenberg and Celinda Lake, was particularly focused on getting non–college educated women to the polls. According to EMILY's List, forty-nine percent of the women who had voted Democratic in 1992 didn't bother to vote or went over to the Republicans two years later. Overall, fifty-nine percent of those who dropped out between 1992 and 1994 were women. The historic gender gap—women giving a higher percentage of their vote to the Democrats—only worked in the Democrats' favor if women voted in great numbers. There had been much talk in political circles after 1994 about "angry white men"—men who shifted to the Republicans in 1994. EMILY's List was making the point that there were angry white women as well.

Several environmental groups combined under their communal political arm, the League of Conservation Voters. The L.C.V. puts out a list of the "Dirty Dozen"—Members of Congress with the worst environmental records, as well as a scorecard. In 1996, they also mounted an "independent expenditures" effort, for the purpose of raising and spending more money than allowed for PACs under the campaign finance law. They were particularly interested in about a dozen House races—especially that of the highly controversial Helen Chenoweth, Republican of Idaho. The other major environmental group, the Sierra Club, also set out to raise unprecedented amounts, to concentrate on Republicans with poor environmental records, particularly those in races on the West Coast, where the environmental movement was especially strong. It targeted in particular Andrea Seastrand, Republican of California.

Both groups made a special effort in Washington State. Philip Clapp, of the Environmental Information Center, a legislative and political clearinghouse for environmental groups, said, "A lot of places that labor is going into have suburbs that labor doesn't get to, but environmentalists do." He listed Randy Tate's district as an example of where blue-collar workers are also environmentalists. The environmental groups met regularly to coordinate their efforts. (These groups had also gone into the Oregon special election.)

Earlier in the year, the AFL-CIO and its allied groups held two long meetings at the 16th Street headquarters to talk about who was doing what, to get a feel for the important contested districts.

The White House, in fact, put together a national steering committee consisting of representatives from the Clinton-Gore campaign, the Democratic National Committee, the AFL-CIO, the National Education Association, and EMILY's List. The group met semi-regularly at the Democratic National Committee headquarters to discuss what priority should be given which states, which of this coalition's partners were actively organizing in which states, who was doing what about direct mail or get-out-the-vote drives—a former campaign official explains, "all with a view toward accumulating enough electoral votes in November." This raises the issue of whether these groups, by coordinating their expenditures with the Clinton-Gore campaign, were in effect making illegal contributions to the campaign under the federal election law.

If a number of these activities didn't cross the line of prohibited coordinated political activity on the part of these groups, or partisan activities by people supposedly conducting nonpartisan "educational" or "issue advocacy" activities, they appear to have come at least within hailing distance of it. In fact, the interlocking nature of these groups, like that of their Republican-oriented counterparts, made a mockery of the election laws.

For example, to keep its "issue advocacy" program clean, the AFL-CIO wasn't supposed to be talking about it in any detail with the Democratic Party election committees. But it was perfectly okay for the Party committees and the labor federation to talk specifics about where labor should spend its *PAC money*. The discussant with the political committees for the PAC and the non-discussant for the "issue advocacy" effort could be the same person—and often was. A Democratic Party operative said, "The thing that made it easy for resources to be placed well was there were a lot of discussions with organized labor relative to targeting PAC money and those targets turn out to be the same that they would make other efforts in." So Steve Rosenthal talked to Democratic Congressional Campaign Committee officials about the status of races of interest to the AFL-CIO's PAC, COPE, which as political director he was also in charge of, at the same time that he was chief strategist for labor's "issue advocacy" effort. (Rosenthal did insist that the ads themselves were drawn up and placed by a separate office in the 16th Street building.) The same thing went on all over town, with both parties' political committees. Matt Angle, the executive director of the D.C.C.C., said, "One of the jobs of the political committees is to communicate with the PAC community and give them our views on the competitive races." There didn't have to be conversations about how much to spend on ads in a specific place. "To tell you the truth," the Democratic operative said, "it didn't have to get to that level to get the desired effect. The point is we all knew who the vulnerable Republicans were—and who the vulnerable Democrats were." He continued, "We can say let's all get together and pool our resources and we can say which districts we have a shot at. We can say to labor, 'We hope you'll contribute to X,' but we can't enter into a formal arrangement on this, and they can't say they gave someone the money because we asked them to."

These distinctions, the operative admitted, "defy human nature."

At the center of the network was a man sitting in House Minority Leader Dick Gephardt's Capitol Hill offices. Tom O'Donnell, Gephardt's chief of staff, a rangy, bearded, forty-five-year-old sandy-haired man and a pol to his toes, kept in touch with all of these groups. O'Donnell worked very closely with the D.C.C.C., regularly going to meetings at its offices near Capitol Hill. He also talked frequently with Steve Rosenthal as well as the political directors of individual unions. And he was in contact with the environmental groups active in the election and EMILY's List. Both O'Donnell and labor, as well as others, relied heavily for their targeting decisions on Mark Gersh, the Washington director of the National Committee for an Effective Congress, a group that does demographic research for Democrats and works for (and makes contributions toward) the election of liberal and moderate Democrats. The N.C.E.C. also conducted polls in some thirty to forty districts, to assess Republicans' vulnerability. And O'Donnell was in regular touch with George Stephanopoulos, a former colleague in Gephardt's office, and Doug Sosnik, the White House political director. Thus O'Donnell wove a tight web of interconnections and shared information. There were, of course, tremendous stakes in this election for Gephardt, who stood to be Speaker if the Democrats took back the House.

———

In this context, the terms "independent expenditure" and "issue advocacy" advertising have no meaning. The search on both sides, and by outside reform groups, for literal violations of the law missed the point of what was going on. Washington sometimes gets bogged down in literalism, looking for a smoking gun in a room full of smoke. It defies common sense, and available evidence, to suggest that, one way or another, like-minded groups on both sides weren't coordinating their activities, or that the outside groups and the political parties didn't act in concert with each other. Even if they didn't have technically forbidden meetings or conversations—and the representatives of some groups, on both sides, were at pains to insist that they didn't—those particular forms of collaboration weren't necessary, and it's not even clear what's technically forbidden.

On each side, the various participants swim in the same pond of pollsters, ad-makers, and consultants. They all had access to the same information—public (newsletters) or private. Though a group carrying out an "independent campaign" isn't supposed to coordinate timing of ads with the candidate's organization—"You go this week and we'll go the next"—the media buyers could simply check time availabilities in the markets where the ads would be placed to find out who's doing what. Vin Weber, the Republican former Member of Congress and now a consultant-activist, says, "The kind of wall of separation that is envisioned here is not really possible in a free society."

The war was without precedent, and it was total.

Chapter Nine

FUNDRAISER

ON THE EVENING OF MAY 29TH, Grover Norquist is holding a fundraiser for Randy Tate at his red brick Victorian townhouse on Capitol Hill. About eighty people are here, most of them younger members of the conservative movement. The charge is $50 per person. Tomorrow there will be a breakfast for Tate with PACs, which will be more expensive. Several of those here work on Capitol Hill, others in pro-life organizations or in one of the conservative think tanks. The pollster Kellyanne Fitzpatrick is here. (She rents an office in Norquist's Dupont Circle domain.)

David Rehr is here, friendly and eager as ever. Though Tate refuses to take money from the alcohol industry, he has allowed Rehr to help him with personal contributions—about a thousand dollars in this election cycle (the maximum an individual can give). Someone with the Heritage Foundation says that a lot of the people here "like to drink beer and eat Chinese food and talk politics at Grover's house." He adds, "Grover is a microcosm of the conservative movement. Every battle we've been through for the last ten years, Grover's been part of. We used to be a small group of paranoid nuts. Now we're a real movement."

Norquist's house has the attributes of a postgraduate bachelor pad. His brother, now in Army Intelligence in Europe, stays there, and another friend rents space in the large quarters. The furniture is serviceable. On the mantle over the fireplace is a picture of former

Yugoslav leader Marshal Tito, with the glass cracked; a second and larger signed portrait of Tito is to the left of the mantle. ("I liberated it from the Yugoslavian foreign minister's office in what's now Macedonia, because they were about to take it down," Norquist says. "It's war booty. I was working in Albania against Tito and I crossed the border because we were smuggling money, cars, and food across the Albanian border to help the democratic Albanian forces.") Around the place are campaign buttons and posters spanning the ideological spectrum, including a framed portrait of Lenin. Bowls of lukewarm Chinese food are spread on a dining room table; beer is stashed in ice bins in the dining room; wine and liquor are available from a bar in the poster-laden kitchen.

Norquist's own, huge room is a third-floor aerie, covered wall to wall, and much of the ceiling, with posters, plaques, buttons, bumper stickers, nameplates of some of the most liberal House members, and pictures of Norquist carrying guns—an AK-47 in Afghanistan, an assault rifle in Angola. (He keeps a shotgun in a closet.) A spiral staircase in the room leads to a rooftop view of Washington. There are pictures of Norquist in Bulgaria, standing in front of a communist's car that is being burned; Norquist with Ronald Reagan; an autographed photo of Jonas Savimbi. While showing the room to me and a friend in the course of the party, Norquist pedals an Exercycle. Or he takes time out at another point during the party to talk on the phone to a radio talk show, something he does methodically to spread the message. His collection of gewgaws contains bumper stickers and posters (some of them verging on the sick joke) about Whitewater, in which Norquist has an absorbing interest.

Norquist's mind is in a constant whir, making new connections between subjects, events, and people. There remains something of the graduate student in him—he comes across as the brilliant young man, not quite a grown-up, a boy-genius who lives within his own universe, spewing creativity. His sense of humor and his charm and his zeal and imagination, and his brains, have taken him a long way. If Norquist were more like your average driven young Washingtonian—more drive than imagination and at least a little bit dour (Washington is filled with driven, humorless people)—he wouldn't be where he is in the firmament.

At a time when many House members were worried about the effect of Gingrich's unpopularity on their reelection chances, and some were deliberately setting distance from him, Randy Tate remained delighted to have Gingrich's public help, and when I saw him a few days before Norquist's party he was still excited about a visit Gingrich had paid to his district the previous weekend. "We had the biggest turnout anybody can ever remember at a political event in that county," Tate said. On Sunday, May 19th, Tate related, Gingrich had attended a $25 dessert social at 5:00 P.M. and participated in a $500 opportunity to have a donor's picture taken with Tate and Gingrich at a reception followed by dinner. Those who could make do without the photo paid $150 for dinner only. "It's typical to have two or three different things," Tate said, as he sat in his office in the Longworth House Office Building the following Friday afternoon. "That's how you can maximize your resources." Gingrich raised at least $100,000 for Tate on that visit. (Boeing, and Microsoft, which is in a neighboring district, bought tables for Tate's dinner with Gingrich.)

Tate was pleased to say when I saw him in May that as of March 30, 1996, he had raised $536,000 and still had $335,000 in the bank.

Tate was confident in other respects. "If we do all we need to do," he said, "go out and work up the grass roots, have a clearly defined message and run on issues that people think are important—balancing the budget and reduce taxes on working families and allow IRA's for first-time home buyers or a college education" (proposals Clinton, too, had made), "I'll be all right." He thought his strengths were "message, mechanics, and money," but he considered "mechanics," his grassroots campaign, "probably my biggest strength." He had volunteers willing to stand in the rain at 6:00 A.M. with yard signs to be seen by workers on their way to Boeing. Tate himself spent a great deal of time going door-to-door with leaflets, talking to voters. "Our campaigns are very labor-intensive," he said.

When Tate is asked by people in Washington State about Gingrich and the "extremist" Republican Congress, he said, "I make the point, if you want to vote against Newt Gingrich, move to Marietta, Georgia"—Gingrich's district. Tate, still enthused, said, "That fifteen hundred people at my event last weekend were there because they support our agenda, of a balanced budget, reduced taxes, and reform of Congress. The response was incredible. I can't underline that enough."

Tate was slightly cocky but not unpleasant, and there was one cautious note: "I have to be sure we focus on the right issues," Tate said. "My opponent would like to talk about Medicare cuts and tax cuts for the rich, and say that Randy Tate is a 'soldier for Newt Gingrich.' "

Tate believed that a large number of labor members were for him also, despite his championing of a piece of legislation about collective bargaining that labor particularly opposed, and despite his opposition to raising the minimum wage.

Tate admitted to being a little bit worried, but said, "I've found that if we get the message out and work the mechanics and raise enough money, I'll win."

On the day of Norquist's party for Randy Tate, I attended his usually private regular Wednesday morning meeting. About fifty people had gathered in Norquist's conference room on this rainy morning. Norquist presided, sitting at the head of a long table. The first subject he brought up was the political implications of the Whitewater convictions in Arkansas the day before—their impact on House and Senate races. Peter Roff, the political director of GOPAC, an excitable young man in shirtsleeves and suspenders, pointed out that the lieutenant governor, a Republican named Mike Huckabee, "was our Senate candidate" for the seat being vacated by Democrat David Pryor, who was retiring, and he was "odds-on to win." But, since Jim Guy Tucker, the convicted governor, had resigned, "the difficulty," Roff said, was that Huckabee might stay in the governorship and not run for the Senate, which might then deny Republicans a pickup of a Senate seat. The conservatives were also concerned about losing the lieutenant governorship. (In November, Republicans won all three offices in Arkansas.)

Norquist was interested in another aspect of the convictions. "The whole Whitewater thing now opens the possibility of further prosecutions."

"The universe of people who would open their mouth has now exploded," another man said.

Roff, of GOPAC, then spoke about the Mena Airport, a supposed Arkansas site of gun- and drug-running to and from the Nicaraguan Contras while Clinton was governor, which plays a large role in Clinton's opponents'—left and right—conspiracy theories. (Though little has been proven about the airport, the C.I.A. did tell a congressional committee that it had a presence there but said it wasn't engaged in such activities. Clinton has denied having any knowledge about what was going on there.) Roff referred to "the two kids who were killed and found by the railroad tracks because they had seen drugs being loaded and unloaded at the Mena Airport"—a story that had been circulating among Clinton opponents.

A number of people in the room were quite familiar with the Whitewater case. One speculated that Susan McDougal—a former partner in Whitewater with the Clintons who had just been convicted—would now tell Kenneth Starr, the independent counsel, some useful things. (Actually, she went to jail for refusing to do so.)

Norquist speculated that Tucker would be "pressurable, because his wife might be vulnerable to charges." (In fact, Mrs. Tucker hasn't been charged with anything.)

Roff cautioned the group, "We shouldn't get sidetracked into thinking that there is a silver bullet for us against the White House and the liberals." He added, "That may be, but that doesn't mean we should ease up on our work against the liberals."

Norquist asked, "This case does what to the Senate investigation?"

Someone replied, "It gives it a big boost."

Norquist smiled, but commented, "We don't need to talk about this too much; we need to focus on our issues. Every day that Clinton has us talking about Whitewater, we're not focusing on taxes." He joked that perhaps Clinton was deliberately diverting their attention.

Mike Hammond, who was running in a New Hampshire primary against a moderate incumbent Republican congressman, Charles Bass, addressed the group, seeking its support. Hammond argued strenuously that Bass was "a liberal."

Norquist asked, "Has Bass been bad on guns?"

"He's been bad fifty percent of the time," Hammond replied.

Norquist made a point of being willing to have people in who make primary challenges against Republicans, even if he wasn't wild about the candidate, which appeared to be the case in this instance. (Bass won the nomination and reelection.)

Norquist, working from a set agenda of people to address the group this day, asked a representative of a large corporation (who did not want to be named) what he was hearing from the corporate community about the upcoming elections.

The corporate man replied, "The mind-set is that Clinton's going to win. Corporations are in a herd instinct. They think in their heart of hearts that Dole is a war hero, but they don't think he can win." He added, "Corporations have a terrible record about House races. They're managers, not leaders."

Norquist asked, "Is Forbes showing up in people's districts? Is he doing his job?" (Steve Forbes, who by now had pulled out of the race, was going to congressional districts to campaign for candidates for the House.)

The corporate man replied that he was.

Horace Cooper, a black man in his thirties, an aide to House Majority Leader Dick Armey, talked about what was going on on Capitol Hill. He said that it looked as if the administration wasn't going to respond to a subpoena from a House committee for documents on the controversy over the firing in 1993 of all seven holdover employees in the White House travel office—with questions about Mrs. Clinton's role—and that the committee had already voted to issue a contempt citation against the White House, and the House would have to vote on it.

Norquist asked, "If you hold this vote and the Democrats vote against the contempt citation and the papers are incriminating, isn't that damning?" (The White House turned over some papers in early June; one document, on Billy Dale, the former head of the travel office, provided the tip-off that the White House Office of Personnel had requested the F.B.I. files on former employees.)

Mark Rhoades, a soft-spoken former Illinois state senator who has his own public relations firm housed in the Americans for Tax Reform complex, and does some PR for A.T.R., commented, "Clinton has moved to coopt us on various issues—same-sex marriages [Clinton said he'd back a bill pending in Congress to give states the right not to recognize such marriages], the Wisconsin welfare plan." (Clinton approved the state's stringent new plan, which would end guaranteed welfare.) Rhoades asked, "How soon can we get these poison-pill bills to him to either sign or veto?" The idea, gaining strength among Republicans, was that Congress should send Clinton some bills—on welfare, immigration, and other topics—that would force him to make difficult decisions on whether to sign.

Under questioning by Norquist, Armey's aide said, "The Democrats most want to be in session close to the election." (House Republicans had been urged by their political advisers to get home as early as they could in the fall, in order to campaign. In 1994, the Republican minority kept the Democrats in session until quite close to the November election, leaving them more exposed to their challengers.) He also said that now that Trent Lott had taken over from Dole as Senate majority leader, "You're probably going to see a more outspoken leader in Mr. Lott." But, he lamented, "not a different outcome, because you still have seven Republicans who are moderates." So, he added, "on issues in the vanguard of the revolution" the outcome would still be uncertain.

Norquist asked, referring to such moderates as William Cohen, of Maine, Nancy Kassebaum, of Kansas, and Mark Hatfield, of Oregon, who had announced their retirements, "Win, lose, or draw on the Presidency, are we not better off in the Senate with the change of leadership and the retirees?"

Peter Roff, the GOPAC man, volunteered that "we're taking over South Carolina." Norquist asked eagerly, "Do we have a shot at the North Carolina state senate?" Roff said they did. (In November, the Republicans failed to take over the North or South Carolina state senates.)

Someone announced a fundraiser for James Miller, a conservative who was challenging the more moderate incumbent Republican Virginia senator, John Warner. "So we can finally have a Republican from Virginia in the Senate," he added, to cheers and applause.

Norquist reminded the group about his fundraiser tonight for Randy Tate.

Jim Lucier, who handles several areas for Americans for Tax Reform, including telecommunications, encryption, and privatizing Social Security, and whose father had been an important adviser to Jesse Helms, spoke about "the Japanese revolution"—a "pro–free market force in Japan trying to overthrow the establishment," which, he explained, was comprised of "the bureaucratic, corporate anti-market forces that have controlled the governing party." A man of Japanese heritage, Hiroshi Takei, who is with the Asia Forum Japan, a think tank trying to build an American-style party in Japan, was to address the group. Lucier explained that the Asia Forum Japan is for tax limitation and deregulation in Japan. (Mark Rhoades explained to me later that Norquist's group brings in people from all over the world who want to start an anti-tax movement.)

Norquist reported on moves in state legislatures to require a two-thirds vote to raise taxes. Roff talked some more about state legislatures "we might take over."

———

Then the group got into a discussion of an issue, important to many people on the right but on which they are philosophically divided. A woman from Capitol Hill spoke in favor of a tax credit for gifts to charities, a proposal favored among some conservatives as an alternative to government programs. (This direct reduction from the taxes one owes would be a greater benefit than the current tax deductions for charitable contributions.)

Norquist was skeptical, saying, "You'd be nationalizing instead of privatizing," and pointed out that the group is split on the proposition. He was worried, he said, "about the greater danger of having the federal government gain power over private charitable organizations, because they would be getting money almost directly from the federal government." He asked if the Christian Coalition had a position on this.

"Not yet," came the reply from the Christian Coalition representative.

Armey's man said, "It's not either-or. We're looking into how to do this. The House Republican leadership and the Dole people are excited about this because it's an example of how to work out ideas for solutions right now. If we take this off the table, we're left with standard root-canal policies. It'll help us with voters who don't think we're being positive." (The idea, much discussed, didn't reach fruition before the election, but, Norquist said later, "It's a good idea to have out there because it starts a debate about whether charity can be better run by private institutions than by the state.")

There was a lot of citing of the French observer Alexis de Tocqueville, who in his writing about America in the 1830s praised the existence of private associations to help people and bring them together over their common interests and to make civic improvements, instead of turning to the government. Norquist says conservatives are big fans of Tocqueville.

Another man in the room called the proposal for tax credits "a dangerous idea." He asked, "Who approves the groups? It will go to the Children's Defense Fund. Why do we want the federal government establishing a conservative federal policy?"

There was a report about what was going on in Arkansas from

someone who said he was in touch with the Republican National Committee, which he said was watching the situation closely. Norquist asked whether the Arkansas state troopers work directly for the governor. He was interested in whether, now that Tucker had been convicted and there was no longer a Democratic governor, and therefore there was no longer pressure on them to keep quiet about possible misdeeds on the part of Clinton or Tucker, "The troopers might feel freer to talk."

A woman from Consumer Alert, a market-oriented consumer group, passed around copies of an article disputing recent reports that a statistical drop in the sperm count among men might be caused by chemical pollutants affecting hormones. To the assembled group, this was an example of "the left" using "phony" science in order to bring about more regulation. She asked for the group's help in highlighting what she saw as this distortion.

At Norquist's party for him, Randy Tate addresses the crowd from the stairway, telling it, "My district is probably the most targeted district in my state." He says, though, that "people in the grass roots are very fired up." He relates Gingrich's visit to his district. Norquist interjects that "Speaker Gingrich was really jazzed up by what's going on in Randy's district." Tate points out that his opponent is a trial lawyer—to boos—who had supported a state health plan like the Clintons' plan. Boos and hisses.

A young woman says to Tate, "I just want to thank you on behalf of the pro-family groups because you brought to the attention of the leadership what the AFL-CIO is up to."

Tate says that Republicans are winning on Medicare when they make the issue " 'Do you want it preserved?' " and that the environment wasn't showing up much as an issue. He told the group, "Our message is better than their message: local control, local management."

Chapter Ten

OVERBOARD

BY EARLY SUMMER Republican House members and Party leaders
were becoming increasingly frustrated with the Dole campaign, and
worried about its effect on their effort to retain control of the
House. Dole just couldn't gain altitude, and his candidacy now
seemed to seriously threaten their hold on the House. Bill Paxon
had been predicting a Republican pickup of twenty House seats,
and though Paxon continued to sing this song, other Republicans
were privately more pessimistic. (Similarly, earlier predictions of a
Republican pickup of seven Senate seats were now being privately
downgraded to two or three.)

The period from spring to early summer wasn't at all a good
time for Dole. After he wrapped up the nomination, he seriously—
and puzzlingly—miscalculated in thinking he would follow that with
demonstrating to the country his leadership and ability to govern
from the Senate floor. So, after the South Carolina primary, Dole
announced that he was taking his campaign into the United States
Senate. He appeared to have completely forgotten how, toward the
end of the 1994 session, using Senate rules that make majority control of the Senate difficult to enforce, he had tied the Democratic
majority in procedural knots, preventing it from being productive
as it went into the election. But the Democrats remembered.
So Dole's return to the Senate was defined by a series of reverses
on legislation and his being boxed in by Senator Edward Kennedy,
of Massachusetts, and House Minority Leader Tom Daschle. Any

time Dole tried to bring up the rollback of the gasoline tax, the Democrats countered with proposing an increase in the minimum wage. Dole was engaged not with Clinton but with Daschle and Kennedy.

The more Dole tried to govern from the Senate floor, the more the Democrats made sport of him (and ran ads about the "Dole-Gingrich Congress") and the more he looked like the Washington "insider" he was trying to pretend he wasn't. "His head is becoming very well known," a Dole campaign aide said. Besides, astonishingly, the Republicans had no specific legislative plan. "Therefore," a Republican strategist said, "you couldn't prepare a message."

Worried Republican leaders and consultants were concluding, as Don Fierce, the Republican strategist, put it, "This is a fool's game." The subject of whether Dole should stay in the Senate was discussed at a meeting in late April, in Gingrich's office, attended by Dole campaign officials and Party leaders, including some governors.

A week later at a strategy meeting at the Dole headquarters of a number of his campaign officials, Don Fierce said, "Before we start, we should talk about whether he should stay in the Senate. How many think he should?" Not one hand went up.

Other accounts to the contrary, Dole actually resisted the idea of giving up his role as Senate leader and retiring from the Congress (the spun version was that it was his idea, and that he had sprung it on the others). Dole had to be persuaded to leave the Senate—by R.N.C. chairman Haley Barbour and Scott Reed, his campaign manager. Barbour first brought the matter up with Dole on May 4th. Dole said he was thinking about it. A Republican source said, "Barbour and Reed felt that Dole was in an untenable position. He was reluctant. But they had to get him off the floor of the Senate, get him to stop using the symbols and the language of Washington. The language and symbolism were inconsistent with 'changing America.' Staying in his role had him thinking minutiae, details. That's why legislators make poor Presidential candidates." He added, "It was difficult for Dole to do, even though it was logical."

Dole's departure from the Senate, on June 11th, caused a minor improvement in his ratings, but then the polls settled back into the double-digit lead for Clinton that had been prevailing for most of the year.

Even Clinton's considerable problems during June didn't help Dole. The revelation that a Democratic knockabout named Craig Livingstone had, as head of the Clinton White House personnel security office, obtained the F.B.I. records on more than four hundred people who had served in previous Republican White Houses was greeted by the Republicans as a wonderful gift. They had begun to give up on Whitewater doing a sufficient amount of political damage to Clinton before the election. Among the questions raised in the case of the F.B.I. files were why Livingstone and Anthony Marceca, his sidekick, had asked for them and what they did with them—or why in fact Livingstone had been made head of that office. The whole thing could have been, as the President claimed, an "honest bureaucratic snafu," or it could have been a byproduct of Mrs. Clinton's deep suspicion of "holdovers"—ushers, Secret Service, and the like.

Urged on by Gingrich, William Clinger, of Pennsylvania, the chairman of the House Government Reform and Oversight Committee, held hearings on the matter, but made little headway.

A Republican strategist said to me at the time, "There is a feeling that there are multiple problems for the administration that are coming together very soon, and reaching a critical mass. And there's an effort to get the facts together and get them out—with a political spin, of course." He added, "Politically there has to be some distance. If Party people speak on it, we discredit the ongoing hearing process. We want the hearing process to go forward."

The next blow came when, on June 19th, Bruce Lindsey, Clinton's closest aide, his traveling companion and confidant, was named an unindicted co-conspirator in a trial taking place in Little Rock of two Arkansas bankers, involving contributions to Clinton's 1990 gubernatorial campaign. (Both were acquitted on August 1st.) Also during June, the special Senate Whitewater committee issued its report, and though chairman Al D'Amato, of New York, one of the less charming of legislators, had managed to damage himself through his heavy-handed and repetitive approach, the report, spread out in the papers over several days, kept the subject of Whitewater alive. The report, even if partisan, did raise some questions about the Clinton White House's, and Mrs. Clinton's, behavior since taking office.

Dole's continuing ineptness turned out to be quite costly in ways essentially unrecognized at the time. Within a period of little over three weeks in late June and early July, he had stumbled on the issue of whether smoking was addictive (and, resisting his staff—he was tired of being "handled"—wouldn't drop the subject); managed to anger both the N.R.A. and gun-control advocates by making a murky, legislatively sliced statement about whether the assault weapons ban should be repealed (he meant to say that he didn't think it should be, but then fudged his statement); pleased no one with an attempted compromise on the abortion statement in the platform, which was an about-face from a position he had taken not long before.

The Dole campaign had hoped to get two sensitive issues—gun control and abortion—out of the way in a single week. Things didn't turn out as they had hoped.

Dole had told the N.R.A. in a letter on March 10, 1995, that repealing the assault weapons ban was "one of my legislative priorities." (His campaign staff said this had been signed by an "autopen," which was a pretty lame explanation.) In fact, he and his campaign had decided to show that he was independent of the N.R.A. by a last-minute addition to a speech on July 9th to the Virginia State Police Academy in Richmond, questioning whether the assault weapons ban should be repealed.

Tanya Metaksa tried to keep the peace with the Dole campaign and also within her own organization by saying that "I didn't hear him say that he would veto a repeal of the gun ban should it get to his desk"—as President. But two days later, Dole said, "I'd probably veto it." As Metaksa's N.R.A. constituency became impatient with what they saw as her temporizing, she was left with no choice than to break with him openly, saying that the N.R.A.'s three million members were "disappointed and disillusioned" with Dole. She noted that when the N.R.A.'s board met in early September to decide whether to endorse Dole, "I'm sure they will take everything into consideration." She indicated that the N.R.A. would focus on the congressional races instead: "Our members are asking us to help them elect a Second Amendment majority in Congress."

When I spoke with Metaksa at the end of that week she said, "The reaction is coming in fast—phone calls, letters, faxes, e-mail. What Dole has done is ask three million volunteers to leave the playing field. In '94 our members were involved in ten thousand elections. This year we'll be just as involved in ten thousand minus one."

Dole's apparent turnabout on the assault weapons ban quickly became the subject of much talk among the groups on the right. Grover Norquist said to me in a conversation, "This doesn't just affect gun owners. The pro-lifers look at it and say, What does it mean to have a pledge from him? Anti-tax groups wonder whether it means he'd keep the pledge." (Dole had signed Americans for Tax Reform's no-tax-increases pledge on April 7, 1995, the same day that he announced his candidacy for President. There are photographs of Norquist holding the document as Dole signed it.) Norquist said, "The damage here is to his credibility, not just on guns."

As Norquist understood, motivating these groups and getting enough turnout was the heart of the matter—for Dole as well as for the effort to keep Republican control of the House and guarantee the realignment. "The danger to Dole is not that anti-taxers or pro-lifers or gun owners will turn around and vote for the Libertarian Party or the Reform Party, but that they'll put all of their resources into saving the House and the Senate," Norquist said. An increasing number of conservative groups were deciding to do just that, he said, adding, "That Dole isn't making it easier to work with his campaign strengthens the trend that was already there."

Dole was alienating the Republican Party's "base" groups—the

N.R.A., the religious right—without making much progress at the center, which Clinton had largely coopted. When Dole did try to move to the center, the "base," which had been suspicious of him all along—he had never been a "movement conservative" and after the 1994 election but before he signed on to the Contract (to keep Gingrich's, and Gingrich's constituency's, support during the primaries) he had made some snide remarks about it—turned against him. Dole often cited Richard Nixon's advice to him to run for the nomination on the right and then move to the center. But the right in Nixon's day was a far less conservative and militant collection than now. Furthermore, Dole moved to the center before he had secured "the base." This was the subject of one of the arguments between Barbour and Dole campaign officials, who figured that the base had nowhere else to go. But what these people could do was stay home. This was the difficulty of operating within the Republican Party under any circumstances; it would take a politician of more skill than Dole to work one's way through it.

The danger to the Republicans was that the energy of the coalition that elected a Republican House in 1994 wouldn't be as great as before, because, as one Party strategist put it, "It's not clear to them what Dole's going to do." Validating Clinton's campaign strategy, Don Fierce said, "When Clinton takes school uniforms, when Clinton points to mother Hillary and daughter Chelsea, and takes Tommy Thompson's [Republican governor of Wisconsin] welfare program, and adopts the balanced budget—when he takes our agenda and makes it his agenda, the base isn't charged the way it would be if he opposed those issues." He added, "Grover's group was activated in '94 toward a common objective. They are nowhere near as activated nationally—for Dole—as they were in 1994."

Things reached such a turn that on July 11th, a highly frustrated Haley Barbour sent Scott Reed a tough memo, saying, "There is no perception or recognition that the campaign has a message." He urged that Dole talk about taxes for five days—Party leaders were despairing of Dole's ability to talk about a single theme for more than a day—and said, "Our news message doesn't support or even relate to our advertising message." As for what Dole was doing to the base groups—who were needed for the congressional as well as the Presidential campaign—Barbour said, "Most people see the second bite at the abortion apple [another attempt by Dole to compromise] and the assault weapons ban remarks as planned efforts to stiff-arm the Christian Coalition, Right-to-Life and N.R.A. groups." He went on, "Jabbing base voter groups going into the convention . . . makes it more likely that contentious issues will be highly visible and prominent at the convention. . . . So my last piece of counsel is to quit this strategy."

"We were demobilizing our Party," a Republican official said later.

Privately, Gingrich, who had tried to stay loyal to Dole, was becoming increasingly agitated about the state of Dole's campaign and worried that if Dole lost to Clinton by seven points, normally considered a landslide, the Republicans would lose the House. Other House Republicans were increasingly frustrated as well. They came back from the July 4th recess "pretty down in the dumps," Eddie Gillespie, the R.N.C. spokesman and strategist, said, "especially over tobacco."

Gingrich had already taken it upon himself to play a major role in the Dole campaign. (It was his intervention that caused Dole's comments on the assault weapons ban to be murky; he worried that Dole's planned statement simply saying that repeal of the ban was no longer necessary would be damaging to House members who earlier in the year had voted against the repeal. Dole had been blindsided by the House vote.)

To try to get better coordination between the Congress and the Dole campaign, and to assure that he had a strong role in both, in mid-March Gingrich started convening a meeting every Wednesday night in Haley Barbour's office at the R.N.C., near the Capitol, attended by Barbour, Scott Reed and a couple of others from the Dole campaign, Eddie Gillespie, Joe Gaylord (Gingrich's close political adviser, paid by outside groups), New Hampshire Governor Steve Merrill, and Don Fierce. The Wednesday night meetings were to be kept a secret. In an early one, Gingrich proposed that the Republicans run as "Team GOP." The thought, which had come out of Gingrich's meetings in Atlanta, was that the Republicans would run as the conservative party and paint the Democrats as the liberal party. He pushed the idea that Dole run against Clinton as Bush had run against Michael Dukakis. But Clinton had taken many steps to make that difficult. Scott Reed considered dealing with Gingrich a pain but something he had to do. But he rejected "Team GOP."

The meetings got off to a bad start. At one of the early ones, the Dole campaign representatives bluntly told the others that the congressional Republicans were damaging Dole's effort. The real worry of the other Republicans, of course, was that *Dole* would bring *them* down.

Every Wednesday night, Gingrich showed up with a memo containing new ideas for the campaign. Gingrich considered himself *the* communicator for the 1996 House elections. (In the meeting in Atlanta earlier in the year, Gingrich, working at an easel, drew a box and called it "communication." Underneath, he wrote "Newt.")

The fact that Gingrich had—as he knew—made big mistakes in 1995 discouraged him not at all from attempting to be *the* Republican strategist in 1996. Nor was he becoming any more of an asset to House Republicans who were in tough reelection fights. A *Wall Street Journal* poll in May said that by 55 percent to 32 percent voters were less likely to support a Republican who backed Gingrich and his policies.

Once he had established the Wednesday meetings, Gingrich—to show everybody that he was on the inside, and to bring House and Senate Republicans into the picture—convened meetings on Thursday mornings. That group was made up of House and Senate members, some of them former state chairs, whose political judgment he respected, plus Haley Barbour, Eddie Gillespie, Scott Reed, and a couple of governors. A Gingrich ally said, "There was a deep desire to get information out of the campaign: what are we campaigning on, what's the message, what do you want us to do."

At a Wednesday night meeting in June, the participants were in despair. They agreed that voters hadn't been given a "third reason to vote for Dole"—the two existing ones being "I hate Bill Clinton" and "I'm a Republican." Gingrich urged the Dukakis strategy once again. "I think Clinton has outmaneuvered us," one attendee argued. The Republicans used to win on "wedge" issues, he said, but "we aren't getting traction on wedge issues. We can't get the wedge on welfare, we can't get the wedge on crime, we can't get the wedge on taxes, we can't beat him on the budget, and I don't think we have the right candidate to drive the wedge. We have a Midwestern moderate Republican." They couldn't run against Mrs. Clinton's health care plan (as they had in 1994), they acknowledged, because Clinton had preempted that by saying that he knows the proposal was too complex, that he's for incremental changes now.

In July, Scott Reed decided that the Wednesday night meetings were a waste of time, and refused to attend any more, in effect shutting them down. Gingrich realized that he wasn't being listened to, that he was, at best, being humored. The Thursday meetings were soon shut down as well; Scott Reed told Gingrich that he didn't think they were productive, either.

The Dole campaign still wasn't getting anywhere. It was engaged in a protracted—and much leaked—argument over the size and nature of his promised tax cut. His scheduling remained bizarre—Alcatraz in California and a rock-and-roll museum in Cleveland (where he couldn't name his favorite group). His advisers had been debating at length how to deal with the "character" issue against Clinton, with many concerned that an attack could come off as partisan and not help at all. A Dole adviser said in early July, "We don't do it because it doesn't work. We'll do it through third parties—Rush Limbaugh, Bill Clinger, the *Washington Times* [a conservative paper], the *Wall Street Journal* editorial page."

Almost unnoticed in the midst of the chatter about Dole's missteps on tobacco, guns, and abortion, the House Republicans took a step on Thursday, July 11th, that amounted to throwing their Presidential candidate overboard. They decided to take up and pass a separate welfare reform bill. Until then, at the behest of the Dole campaign, the welfare bill had been linked to a proposal to turn Medicaid over to the states and cut its rate of growth in half—which would make it easy for Clinton to veto the whole thing because of his opposition to the changes in Medicaid. (The linking of the two proposals was not done, as was widely reported, at the behest of the Republican governors, who knew that the Medicaid proposal would keep them from getting the welfare bill they wanted.) The Republican leaders' decision to separate out the welfare bill was made despite strong efforts by the Dole campaign to block such a move. It signalled the end of the months-long debate among Republicans on Capitol Hill over whether to cut loose from Dole lest he cost them control of the House. It was also a conscious gamble by the congressional Republicans that they would be giving Clinton an opportunity to sign a welfare reform bill, eliminating an issue against him. Dole himself felt strongly that he needed the welfare issue against Clinton. But the House Republican leaders were eager to remove the two biggest issues Clinton had against the Republican House— that it was "extremist" and "do-nothing." House Republicans had become increasingly determined to proceed with a welfare bill. "We were at the bottom of tobacco," Scott Reed said later. "They were worried about the state of our campaign and our ability to carry a message."

Gingrich had given the Dole campaign his word that he would block a separate welfare bill, but he was run over by the other House leaders, in particular Armey, who told Gingrich that he would oppose him on this in the next leadership meeting.

Trent Lott, the new Senate majority leader, was very much in favor of the strategy of passing legislation, regardless of what the Dole camp thought. Lott, a smart and aggressive legislator, and Dole had never had a warm relationship—Dole had supported Alan Simpson for whip in Lott's successful attempt to take Simpson's job—and Lott wasn't reluctant to thwart Dole on welfare. To Dole allies in the Senate who questioned this approach, Lott explained that he had to do it because of the House Republicans' panic.

Clinton had vetoed a welfare bill in 1995, saying that it cut food stamps and other assistance to the poor too severely, but he had gone along with the bill's five-year limit on being on welfare and the elimination of the entitlement status of the welfare program— that people in certain economic circumstances were guaranteed assistance—that had held since the New Deal. The Republicans then put essentially the same proposal in their large omnibus budget bill—which Clinton vetoed on several grounds in his great political struggle with the Republicans over the budget. This had allowed Republicans to argue that Clinton had vetoed a welfare reform bill "twice," and to mock his ambiguous 1992 campaign pledge to "end welfare as we know it." Clinton had passed up the opportunity to push welfare reform in his first two years in office, though in early 1994 he did offer a bill—one that was quite different from the Republican proposals. Clinton proposed a five-year limit, but his bill also contained ten billion dollars for job training, and it preserved the principle of entitlement. The Republicans, particularly the House Republicans, were intent on ending the entitlement—this was at the heart of Gingrich's assault on the New Deal, his critique of "the welfare state"—and their bill forced able-bodied people to go to work within two years. Welfare was, in the words of one Republican congressional aide, "ground zero" in the struggle over the federal government's role.

The House Republicans' decision to go ahead with a separate welfare bill came during the same week as Dole's bungling on the assault weapons ban. A Republican strategist said, "The general House disgust with Dole had grown and grown—to the point where it boiled over." After holding off for a while, Haley Barbour now championed the strategy of the House Republicans helping themselves—regardless of what the Dole people thought. Enough is enough, Barbour decided. This was not to be the only time that Barbour—a stumpy man with a slow Mississippi drawl and a killer mind—when faced with a choice between retaining control of the Congress or trying to save Dole, chose the Congress. Barbour would argue that these were compatible goals, but after a certain point—when it came to important decisions about allocation of resources or whose political exigencies should have supremacy—they weren't. Gingrich had held out, trying to protect Dole, but in the end, in a leadership meeting on July 11th, he accepted the fact that the other House Republican leaders would insist that the House take up the bill anyway.

To mask what was really going on, Tony Blankley, Gingrich's press secretary, called John Buckley, the communications director of the Dole campaign, and suggested that Dole send a letter to Gingrich asking that House Republicans pass a separate welfare bill, and the Dole people complied. But within days, Dole campaign officials were telling reporters that they had been forced into sending the letter—thus blowing their own cover.

On Tuesday, July 16th, Barbour handed Scott Reed another memo and said, "Here's the themes we're going on. You can do what you want, but this is what we're going to say." The memo urged the themes of lower taxes, higher incomes, and better jobs; "the courage to choose right over wrong to end decades of moral decline" (stressing drugs); balancing the budget; that "Bob Dole doesn't just say anything to get elected; that the Republican Congress had kept its promises." (The last point was debatable.)

Reed said that there were some things in the memo that the Dole campaign had already agreed to. "Fine," Barbour said. "But we're not waiting for your message any longer. We're going with what we've got."

Chapter Eleven

ENDANGERED II

IN MID-MAY, I dropped in on Greg Ganske and Peter Torkildsen (as well as Tate, just before Grover Norquist's fundraiser for him) in their Capitol Hill offices, to see how they were doing. Both were worried about the ads being run against them, but expressed confidence nonetheless.

Ganske had voted against repealing the assault weapons ban, and for the ban on partial-birth abortions. He voted for the minimum wage increase. "The major thing that's going on around the country is the disinformation in the media about Medicare," Ganske said. He showed me a calendar on which he had marked, within a single week, ads in his district on Medicare by not only the AFL-CIO but also Citizen Action, a consumer group; and ads on Medicare and the environment by the Natural Resources Defense Council, an environmental group. "It's always Medicare and the issue du jour," Ganske said. "They're attacking 'those radical extremists who wanted to cut Medicare.' " He charged the groups with "obvious coordination."

Ganske said that his opponents would "have a hard time" linking him to Gingrich "because I took independent stands last year." He showed me an ad his campaign would run the following week, which stressed the word "working"—Ganske "working to save Medicare . . . working for clean air and water and working for our children and grandchildren for a balanced budget." It showed a picture of Ganske with his father and with his own family (he has three children), and made frequent use of the logo "Independent." "It's becoming important that the freshman class in particular reconnect with the voters," Ganske said, emphasizing that they should show that they have families, to give them a more human appearance.

In fact, the freshman class was by now, for the most part, a chastened lot. Its members recognized that their "revolutionary" zeal in the first year had been costly; so they eased up in their demands and were more willing to compromise—a word they had once treated with disdain. They now realized that it had been too much to demand the elimination of four Cabinet departments, so now they settled on trying to kill just the Commerce Department, which they saw as unnecessary and costly and interfering in the free market. (The other three departments they had wanted to kill were Education, Energy, and Housing and Urban Development.) Sam Brownback, one of the formerly militant freshman leaders, who had led the move to eliminate the four departments, told me in May, 1996, that the effort now was "to say we can run the Congress and make it work, rather than a dramatic strategy of downsizing the government and decentralizing." Brownback said, "We were trying to get a lot done fast and we should have tried to get a lot done slow. We outran our blockers. Now, we're going to get through what we can get through. We've got to convince the American public that we can govern."

Despite his perturbation over the ads against him, Ganske maintained that they had had one positive effect: "All of these ads back home are really starting to get the Republicans riled up, and we have seen a large increase in both spontaneous donations and also response rates to our mailings. And I believe that the troops are starting to get energized."

Peter Torkildsen was pleased that a recent poll in his district put him substantially ahead of John Tierney, his opponent. But he added the caution that he was one of the AFL-CIO targets, that his was a swing district, and that a generic poll question for his race—would the person vote for a Democrat or a Republican—gave a

Democrat thirty-four percent and a Republican thirty percent. "So Tierney has a thirty-four percent base," Torkildsen said.

Acknowledging that "it's not impossible for my race still to be close," Torkildsen said that while his constituents had "a generally positive view of what I've done, they're not aware of the particulars. I have to do more about that."

The second thing, he said, was he had to "let them know about my independence." He pointed out his vote against repeal of the assault weapons ban (though he had voted both for and against the ban itself in 1994). "I thought it was a bodacious decision for it to even be brought up this year, because it wouldn't become law since it wouldn't pass the Senate," Torkildsen said. He also noted that he was one of the few Republicans to vote against the ban on partial-birth abortions, and that he supported the increase in the minimum wage—"I'm voting with the rebels," he said. He did also vote for the minimum wage bill's provision to change collective bargaining. So Torkildsen was carefully slicing it down the middle, and the question was whether that would work.

When the unpopularity of the Gingrich Congress comes up in his district, Torkildsen explained, "I say that on every issue I voted on its own merits," that he had voted against cutting school lunches and other nutritional programs for the poor, against killing public broadcasting or the National Endowment for the Humanities or the National Endowment for the Arts.

Tierney, he said, was using Gingrich against him, and attacking him for having voted to make Gingrich the Speaker. (The vote for Speaker is ordinarily a procedural vote with no party member breaking ranks.)*

I asked Torkildsen if he had invited Gingrich to his district. "I haven't asked him recently," Torkildsen replied. "I asked him last year but he didn't make it, and I haven't asked him since."

He smiled.

*This changed, of course, in January, 1997, when Gingrich was in trouble over ethics.

Chapter Twelve

SAN DIEGO

As the Republicans gathered for their Convention in San Diego in August, the major forces within the Party arrived with varying agendas. The right's conflicted with Bob Dole's.

Dole's priorities were to continue his march toward the center, to establish himself as a credible candidate, and to leave the impression with the public that the Republican Party was a reasonable, mainstream party. The convention management—representing the Dole campaign and the Republican National Committee, with outside help from the Washington lobbyist Kenneth Duberstein and Michael Deaver, Ronald Reagan's former image meister—was bent on erasing the memory of a harsh, intolerant Republican Convention in Houston four years earlier. The result was one of the most strictly controlled conventions ever, suggesting that the last thing the Party wanted to do was debate ideas. But others had other thoughts.

Ralph Reed's priority was to maintain, or even enhance, the power of the Christian right within the Republican Party, and his own pre-eminence as the leader of those forces. Reed and David Rehr, Grover Norquist, and Marc Nuttle had a particular lens through which they viewed the Convention and what Dole did there: Would it help or hurt the Republican House? (Tanya Metaksa, of the N.R.A., didn't attend the Convention. Her public explanation was that she had a family emergency, but the real reason was that she had already split openly with Dole, and it would have been awkward for her to be giving interviews there. "I decided not to become a lightning rod," she told me later.) Vin Weber, the former congressman now co-chairman of the Dole campaign, met with N.R.A. officials before the Convention, who told him that they wouldn't support Dole but that whomever Dole chose as a running mate could affect turnout for the Party as a whole.

In the week before the full Convention officially opened, during which the platform and the rules were being considered, the atmosphere in San Diego was glum, even funereal. Dole's bungling campaign had discouraged the Party faithful. He was still trailing Clinton by double-digit figures. Even the sheer beauty of the place couldn't revive the Republicans' spirits.

Coming into the Convention, Ralph Reed had a problem. Though he had issued a statement approving Dole's latest compromise on abortion, hammered out on Friday, July 12th, other pro-life forces weren't happy with it. That compromise had eliminated from the proposed abortion plank—which reiterated the Party's call for a Constitutional Amendment prohibiting abortion—language that expressed "tolerance" for those who didn't share the pro-life view, and stated it as a general principle elsewhere in the platform. But it did specifically mention abortion and the death penalty as examples of issues on which tolerance should be practiced. In accepting this latest change, Dole overruled his earlier position that "tolerance" be in the abortion plank itself. "It's not negotiable," Dole had said. But the pro-life forces objected strenuously, and it turned out to be negotiable. Once again, Dole had tried but failed to impose a solution that would help him expand his reach to the electorate.

In a conversation in San Diego, Ralph Reed said he had told the Dole campaign that his approval of that compromise was conditional—on whether the other pro-life leaders agreed. Scott Reed, Dole's campaign manager, had told him that Dole needed a successful end to that particular week (the one when he was in trouble on the assault weapons ban, and tobacco), to generate positive news stories over the weekend. Ralph Reed said to me in San Diego, "What good would it have done to express doubts about it? I figured, give him a good news day and if we needed to fix it in San Diego, we'd fix it."

After Reed agreed to the compromise he learned overnight, he said, that Gary Bauer and Phyllis Schlafly, of the Eagle Forum, had doubts about it. So he, Bauer, and Schlafly started conferring by phone the next day. On Monday, they conferred again, this time with Bay Buchanan, Pat's militant sister, who was also in on the conference call. These calls, which came to include other pro-life leaders, were a test of the delegate strength of each leader, as well as a test of their collective strength against Dole. So, a few days before the Convention, Ralph Reed told Scott Reed that he was going to fight the compromise. The two men kept an open line to each other. "Scott has an ongoing relationship with Ralph," a Dole adviser said. According to Scott Reed, the two men talked once a week throughout the summer and fall.

Ralph Reed's problem—one that he had had all year—was that while he was trying in one form or another to give Dole some room on abortion, he couldn't be caught out by the other pro-life leaders, or accused by his own constituency of selling out. Grover Norquist said, "Ralph is in a complex situation because he can't seem too 'reasonable' on abortion or he gets flouted on the right by Gary Bauer." Reed's having helped Dole win the nomination had already caused him problems with the rest of the conservative movement, who felt he had become too mainstream. According to several people who took part in the discussions between the pro-life forces and Dole representatives and other Party officials in San Diego, Bay Buchanan—who had to get something out of the Convention for her brother, who could still cause trouble—was the most adamant, which affected Schlafly, which affected Bauer, which affected Reed. One participant in the negotiations said, "We'd get somewhere with Ralph or Phyllis or Gary, and Bay would say 'sellout,' and they would back off."

In the rolling negotiations that proceeded through Monday of the week before the Convention, the Dole representatives agreed to drop any direct connection between the words "tolerance" and "abortion," and substituted a general statement saying that the Republican Party was "the party of the open door," and recognizing "that members of our party have deeply held and sometimes differing views." It also said elsewhere that the American people are "a diverse and tolerant people."

Ralph Reed said later that he had no objection to the word "tolerance" being in the platform; that in June, using a laptop, in the course of the Republican state party convention in San Antonio, Texas, he had in fact drafted a freestanding tolerance plank that had become part of Dole's earlier compromise.

Dole, in Washington, watching the platform proceedings on C-SPAN, blew up. He was unhappy with the compromise his team had worked out with the pro-lifers, and furious that the pro-lifers held a press conference Monday night claiming victory. The press interpretation, inevitably, was that these groups had defeated him. He was hearing complaints from California Governor Pete Wilson and other prominent pro-choice Republicans. Dole argued strenuously by phone to his team in San Diego that the deal should be reopened. Once again, he was being a legislator, trying to craft cloakroom deals on an open stage, with a lot of het-up actors, and a vast press audience. He demanded, once again, that his representatives at the Convention insist that a reference to differing views on abortion be put in the abortion plank. "They all thought they were going to be fired," offered one person close to the discussions. Dole's people in San Diego tried to persuade him that his choices were the compromise they had just reached or a messy floor fight, and that the subject of abortion shouldn't be hanging over the Convention when Dole got to announcing his running mate, set for later that week—and ultimately he was convinced.

The platform battle over the abortion plank was widely interpreted as another blow to Dole's leadership and prestige. The news about that fight overtook the story of Dole's economic program, announced with great fanfare in Chicago on the same Monday that the abortion struggle was taking place in San Diego. The Dole forces had hoped that his decision to call for a fifteen percent cut in income tax rates would dominate the news going into the Convention. Vulnerable though Dole's economic program was to criticism that he didn't come close to paying for it—though he said he would also balance the budget—the tax proposal was to be the substantive centerpiece of Dole's campaign, a surefire means of winning votes.

The problem, Grover Norquist said when we talked during the pre-convention week in San Diego, was that Dole didn't comprehend the changes that had taken place in convention politics. "Dole thinks it's '68, when the candidate could pick up the phone and dictate the platform," Norquist said. He pointed out that the 110 members of the platform committee were elected from the grass roots up in their own states. But Dole didn't understand much about grass-roots politics. Once again, he had been tripped up in trying to apply the lesson from Richard Nixon—run to the right to get the nomination, then move to the center—to a different era. When Nixon was first elected President, in 1968, the outside groups that now dominated the platform proceedings didn't even exist as such, Norquist said. He said that Nixon himself had encouraged the rise of the "New Right" by taking actions—wage-and-price controls, the opening to China—that convinced the right that it couldn't trust the Republican Party.

Further, Dole didn't understand the nature of his own delegates—that would-be delegates had been urged, by Bauer and Reed and Schlafly to sign up with certain candidates in order to get to the Convention and promote the conservative agenda there. So, many signed on with Dole as the most likely train to reach San Diego, if not their preferred one. "Ninety percent of them are Dole delegates," Norquist said, "but nobody was there because of Bob Dole." He added, "If you have a bottom-up movement, the leader can't dictate."

The anti-abortion groups had made sure they had a majority on the Individual Rights and Personal Safety subcommittee that reflected their views—Ralph Reed said that his organization had been at work on this for six months. And they had enough support in the Convention to force a floor fight over abortion—the last thing that the Dole forces wanted. Reed had warned the Dole camp that if the platform wasn't fixed, there would be a floor fight.

Ralph Reed saw the change in the abortion language in San Diego as a major triumph. He said, "For the first time since the pro-life plank went into the platform in 1980, the victory was not by the nominee but the grassroots religious conservatives who were on the committee. That's a huge step forward."

When Reed and I talked, a few days after the abortion issue was settled, Dole had already remarked that he hadn't read the platform (telling the San Diego *Union*, "I'm not bound by the platform"), and it had become clear that the platform, and in particular the abortion plank, would receive scant mention from the Convention podium. Given these developments, I asked Reed what his "victory" had actually availed him. Reed, the long-sighted strategist, had an immediate and blunt response: "It sends a signal to the future nominees that 'Boy, I better not mess with that one. I better not pull the grass up from underneath that lawn mower without turning it off first.' "

In this conversation, which took place after Dole had made his surprise choice of Jack Kemp as a running mate—a move that much pleased the right—Reed made no bones about the fact that his primary concern remained keeping Republican control of the House, and he gave it newly expressed urgency and new implications. (While we were talking, over lunch, Reed interrupted several times to express excitement over seeing Bo Derek at a nearby table.) He said, "From the standpoint of the long-term institutional interests of religious conservatives, holding the Congress is still paramount. It is as important to our survival and long-term prosperity as holding the White House is to the liberals. To the liberals, losing the White House is everything—if they do, they're cooked, and they know it."

Reed added, "The religious conservative movement hasn't focused on the White House very much. But if Dole and Kemp come roaring out of this Convention, as they could, groups like ours might begin to focus on the Presidency more than they have.

"But if this Congress is reelected it will be the first Republican Congress to serve more than one term in sixty-eight years—it's a historic achievement. If it's defeated, people will say the Republican Congress was a fluke, that it said nothing about the long term, about the size of government, about the social issues.

"If this Congress is not reelected, we believe not only will we be unable to move the social agenda on Capitol Hill, but Democratic groups and a Democratic Congress would try to exact retribution. That's very important to us." Reed cited previous congressional hearings on various outside groups, meant to be intimidating, and sometimes successfully so. And his own group already had a Federal Election Commission suit pending against it. (In late July, the F.E.C. charged that the Christian Coalition, as a corporation, had illegally coordinated efforts with, and made expenditures directly or through state affiliates to, certain Republican campaigns, including George Bush's reelection in 1992; Jesse Helms's 1990 reelection to the Senate; Oliver North's unsuccessful 1994 campaign for the Senate; and that of J.D. Hayworth, of Arizona, now a Republican freshman. The F.E.C. counted the voter guides for these elections as among the illegal expenditures. The commission had split over whether to also sue the Christian Coalition for failing to register and report as a political committee.) Should the Democrats retake the House, Reed's prominent role in politics, especially House elections, could well draw Democratic fire.

Reed's detailed interest in Republican races came across as he spoke of his pleasure that religious conservatives had done very well in five primaries that had taken place the week before the Convention. In Kansas, Sam Brownback, the conservative freshman, won the primary fight to run for Dole's Senate seat, defeating the establishment Republican, Sheila Frahm, who had been appointed by the governor to temporarily take Dole's seat. In fact, Reed pointed out, all three Republican candidates, for the House as well as the Senate, in Kansas who won the primaries were pro-life. Reed said that the Christian Coalition did mailings, engaged phone banks, and sent out a half-million voter guides. Grover Norquist said that the Christian Coalition's voter guides "were very strong." In all, the Christian Coalition distributed ten million voter guides in the primaries. Norquist himself got involved, too, mainly making radio appearances. The importance of helping in the Kansas races was discussed at one of Norquist's Wednesday morning meetings, and Norquist also sent a letter to the groups in his coalition, urging them to get involved. Reed was also pleased that in Georgia, Guy Millner defeated Johnny Isakson for the Republican Senate nomination. Christian Coalition voter guides had been distributed.

While much of the focus in San Diego was on the abortion issue, other platform subcommittees, at the behest of a coalition of economic and social conservative groups, were adopting proposals that also reflected the Party's rightward march. The platform called for (as Dole had) giving parents vouchers with which to exercise the right to choose their children's school—an issue popular among conservatives; welfare reform (going further than the bill recently passed by the House and the Senate); a simpler and flatter tax code (but not necessarily a flat tax) in addition to Dole's fifteen percent proposal. Sweeping aside a Constitutional guarantee (in the Fourteenth Amendment), it proposed to deny automatic citizenship to children born to illegal immigrants. Grover Norquist said that the platform "is more radical than the Contract." Henry Hyde, a conservative Republican congressman from Illinois who was the chairman of the platform committee, remarked to me that on a conservative scale of one to ten, the Houston platform was a six, and the San Diego document was an eight. Thus, the Party that wished to avoid the spectre of Houston produced a platform potentially more inflammatory than the one adopted there.

Grover Norquist had a very busy schedule in San Diego. He got a few things put in the platform: a call for building the museum, along the lines of the Holocaust Museum, honoring the victims of communism that the Congress had already voted to authorize; a denunciation of an idea floating around the U.N. that it pay for its costs by taxing international flights and other international transactions, rather than rely on countries to pay their assessed dues (the U.S. was one billion dollars in arrears). "It sounds great: stop the U.N. from taxing U.S. citizens," Norquist said, smiling. He had suggested that there be a floor fight on tax policy, beyond Dole's fifteen percent proposal, to show that the Republican Party had ideas, but predictably was overruled by the Convention management. He helped Ralph Reed and the others in the abortion fight. He helped the conservative forces on rules changes. And he went from party to party, meeting to meeting, to spread the anti-tax gospel, and, of course, to build his movement.

On Friday, shortly before noon, Marc Nuttle, looking perturbed, is rushing across the lobby of the Marriott Hotel, on his way to the Convention Center next door. He's planned three events—two lunches and a brunch—in a large room for receptions on the floor above the Convention Hall, to promote small business as well as discuss economic issues such as taxes. They were to be financed by Koch Industries, an oil and gas company that's the second-largest privately held business in America, but were also billed as National Federation of Independent Business events. The forums are to be a show of strength and an organizing mechanism: other special interest groups as well as representatives of the state delegations will be invited to them. Nuttle is anxious to check the progress of his project to produce a depiction of a small town in the room, and about whether, now that Jack Kemp has been all but officially named as Dole's running mate, he will appear, as scheduled, at one of Nuttle's events.

At the Convention Center, Nuttle's small town is making progress. The ballroom-size room is decorated with gaslights, street signs with such names as "Main Street, U.S.A."—"I like that," Nuttle says—and a replica of a hardware store. Nuttle has prepared talking points for some Convention speakers, and takes part in the regular 8:00 A.M. meetings of the Convention staff.

I ask Nuttle about the role of the 35,000 state groups he told me about earlier when he described the efforts he would be making at the Convention. He says they "are all the more important" since the Dole campaign isn't going to have a coalition division. Because of the decline of political parties, Nuttle says, these groups—property-rights groups in the West, tax-reform groups—have taken things into their own hands. Nuttle says that because the Dole campaign wasn't doing it, he will teach these groups "how to communicate their message in a way compatible with the campaign's own theme and message." Nuttle says of the 35,000 groups, "That's a lot of groups that look to me for direction."

Nuttle's current analysis is that in a "worst case" the Republicans will lose seven House seats, and at best will pick up five. This is less optimistic than the current official pronouncements; Bill Paxon, the House Republican campaign committee chairman, is still saying that the Republicans will pick up twenty House seats. Nuttle, like just about any Republican one encounters, is delighted with the choice of Kemp.

The sudden transformation of the mood in San Diego has been remarkable. Like just about everyone else, Nuttle says that Kemp will "energize" the Party: that means not necessarily cause Dole to win but give him a better shot, and get more people to the polls and therefore strengthen the Republicans' chances of holding the House. The personable Kemp, the sentimental favorite of several Republican Conventions past, is liked by people on the right and in the center; conservatives see him firing up the base; moderates see him expanding the Party's reach to urban areas and minorities, in which Kemp had long shown an interest. About two weeks before the Convention, Kemp was depressed because he hadn't even been asked to speak. That Dole chose him also speaks well of Dole, since the two men have never much liked each other, and gives many Republicans more faith in him. (Kemp, in a peculiar display of timing, endorsed Steve Forbes, a fellow supply-sider, after Dole had effectively wrapped up the nomination.) A close friend of Kemp's says Kemp was "stunned" that Dole had asked him, that he hadn't taken it seriously when Scott Reed started to talk to him about the possibility. Now the question was whether Kemp would show more discipline than in the past (in particular his 1988 run at the nomination). But at the moment, the Republicans gathered in San Diego, in their surprise and happiness, aren't thinking about that.

Grover Norquist says of the choice of Kemp, "It's one more thing that helps us hold the House."

The multitudinous events in San Diego, a great percentage of them sponsored by corporations or trade associations or law firms, made this political ritual into a bazaar. The phenomenon wasn't new, but in San Diego it was taken to ever-greater excess. Events sponsored by the campaign committees, such as the congressional election committees, were underwritten by interest groups. Some of them were given especially for the largest donors, to keep them happy and help them amortize their gifts. Access and gratitude were being purchased all over town, often simultaneously.

The hectic schedule included breakfasts, brunches, receptions, lunches, dinners, late-night events, that went on back-to-back, and concurrently, every day. Many of them were organized around an important politician's body. U.S.T. Public Affairs, Inc., a lobbying group for the tobacco industry, and the Mortgage Bankers Association held a luncheon on a boat for Senator Christopher Bond, of Missouri, a major figure on the National Republican Senatorial Committee. The natural gas industry held a party for Alaska Senator Frank Murkowski, chairman of the Energy and Natural Resources Committee, and also one for John Boehner, the chairman of the House Republican Conference (which includes all House Republicans). The Chicago Mercantile Exchange held a reception for three Illinois congressmen. The Pillsbury company held a "salute" to the Minnesota delegation. Patton Boggs, a major Washington law firm, held an afternoon event at a restaurant in San Diego's historic Gaslamp Quarter. The roofing industry also held a party in the Gaslamp Quarter. The Oklahoma-based Kerr-McGee oil and natural gas company held a breakfast for Oklahoma Senator Don

Nickles. GTE, a major telecommunications company, held an ice cream social for Missouri Senator John Ashcroft. The Food Marketing Institute, which represents mainly chain grocery stores, gave a breakfast for Arizona Senator Jon Kyl and his wife. The American Trucking Association gave a luncheon for Senator John McCain. And on it went. Haley Barbour had issued orders that the House and Senate campaign committees weren't to raise money at the Convention—if there was money to be collected in San Diego, it would be done by the Republican National Committee.

Sitting out on the balcony of his Marriott suite on Sunday afternoon, his feet on the railing, Bill Paxon was, as usual, giving off cheerful confidence. (There was plenty of activity in his suite. His wife, Congresswoman Susan Molinari, was to give the keynote speech, on Tuesday night. Their three-month-old baby was with them and was displayed on television while Molinari spoke.) Paxon was pleased to hear that Randy Tate wasn't coming to the Convention, and that Ganske and Torkildsen would be here only briefly, because, he said, he had urged his targeted candidates to stay home. "If you work your district while the Convention is going on," Paxon said, "you can get enormous press. You're asked for your reaction by the local press." He said that Tate was "the best example of all, better than any, at meeting the challenge." Paxon said, "He has one of the toughest districts. I told him he's going to be the poster boy for doing everything right—he's aggressive, he's home every single weekend." Peter Torkildsen is attending only a few events here so as to spend semi-vacation time with his wife of seven months. He's also going to events given for the bigger fat cats, so as to meet potential new donors. Greg Ganske is to come later for a couple of days.

Paxon had been a strong advocate of the strategy of having the House pass bills so that the Republicans could claim that they were a "do-something" Congress—but he had been opposed to giving Clinton a chance to sign a welfare bill. In the past two weeks, the House had passed measures on the minimum wage, terrorism, health insurance, and tax breaks for small business. "I don't think it can be overstated how important that last two weeks was," Paxon said. Also important, Paxon said, was the decision in June that the National Republican Congressional Committee would spend eight million dollars on television ads. "A lot of our freshmen were feeling very beleaguered—that the cavalry wasn't arriving to help," Paxon said. "Newt and I got impatient that our so-called corporate friends weren't coming to the rescue." "The Coalition," which was established this year to offset the unions and included several business groups and was managed by the U.S. Chamber of Commerce, hadn't raised much money thus far.

In a novel interpretation of the laws, the N.R.C.C. decided, on the advice of counsel, that it could spend its own corporate donations, known as "soft money," on "issue advocacy" ads. Even Paxon conceded that soft money couldn't legally be spent directly on federal elections, but, according to the new theory, soft money could be used on such ads if it was paired with "hard money"—the limited contributions by individuals and PACs under the campaign finance laws. This took "issue advocacy"—supposedly a nonpartisan "educational" activity—to a new place—the party campaign organizations themselves. "Soft money" means contributions of union dues and corporation treasury funds ordinarily not legal in federal elections, and by individuals beyond the legal limits for federal elections. This spending device originated in an advisory opinion by the Federal Election Commission, in 1978, that a party could conduct certain generic "party building" activities, such as get-out-the-vote drives, using a combination of soft and hard money. The F.E.C. then compounded the problem in its regulations governing what percentage of spending on mixed federal and state political activities could be paid for with soft money: the states being allowed to use a greater percentage than the national parties. This opened up a huge loophole—which kept expanding as the parties became more creative. By funneling soft money through the state parties, which could spend a higher proportion of soft money on ads, the political parties got more mileage with their money. They could make "cookie cutter" ads (the same for each congressman but with the name changed), ostensibly paid for by the state parties. The uses of soft money took on an ever-widening definition, and the raising and disbursing of it developed into a major national activity out of the parties' headquarters.

By 1996 soft money had grown into a monster, overwhelming the original reform laws, and it was put to uses that were legally questionable. In 1996 all four congressional campaign committees, plus the national parties, used soft money for "issue advocacy" ads for candidates for federal office, paid for with a mix of hard and soft money, thus using soft money for individual campaigns for federal office. This was supposedly prohibited by law.

The "Watergate reforms" of 1974 ostensibly got rid of the ability of big-money people to buy access and ambassadorships—and perhaps policy. But once the soft-money loophole was discovered, and was constantly widened by both parties, such things became commonplace again. Except at a higher price. The discovery of personal donations of $50,000 during the Nixon period was shocking; now $200,000 is no big deal. Now the Republicans sell "season tickets"—pay once and get invited to all the big events, sit in a skybox at the Convention, get one's picture taken with the Party's nominees, and get help in seeing the right people in Washington— for $250,000. (This outstripped the Republicans' "Team 100"— people who give $175,000 over a four-year period.) The *New York Times* said that seventy-five corporations or individuals gave $250,000 or more to the Republicans in 1996, while the Democrats hauled in forty-five contributors who gave $250,000 or more. All four congressional campaign committees sold access packages.

Going into the 1996 elections, there were still some limits observed on how soft money could be used. But as the election went on, both the Democrats and the Republicans blew those limits away. In a major departure from how the campaign laws were supposed to work, both national parties used soft money for ads supporting their Presidential candidate; moreover they did it under the direction of the Presidential campaigns, undermining the argument that these were "issue" ads. (Even if they had been, this use of soft money was a departure.) "Issue" ads for both Clinton and Dole were prepared, written, and produced by their own campaign apparatus. To insist that these ads were nonpartisan—as the parties brazenly did—was ludicrous. Clinton campaign ads were discussed and chosen at the regular Wednesday night political meetings in the White House residence, which were attended by Clinton and his political advisers, top White House officials, and also Cabinet officers who had been in politics.

To pay for its new round of ads, the N.R.C.C. got the needed hard money through what Paxon described as "prayer meetings" with other Members of Congress, persuading them to part with some of their own campaign funds. Like some other Republicans, Paxon both complained about the labor ads and brushed them aside as a waste because they had been begun so early. Also, Paxon predicted that the N.R.C.C. would outspend its Democratic counterpart three-to-one.

The contest for the House was, for both sides, Armageddon: winning was far more important than observing laws that the Federal Election Commission would probably never get around to enforcing anyway. Even if it did, the cynical calculation went, the election would be long over. The F.E.C., its members evenly divided three-to-three between the two major parties, is designed to not make decisions.

On Sunday evening, a delighted Newt Gingrich is watching dolphins dance and leap about at San Diego's famous Sea World. This aquatic show is the first part of a "Salute to Newt" put on this evening by the N.R.C.C. The audience, eating popcorn that has been handed out, is seated in bleachers, on special white plastic commemorative cushions (with dancing elephants and balloons) that are among the souvenirs of the evening. David Rehr is here, along with his wife, Ashley, who works for a House committee. Rehr, too, is excited about Dole's choice of Kemp—announced last night from Dole's home in Russell, Kansas—telling people, "It will get the base pumped."

Gingrich has seemed almost manic at this Convention. Though as a result of his office he is to officially preside over the Convention, the plan is that he will be barely visible during the televised proceedings. He has been all over the place, campaigning in two nearby congressional districts and holding a pointless press conference Friday afternoon to laud Dole's choice of Kemp, a close colleague when Kemp was in the House. Gingrich seems determined to reestablish himself as a major force, not be seen as an extremely unpopular national figure who could be costing some Republicans their House seats, or one with an ethics cloud over him, not someone that his Party prefers to keep in the attic. His activities are an act of defiance. After the dancing dolphins show, the dinner, held inside a large tent, is attended by numerous donors and some members of the House. Its chairman is the local congressman, Randy ("Duke") Cunningham, a highly decorated pilot in the Vietnam War and a trainer of "Top Gun" pilots. The party favors, donated by CBS, are elephant-shaped metal frames containing a photograph of Gingrich and Candice Bergen. (He once appeared on *Murphy Brown*.) In his own speech to the dinner, Gingrich once again complains about the treatment he has been given by the press; introduces his wife, Marianne, who he says has been vilified; lauds the Republican House for just having passed some legislation; and expresses his confidence that the Republicans will retain control of it. "This is going to be the most fun Republican campaign since Theodore Roosevelt," he says, adding, "We can relax and smile every day, because we're the folks who are going to do it with you, not the folks who are going to do it to you."

The dinner is over early; dessert is served outside—with a band for dancing—but most of the guests depart quickly so as to make it to yet more parties.

On Monday morning, during the first, and largely procedural, session of the Convention—time had been set aside in case there was a platform fight—Ralph Reed is seated on the convention floor in the Virginia delegation, with his wife, Jo Anne, who has short, strawberry blond hair and is wearing matching flowered shirt and shorts, with a necklace with a diamond-studded heart-shaped pendant. He looks dapper in a well-fitting gray tweed suit and a black and white striped tie. He is surrounded by a large crowd—a celebrity now. Like any other pol, he claps people on the arm and says, "How are ya, howya doin?" After signing some autographs he says, "Gotta get out of here."

When I ask him, outside the hall, what he had been doing on the convention floor, he replies that he had been talking to Trent Lott, some governors, and had gone "to delegations where we're particularly strong." He tries to reach the Christian Coalition's "war room" on his cell phone—in contemporary politics, even the Christian Coalition has a war room—but can't. There are so many cell phones here that the channels are overloaded already. He says, "We think the traditional-values, pro-family movement needs to be the most advanced in the country. We're not going to rely on tin cans any more."

The Christian Coalition's sophisticated communications system was intended as a warning to the Convention managers: if there was to be a floor battle, Reed was well armed. Reed also planned to use it for stopping rumors and cueing the Coalition delegates when to cheer (for example, when Dan Quayle denounced partial-birth abortions).

Someone asks Reed to talk for the Internet about the R.N.C. theme for the day, but Reed doesn't know the theme for the day. Someone else hands him a slip of paper and he reads, "The Republican Party stands for limited government, lower taxes, safe neighborhoods." He tells reporters that he hopes that the speakers on tonight's program, who include Colin Powell, won't be seen as representative of the Republican Party.

The official program of the Republican Convention was an example—and perhaps an inevitable result—of the recent trends in American culture. Almost everything is dumbed down and packaged, is made into a "story." A short attention span is assumed and therefore encouraged.

Mike Deaver, Ronald Reagan's brilliant impresario, has designed the Convention program to fit the fashions of the day. The Deaverization of the Convention was in a direct lineage from Reagan's "Morning in America" ads. The nature of the programming followed directly upon the heavily packaged broadcasting of the Olympics. Nothing is what it seems. Distortions become the norm and reality is turned into human interest stories.

No one (except the candidate) spoke long. Dozens of "Main Street Americans" were brought onstage ("I'm just a regular guy") or in by film and satellite, lest the public tire of "politicians." The "ordinary Americans" conceit suggests that real Americans don't know who they themselves are, or how they feel about things, and have to be told by others presented by the political parties.

The Convention program, designed to deal with Dole's and the Party's weaknesses, was actually one long, slick commercial, and a deceptive one at that. The substance was misleading—suggesting a party of tolerance and inclusion. Though Colin Powell gave a brilliant opening-night speech, in which his differences with the mainstream of the Party on abortion and affirmative action were put to the Party's advantage—what a tolerant group, to let him talk this way (to some boos)—one Party activist said the next day that there was no way Powell would be nominated by this Republican Party. Though Powell and J.C. Watts, a black Member of Congress, were put on the program in prime time, only three percent of the delegates were black.

The power of the Christian right, evident in the platform and in its numbers at the Convention, wasn't reflected on the podium. And not only was Gingrich largely kept out of sight, but Dick Armey and Tom DeLay, the real ideologues in the House leadership, weren't on the program at all. The House freshmen virtually didn't exist. (A reception, sponsored by the Washington law firm Williams & Jensen, the Beer Institute, and Philip Morris, was held for them in a building away from the Convention Hall.) Trent Lott wasn't even given a speaking role, but did perform as part of a singing quartet of Senators he belongs to, entertaining the Convention with its rendition of "Elvira." (Lott wasn't at all happy with this treatment by the

Dole people, and was said to be smoldering about it for some time.) This, then, was to be seen as a political party devoid of politicians, and the "revolutionary" 104th Congress never happened.

Elizabeth Dole's highly praised walkabout—among the delegates, microphone in hand, extolling her husband's virtues—was another step in the de-dignification of the highest offices in the land. Smart and steely, Mrs. Dole was lauded for her technique—a woman had memorized a whole speech and kept her poise while giving it! (She had given the same speech many times before.)

The mood of the Convention itself continued on its upward trajectory following the selection of Kemp, as the week went on. Some Republicans complained about their role as extras, or the ideological blanding of their Party, but most by far were ecstatic about being happy—a mood they had never expected to feel in San Diego. They accepted being turned into automatons for the greater good.

On Tuesday morning, David Rehr and his wife are attending a brunch in honor of the Senate leadership, at the Loews Coronado Hotel, underwritten by the Mortgage Bankers Association of America and the National Association of Realtors. Donors to the National Republican Senatorial Committee who paid a fee of a thousand dollars are invited to all of the campaign committee's events here. The House campaign committee had a similar arrangement for major donors. At the podium, Al D'Amato, the chairman of the N.R.S.C., tells the donors in the audience of nearly five hundred that once they have contributed, "I'm going to come back to you, you see, so you can protect an investment."

On Tuesday afternoon, Grover Norquist and David Rehr are attending a "Meet and Greet" put on by the House campaign committee to introduce people who are challenging incumbent Democrats to the people who might bankroll their efforts. Rehr tells me, "My whole idea of my role here is visibility, bumping into Members of Congress. And some wholesalers are here, they're just kind of around." (Tomorrow, Rehr plans to attend the lunch for Senator

McCain and the ice cream social for Senator Ashcroft.) The "Meet and Greet" takes place in a microbrewery, where beer, margaritas, and Mexican food are served. A placard inside the door announces that this event is underwritten by United Parcel Service, which has one of the largest PACs, the Associated Builders and Contractors, Ameritech, and N.R.E.C.A. (the National Rural Electric Cooperative Association, which traditionally was allied with the Democrats).

Dick Armey turns up to give the challengers a pep talk. "We're going to see a lot of each other," he says.

Grover Norquist arranged that the benediction on Tuesday night of the Convention be given by Rabbi Daniel Lapin (Norquist is amused by the play on words "Rabbi Rabbit"), a conservative activist and talk show host in Seattle. Rabbi Lapin also maintains an office in Norquist's suite of offices in Washington. Norquist told me later, "We wanted *our* rabbi, not any old liberal rabbi."

On Wednesday morning, Norquist has gathered for a breakfast rally a number of anti-tax groups. He tells the roughly hundred people gathered in a meeting room at the Wyndham Emerald Plaza Hotel to "call your radio talk show or write a two-paragraph letter to the editor." He says, "We shouldn't wait for the politicians." Norquist's Americans for Tax Reform has worked up a study of how much of a product's cost comes from taxes (a loaf of bread = 31% taxes) and has produced a page on each one. Norquist tells the group, "We'll get out one a day in September."

Norquist is planning to appear on four radio talk shows today and give interviews to three major papers. He will speak to a Republican lawyers group and to the GOPAC candidate school that is being conducted here. Norquist and many others here are convinced that they are on the winning side of the tax issue—that Clinton, whom they respect as an adept politician, has gotten himself caught out by opposing Dole's across-the-board tax cut. (Clinton instead argues for "targeted tax cuts.")

John Boehner, chairman of the Republican Conference, turns

up to talk to Norquist's gathering, stressing "the importance of groups like you" to get a tax cut passed. But Boehner knows that the people in this group want to go further, so tells them, "This tax cut is just a way station." He says that the American people want a flat tax, and to abolish the I.R.S. The latter has become a battle cry—"End the I.R.S. as we know it"—a meaningless one that Dole favors.

Later that morning, Ralph Reed is conducting a "Faith and Freedom" prayer meeting at a pavilion in Balboa Park. The organ pavilion is huge, imposing. A large Christian Coalition banner is over center stage. The crowd of about three thousand people is being warmed up by some gospel singers. The morning sun is hot. Outside the amphitheater where the audience is gathered, pro-choice demonstrators are marching and chanting. Some policemen look on tensely.

When Reed enters the stage, to applause and cheers, he becomes the public figure rather than the backroom maneuverer. On the vast stage, his body, clad in a dark suit, looks very small, supporting a large head. Arms outstretched, he tells the crowd, in a strong, clear voice, "Let's tell the whole world we're not going to walk away from an unborn child." He says that problems should be solved "not by taxing and spending bureaucrats in Washington, D.C., but from faith in the family."

Reed then tells the crowd, "Let there be no doubt: the Republican Party is a pro-life party and as long as we're here it always will be." He is telling them where their allegiance should lie and also that their—his—efforts haven't been in vain. Obviously referring to Dole, he says, "There are some here who've said they haven't read the platform." But he cites the pro-life section of the platform and points out that it also calls for prayer in public schools and contains other pledges backed by the Christian Coalition.

Reed speaks clearly and with confidence, delivering his message in understandable terms. This is as much part of his job as his back-stage maneuvering to strengthen his organization's political hand.

"To those who say that Christian conservatives are an albatross

SAN DIEGO • 125

hanging around the neck of the Republican Party," Reed cries, "this Party . . . was founded to right a wrong . . . to remove the stain of slavery from this land." Waving his arms to his side, index fingers pointed up, he goes on about the strength of the Christian right. "Some press," he says, "ask, 'Isn't the Christian Coalition destroying the Republican Party?' " He answers by citing the example of Texas, where "we have a majority of the congressional delegation for the first time since the Alamo." His voice rising, he shouts, "If that's destruction, bring it on!" The crowd cheers wildly.

And he concludes, "If you thought 1994 was something, you ain't seen nothin' yet."

On Thursday, the last day of the Convention, Reed was eager to dispel the widely published view that the Christian Coalition had been shunted aside in the Convention itself, its main issue ignored by the speakers, and that he was bothered by the lack of attention. Reed has spent his entire time here trying to be pragmatic without losing his purchase as the leader of the Christian right.

For all his studied nonchalance about how the Convention had gone, Reed still wanted to get prominent mention of "values" issues in the acceptance speeches that night. Kemp, whom Reed had supported in 1988, had called him from Russell, Kansas, on Saturday night. In that conversation and in one on Sunday, Reed had made the case to Kemp that the Convention had to talk about values. Reed also importuned people around Dole.

Ralph Reed had also been called upon by Scott Reed, Dole's campaign manager, to calm the turbulence caused by Pat Robertson's vehement reaction to Kemp's being chosen. There had been bad blood between Kemp and Robertson ever since they opposed each other for the nomination in 1988. And Robertson, who had tried all year to be in the inner circle of the Dole campaign, had assumed that he would be given final say on whom Dole chose. But Robertson, who Dole officials felt was too egotistical to deal with, never made it into the campaign's deliberations, whereas Ralph Reed and Scott Reed were in touch at least once a week.

"Ralph is the person who can talk sense to Robertson," Scott Reed told me. "He's the one who can say 'no' to him."

In a late-afternoon talk on the last day of the Convention, while Ralph Reed munched on Buffalo wings to stoke himself for the evening, he said, "When has a Christian conservative organization ever been named from the podium of a Republican Convention? There's been talk of school choice, there's talk of welfare reform, there's been talk of family values. I understand that Kemp is going to have a strong values element tonight." He continued, "We're fine. We don't want to be mentioned in every speech. We don't want every speech to be about the Coalition; that makes us an even bigger target."

When I asked Reed if that was the point, if he was seeking to be less prominent and thus less controversial, he replied, "No, that's not the point. But it's certainly something to factor into your strategy. I think it's amazing: the media says, or the pundits say, 'Well, Houston was taken over by the family values crowd. They drove people out of the Party and they cost them the election.' So that's what happens when they put us front and center; we get killed. Then when we're not front and center, they say, 'Well, they aren't mentioning them.'

"We certainly don't want Dole to back away from his pro-life position, but we're not asking him to make it the centerpiece of his campaign," Reed said, "The way you win an election is talk about issues that people care about. Part of that is family values, but it also includes the economy, taxes, the budget, crime, and education."

Reed the cool, sophisticated pol understood what Dole had to do to win, and that that included not being seen as the captive of the religious right. Reed was more politically sophisticated than his followers, and had to be careful in what he said publicly about such matters, lest he seem less committed than they expected him to be. His job is not an easy one. But he understood the game. He understood why Dole had said he hadn't read the platform, and why his group's interests wouldn't be front and center in Dole's campaign. And he understood that the press would make a big thing of Dole's saying that he hadn't read the platform, because that's the way it works. It was an interesting line, it suggested a schism, and the press loves schisms, so it pounced on the line. Reed understood that.

Bob Dole's acceptance speech was much criticized, rightly, for its literary quality, but within the Convention Hall, for what that's worth, it was a political success. Literarily, it was a hodgepodge. I was told that Dole himself added to it at the last minute, making it harsher, especially on the subject of crime. In a major and odd contradiction, Dole criticized Clinton (actually, James Carville) for saying that the 1992 election was about "the economy, stupid." Dole chided such materialism before the well-heeled gathering (twenty percent were millionaires), at a convention marked by corporate wining and dining, going right on to extol his own fifteen percent tax cut. Dole's calling himself "the most optimistic man in America" was an obvious false note: Dole's personality may not be as dour as much of the public thinks, but his nature could not accurately be called sunny.

And there was sheer demagoguery—attacking the World Trade Organization (this for the remnants of the Pat Buchanan constituency) and, by name, U.N. Secretary General Boutros Boutros-Ghali. The name of the Secretary General set off an instant roar in the Convention Hall. It was code for racism and a metaphor for a falsehood about foreign policy that had been uttered by several speakers stating or implying that U.S. troops had served under U.N. commanders in Somalia. Dole had been using this line for much of the year, and liked its effect. (The Clinton administration itself had played on the unpopularity of Boutros-Ghali by announcing publicly and prematurely that it would oppose his serving a second term.)

Dole's righteous demand that those who didn't stand firmly for civil rights should use the exits also rang a false note. Dole, who at one time had a strong civil rights record, had turned against affirmative action, which he had once supported, as his eyes turned toward the Presidency. There was no mention of the environment, and only a fleeting, unexplained, reference to education. He inexplicably attacked teachers unions.

The fact that by the time Dole spoke, there had been plenty of talk about his war wound (including a long reference to it by his wife) didn't stop him from speaking of it once again. The lasting damage and discomfort that this left him with, and his constant struggle against this, had to be respected, but Dole, who used to be reticent on the subject, was now milking it, and bordered on engaging in self-pity. It did, of course, offer a useful contrast with the "draft-dodging" Clinton.

Dole did succeed in drawing the larger contrast, the one that could be the key to his winning the election: he painted himself as the plainspoken, truthful, trustworthy man from the American Plains, up against a slick, smooth-talking political con artist. Dole made Clinton's changing of political colors into a character issue, which it was. His joke that he half expected to see Clinton turn up at the Republican Convention was typical of one form of Dole's humor—stinging but not nasty (though he could also be nasty)—but in other respects he went hard at both Clintons, undermining his own effort to achieve new stature in the eyes of the public at large.

But in his acceptance speech Dole came across as forceful, vigorous, and in command—unlike the candidate who had been stumbling around incoherently for months. He painted a new self-portrait. Now he had to maintain it.

The effect in the Convention Hall was very strong, the delegates cheering far more than they had probably expected to.

On the Convention floor, Peter Torkildsen tells me that the upbeat mood at the end of the Convention "definitely helps," adding, "You're never going to get more of a boost out of anything than a Convention. Bush came out of Houston flat. Bob Dole couldn't afford to have that happen."

I ask Torkildsen if he had made some good contacts with contributors here. "Some," he replies. "I'll know in the next few weeks when this is followed up. You don't do a hard pitch when you meet them right now. You follow up when they don't feel as pressured. Whether you're asking for ten dollars or a thousand dollars, it's the same way."

Marc Nuttle tells me on the Convention floor, with great satisfaction, that Kemp did show up for his event.

Greg Ganske, who has barely been here, occupies a seat in the front row of the Iowa delegation, which occupies a choice position on the floor in front of the podium. This is his first political convention. During Dole's speech, he listens raptly, undoubtedly aware that his face might be picked up by the television cameras.

After the Convention, Ganske tells me that ads sponsored by the N.R.C.C. and the Iowa Republican Party (with hard and soft money) on welfare, Medicare, and regulations have been helping. His opponent, Connie McBurney, a former TV weather announcer, has been calling him an "extremist" and put out a poll showing her only seven points behind him. But he thinks, he says, "the moderates in the Party got a major boost"—from the speeches by Colin Powell and Susan Molinari, "and from having a place at the table." (In fact, White House polls showed the image of the Republicans as moderates up by twenty percent as a result of the Convention.)

He tells me that at the end of the summer, he will go to Peru to perform reconstructive surgery on children.

At the end of the Convention, David Rehr, in a very happy mood, is off to sponsor a post-Convention beer party for the N.R.C.C.

Grover Norquist tells me he's very pleased with Dole's speech, and particularly happy that Kemp had said of the fifteen percent tax cut "This is just the beginning." He's been talking to a lot of media today, and now that the Convention is over will join Gingrich for a long schmooze at Gingrich's hotel. Tomorrow he's going to Seattle to help Randy Tate.

Chapter Thirteen

CHICAGO

As the Democrats gathered in Chicago for their Convention, to begin on August 26th, the Clinton forces were more worried than they let on.

The liberal wing of the Party—labor (including teachers unions), blacks, Hispanics, and feminist groups—dominated the Convention delegations (just as the right dominated the Republican Convention), and the Clinton people were concerned that the President's announcement, on July 31st, that he would sign the welfare bill would cause a deep split in the Party, and perhaps an explosion in Chicago. The Republicans had deliberately sent Clinton a bill that would cause him political trouble whether he signed it or vetoed it. (Eddie Gillespie, the Republican National Committee press secretary and strategist, told me, "They tried to write a bill where he'd be hurt either way—that if he signed it he'd make his base crazy and if he vetoed it he'd be going against the mainstream.")

If the Democratic base was unhappy enough, it might stay home, as it did in 1994, weakening Clinton's position against Dole and greatly reducing the Democrats' chances of taking back the House. A disruption at the Convention, which would be heavily covered by the media, wasn't their only worry about the possible adverse political effects of Clinton's signing the welfare bill. The question of what that would do to the Democrats' chances of regaining control of the Congress had been a large consideration in the internal administration debate over whether Clinton should sign the bill.

Clinton's decision to sign the welfare bill was an epochal event—the largest blot on his Presidency thus far. He not only condoned ending the sixty-year welfare entitlement—he had already let that go during his maneuvering with the Republicans in 1995—but the bill also made steep cuts in other benefits for the poor, especially food stamps. The food-stamp cuts were likely to put some people in poverty who were now just above the line. Strict time limits were put on how long people could be on welfare (a lifetime cumulative five years, or less if a state chooses), without providing additional funds for the job training or the jobs that would be needed to put these people to work—Clinton had once proposed both. The poor were already bearing the brunt of the cuts in federal spending made by the Republican Congress, with the President's complaisance. The welfare bill made only limited provision for extra federal help in case of a recession, which could make jobs even scarcer and exceed the capacity of state treasuries. (This was a prosperity-based bill.) Thus, Clinton colluded with Newt Gingrich in removing a cornerstone of the New Deal, or what Gingrich called "the welfare state." This had been Gingrich's highest goal.

Some Clinton advisers felt strongly that he shouldn't sign the bill on the merits, and some even argued that vetoing it would be better politics. (A Republican as sophisticated as Vin Weber thought it so obvious that the better politics for Clinton would be to veto the bill that he was distressed that his fellow Party members had given him the opportunity.) The better-politics argument was that doing such a presumably unpopular thing would help Clinton with his greatest liability, the "character" issue—in particular the question of whether he stood for anything.

The corollary to the "character" argument for Clinton's vetoing the bill was that he was a skillful enough politician to make the case that it was the right thing to do—that he wouldn't stand by while millions of poor and near-poor people were hurt. (The White House didn't want a study of the probable effects of the bill to be done by the Department of Health and Human Services, because they felt sure that it would come out the same way as one done the year before, which said that a million children would be driven into poverty. So, with the encouragement of some administration officials, the Urban Institute, a Washington research organization, did a study—which said that eleven million families would be substantially hurt by the bill.) In the course of the year, Clinton had boasted of having created eight million jobs in nearly four years. There was no way, a worried Cabinet officer told me, that enough jobs could be created to soak up those who were removed from the rolls (and not too dysfunctional to hold a job). Roughly seven million people were already looking for jobs, and now roughly four million women on welfare also had to find jobs. A high administration official said, "The problem is we're expecting people to take jobs that aren't there."

Both sides in the debate argued in terms of what effect Clinton's signing the bill would have on the House races. If he vetoed the bill, Clinton could add it to the bill of particulars against the "extremist" Republican Congress. If he signed it, that very charge—the one that the Republicans were most anxious to shake—would be substantially weakened.

In a meeting in the Cabinet Room some hours before the President announced he would sign the bill, Harold Ickes and George Stephanopoulos argued that signing the bill would not only give the congressional Republicans a boost, but also could cause major disruption among the President's base, and problems at the Chicago Convention. Stephanopoulos also argued that signing it would "cut off at the knees" Democratic challengers for House Republican seats, by weakening their case against the incumbents. But others— domestic policy adviser Bruce Reed, and John Hilley, the head of legislative affairs—argued that vetoing the bill would make it harder to hold onto Democratic seats in marginal districts, particularly in the South.

Labor Secretary Robert Reich argued to Clinton, his old friend since Oxford, that it would be better politics for him to veto the bill. Reich opposed the bill on its merits, but knew which argument might be more persuasive. He told Clinton that every time he had stood up for principle (as he appeared to do in the budget fight) he had gained. Health and Human Services Secretary Donna Shalala argued strongly against signing the bill, and presented a lot of data on who would be hurt by it. She didn't argue that welfare should remain an entitlement, because she knew that that argument was lost. She did insist that the provisions to cut funding for food stamps and ending welfare assistance for legal immigrants (another provision in the bill) would simply throw more people into poverty, and had nothing to do with welfare reform and getting people to work. Shalala said that it was unjust that legal immigrants who had come to this country under the rules, and were elderly or disabled and could not work, would suffer. She maintained that there weren't enough protections for children in the bill, and that "justice ought not depend on geography." Under the bill, the states, which had already been allowed to set the size of their own welfare payments, wouldn't have to offer equal treatment *within* the state.

Before the President called the Cabinet Room meeting, Shalala was involved in the extensive intra-administration maneuvering to try to affect his decision. (One administration opponent of signing the bill said while these discussions were still going on, "It's not a question of how many bodies are on which side. It's a question of how the President sees the politics.") Chief of Staff Leon Panetta and economic adviser Laura Tyson were for vetoing the bill. So was Housing and Urban Development Secretary Henry Cisneros, who said in the Cabinet Room meeting that he could understand the political argument for signing the bill, but that was outweighed by other considerations. "I know what your head tells you about what to do," Cisneros told Clinton in the meeting, "but sometimes we have an objective reality that tells you you shouldn't do what you want to do." Cisneros continued, "The objective reality is people are going to get hurt." Even Treasury Secretary Robert Rubin, who reflected business's interests, told the President that too many people would be hurt if he signed the bill.

In a smaller meeting in the Oval Office that followed the Cabinet Room meeting, Panetta, who had been working on the bill as it moved through the Congress, said to Clinton, "Mr. President, in the end, Congress basically said 'To Hell with you' on provisions that are really going to hurt people." He said that the provisions cutting off welfare benefits for legal immigrants and making severe cuts in food stamps, "will really cut a hole in the safety net." And then he said, "It's tough for me. I'm the son of immigrants. Cutting off immigrants isn't what this country's all about." Panetta pointed out that the cutoff in food stamps to legal immigrants would take place by early October, and could cost the President politically in November. And Panetta made an argument similar to Reich's: he said that by standing firm on the budget, and not caving in to demands to totally wipe out affirmative action, Clinton had benefited politically, and that standing firm on welfare would help him as well.

In that Oval Office meeting, Vice President Al Gore supported the idea that the President should sign the bill. But Gore was sensitive to the fact that Dick Gephardt, his longtime rival and possible opponent for the next Democratic Presidential nomination, had voted against the welfare bill.

Dick Morris, who wasn't in either meeting—he had his own channel to the President—was a strong champion of signing the bill. Morris had been telling Clinton that this was the most important decision of his Presidency, that if he signed the bill his reelection was assured. In one of the Wednesday night political meetings in the White House residence, Morris told Clinton that vetoing the bill would make a fifteen-point race into a five-point race. A White House advocate of the President's signing the bill said, "Dick always seemed to think that the political arguments for signing the bill were enough to carry the day." Morris also argued that a Clinton veto of the welfare bill would breathe new life into a moribund Dole campaign; at last, Dole would have something to say. Signing the bill was of course consistent with the move to the center by which Morris, and now Clinton as well, set so much store. That Morris was amoral didn't seem to give Clinton pause.

Domestic advisers Bruce Reed and Rahm Emanuel had been architects of the strategy all along, and were very much in favor of

Clinton's signing the bill. (And both were to have enhanced roles in Clinton's second term.)

Bruce Reed, whose roots were in the centrist Democratic Leadership Council, of which Clinton had been a co-founder, made an argument Clinton adopted: that if he vetoed the bill now he might not get another welfare bill, that welfare reform might go the way of major health care reform. Reed argued that if the Democrats retook the Congress, with liberals Daniel Patrick Moynihan, of New York, and Charles Rangel, also of New York, becoming chairman of the Senate Finance Committee and the House Ways and Means Committee respectively, the Republicans would block a more liberal bill and prevent passage of anything but a more stringent bill than the one now before the President. He also argued that since Clinton had promised welfare reform in the 1992 campaign, he would have a hard time in the fall explaining why he had vetoed welfare reform legislation three times. Clinton needed to approve the bill, Reed argued, to restore people's faith in government. This was a novel argument that could work both ways. We can fix the bill later, Reed argued. It was also understood by several people that Mrs. Clinton, who didn't participate in the meetings, and said nothing publicly about the welfare issue, might have preferred that her husband veto the bill but wasn't ready to make a big thing of the matter if he felt that for political purposes he needed to sign it. (Mrs. Clinton was far more pragmatic than often depicted.)

A number of administration officials believed that the President's mind was made up before he had his final, well-publicized round of meetings on the matter—that the decision wasn't nearly as agonizing as Clinton made it out to be in his July 31st press conference.

Morris was in fact telling colleagues for at least a week before the final meeting in the Cabinet Room that the President would sign the welfare bill. "He was exulting that it was a done deal," one colleague said. Morris bet a colleague ten-to-one that Clinton would sign the bill.

The polls of course said that people hated the current welfare system. But polls are static, a snapshot of the status quo, not taking into account how opinion might change after someone has worked hard to change it. The predominance of polling in both the Clinton and Dole campaigns was of a new order. A Clinton adviser told me, "Nothing is not polled. Hillary's latest statement is polled. Hillary's standing is polled. Every Whitewater development is polled." (This person pointed out that the more polling that takes place, the more lucrative it is for the pollsters—who recommend the polls and then write the polling questions.) A Dole campaign official said, "We have focus-group government."

Morris was always giving Clinton advice based on polling—but in most cases he had designed the poll. A White House official told me later, "Morris's great skill was to manipulate opinion to a position he wanted by a poll he'd designed."

What Morris didn't understand was that politics should be for the purpose of governing—that governing shouldn't be for the purpose of politics. And much of the time Clinton himself didn't seem to see a distinction.

In his press conference announcing his decision, Clinton said that he would try to fix in the next Congress the provisions cutting off most federal assistance for legal immigrants and making deep reductions in food stamps. But unless the Democrats retook the Congress, it was questionable whether these provisions would be changed. And in talking about seeking changes, Clinton didn't mention fixing the most basic fact that now there was no federal guarantee of welfare. At Clinton's request, Shalala, Education Secretary Richard Riley (who had also opposed signing the bill), Cisneros, and Reich stood within camera range in the briefing room as the President announced his decision—all of them looking like they had just been hit by a truck.

A large amount of rationalizing had gone on about why the welfare bill should be signed—a good bit of it in Clinton's head. A couple of Clinton's advisers have speculated that an important part of Clinton's somewhat mysterious decision-making process is his need to persuade himself that the decision he's making is the right thing to do on the merits. Over time, he will convince himself of this, they said. Another adviser said that Clinton is widely seen as a good "spinner"—persuading the public of his point of view—but that the person he most spins is himself.

When Clinton actually signed the bill, during the weeks between the two Conventions, he said, "We can change what is wrong," and "We shouldn't let this historic opportunity go by." The Democratic congressional leadership was noticeably not present at the signing. (Marian Wright Edelman, president of the Children's Defense Fund, a longtime close friend and ally of the Clintons, issued a statement calling Clinton's signing the bill "an act of shame." Peter Edelman, her husband, was soon to resign as an assistant secretary of Health and Human Services in protest over the bill. In the end, all of the top officials at H.H.S. who specialized in welfare resigned.) Even Christopher Dodd, senator from Connecticut and general chairman of the Democratic National Committee, called the bill "unconscionable."

Clinton signed other bills that same week—the minimum wage bill, the Kennedy-Kassebaum bill making some changes in health coverage—all in the Rose Garden. Also that week came the news that Clinton was going to approve a Food and Drug Administration proposal to regulate tobacco sales and advertising, especially as regards children. (Dick Morris had argued that moving on this front, as well as signing the welfare bill, would please the suburban middle class.) These actions—showing the President being "Presidential"—as the White House intended, stomped on what "bounce" Dole got from his Convention, almost completely eliminating it.

One result of Clinton's decision to sign the welfare bill was in fact anger among the groups likely to be most affected (blacks, Hispanics, women, and big-city elected officials), and other liberals. (In September, an administration official said, "People are very disappointed, ready to walk. If there was an alternative, people would be gone—but Republicans scare them.") A strong Clinton ally within the government said, speaking of the welfare issue, "He walks close to the edge—that's his style." A Cabinet officer said to me, "I'm telling you, it's a powder keg out there." Therefore, a lot of work had to be done at the Convention to mend the Party's base—without making Clinton look too left of center to the swing voters he needed in order to win. His problem was the mirror image of Dole's.

But nothing is simple with Bill Clinton: he and his political advisers didn't mind *some* display of anger by liberal groups over his signing the welfare bill—thus showing the center that he was closer to them than to the liberal base.

At the Convention, officials with good lines to the liberal wing—Harold Ickes, Alexis Herman, the head of White House public liaison, Cisneros, Panetta, and Shalala—spent a lot of time going from caucus to caucus trying to calm people down. Shalala told people that the President and she didn't disagree on the substance of the bill, that the decision to sign it was a matter of tactics. (This might not have been totally comforting.) Democrats were told, If you're unhappy about Clinton's signing the welfare bill, reelect him, because he's the only one who will try to fix it. New York Senator Daniel Patrick Moynihan, who had bitterly opposed the welfare bill, bluntly told people in Chicago that it won't be changed by the Congress.

Hillary Clinton's assignment at the Convention was to try to calm the base over welfare, with women as her particular target. She was well suited to the task and it was a welcome assignment. Mrs. Clinton would be going public more at the Convention than she had since her health care program had gone crashing down in 1994. She was still searching for a role. Since the first of the year she had had successful trips to Eastern and Central Europe, Greece and Turkey, written a best-selling book (and continued her weekly column begun in 1995). Nonetheless she had had a rough year. In January, she had been called before a grand jury in Washington on White-water matters. Publicly, she kept up a brave, almost defiant front, but she was, understandably, deeply upset about the Whitewater developments—many of them involving her, and her lawyer-like, evasive, and even apparently conflicting statements—and the picture of a First Lady entering and leaving a courthouse (in the dark) was a new and unsettling one. As a result of the strident way in which she had handled the health care issue, and the misjudgments involved, she couldn't be seen to be having a role in policy—though she was still a powerful voice behind the scenes. It was a form of purdah, and she didn't like it at all.

In Chicago she went from women's event to women's event, and was hailed as a hero. It was taken as a given that she had run into trouble only because she was a strong and active woman. (That was of course partly the case.) Feminism ran strong in Chicago—in sharp contrast to San Diego.

At a large rally in the Sheraton ballroom on Monday afternoon, sponsored by EMILY's List and the women's divisions of the Democratic National Committee and the Democratic Senatorial Campaign Committee, one of her several appearances that day (the President is taking a train trip to Chicago), Hillary Clinton, dressed in a gold suit, addresses an audience of about two thousand women. ("We're trying to get their energy going," Ellen Malcolm, of EMILY's List, told me.) In her remarks to the women's rally Mrs. Clinton pays tribute to Donna Shalala, who these groups knew had argued against Clinton's signing the welfare bill, and she speaks of the strains in "the life of the everyday woman." She stresses their issues: child care, the budget, crime. She is speaking to the women who didn't turn out in 1994. "It is for those women," she says in her strong, clear, voice, "that Al Gore and Bill Clinton are running"— and she's greeted with huge applause and cheers. "Didn't it feel good to have a President who stands up against the National Rifle Association?" More strong applause. Earlier, at a lunch in her honor at the Chicago Cultural Center, she spoke about Jane Addams and Eleanor Roosevelt, and said, "It does take courage to be in public life." She got big cheers, and she clearly is enjoying these affirming events.

Mrs. Clinton's effort to reassure the base was also evident in her speech to the Convention on Tuesday night. Among the things she said in this first policy address to a national convention by a First Lady, a substantive speech, was, "My husband and I have always felt that all American families should have affordable health insurance." This broad goal wouldn't be reflected in her husband's speech; her comment was both her way of saying, "I'm not backing off," and of winking and nodding to the base about something it favors. Her speech also played heavily on the "family" theme—she talked about her daughter, Chelsea, who had been carefully shielded from the public, more than she had ever talked about her before—and mentioned other protections sought by the middle-class women who were being courted. One was extension of the Family and Medical Leave Act, which gives workers unpaid leave for family illnesses or births, and which Clinton signed into law early in his Presidency (after George Bush had twice vetoed it). She also called for requiring insurance companies to cover forty-eight-hour hospital stays for new mothers. (Her husband mentioned the family leave issue during a stop in Battle Creek, Michigan, the nex hurled proposals from the train each day—on crime, hooking schools up to the Internet, on the environme

The entertaining of public figures by private interest cratic Convention was, if not a tie with, a close secon Diego. The Democrats took numerous opportuniti their candidates for Congress. The House campaign its Republican counterpart, didn't raise money at the Convention, but it did a lot of hinting that contributing was quite in order. The Senate campaign committee had no compunctions about raising money. But, like the Republicans, the Democrats had urged their candidates for House seats to stay home, where they could accomplish more. The fifty-some Democratic challengers who did go to Chicago were included in numerous events involving donors, or potential ones. The generic polls were showing that the Democrats had at least an even chance to retake the House. For the lobbyists, it was a time for investing. The Republican congressional campaign committee had three times as much money as its Democratic counterpart.

Unlike the Republicans, the Democrats were running a national campaign for the House—based on the theme that the Republican Congress was "extremist." If Republicans were passing bills with the Democrats now, the argument went, that was because they had to temper their extremism or face disaster. If the Republicans were given another term, the Democrats maintained, they would return to the ways of their first year. Earlier in the year, the Democratic Congressional Campaign Committee had thought that it would "morph"—transform—the faces of targeted Republican candidates into Gingrich's face. (In 1994, a number of Republican ads morphed the face of the Democratic incumbent into Clinton's.) But it hadn't worked against a moderate Republican in a special election in California (in that case it wasn't credible), and now focus groups—the institutions that really run America—were saying that this device was "too partisan." But the name "Gingrich" or the term "Gingrich agenda" were to be part of every Democratic campaign. "I don't know that we need morphing," a Democratic Party official said.

Another part of the base to be kept happy and active—through Election Day—was labor, which was represented by about twenty percent of the delegates. John Sweeney, the AFL-CIO president, had complained publicly about the welfare bill, and had tried to dissuade Clinton from signing it. But Sweeney had an overriding goal: to defeat the Republicans in the battle over the House.

On the Sunday afternoon before the Convention began, labor's delegates are assembled for a rally in the huge ballroom of the Sheraton Hotel. (There will be meetings of labor subgroups and caucuses all week.) The AFL-CIO has handed out some defensive literature responding to the criticism of its role in the fight for the House: one leaflet cites a poll conducted for the AFL-CIO saying that members want their unions to be involved in politics; it also says that sixty-four percent of union members are more likely to support a congressional candidate who is supported by the

AFL-CIO, and that sixty-seven percent respond positively to the AFL-CIO's campaign "to educate and inform its members."

Sweeney, again dressed in shirtsleeves and suspenders, tells the group, "This is the most important caucus at this Convention." After a few more words he introduces Gore, who gets a big cheer as he arrives onstage like a Presidential contender. Gore has a double agenda here, one for this year and one for four years later. "We're on your side. We need to stick together," Gore tells them, and he jokes about "this two-headed monster of Dole and Gingrich"—to boos. They've turned on the labor movement, Gore tells them, "they want to drive you out of politics"—to loud "NO"s. He goes through issues affecting labor, saying, "Dole and Gingrich believe that OSHA should be NOSHA."

Gore is loose, animated, and funny today, showing traits his friends know but that he has difficulty displaying, or is reluctant to display, in public. (But his jokes about his own woodenness are getting tired.) He now has a whole routine, which he acts out, about the difference his audience will feel on the day after the election if Dole wins or Clinton wins. And for good measure he refers to "the extremist ideology of the Dole-Gingrich party of '96." He implores them, "Recapture the Congress and make Dick Gephardt Speaker." There are some who wonder whether Gore really wants that.

Steve Rosenthal, standing in the back of the room, is pleased. "They're really worked up," he says.

Sweeney, concluding the rally, tells the union members, "Consider where labor was in 1994."

On Sunday evening, there is a reception for Gephardt at the Children's Museum at the restored Navy Pier, on the lakefront. About two thousand people, a great many of them Washington lobbyists, have come to pay their respects. He is, after all, the House Democratic leader, and just might become Speaker. Past donors have been invited. A close associate of Gephardt's says that this is the kickoff of the Gephardt 2000 campaign.

Shortly before noon on Monday morning, in the William Tell Room of the Swissôtel, Gephardt is introducing to the press eleven challengers for House seats. He makes a little speech attacking the Republican Congress. ("We fought their $270 billion cut in Medicare ... rollbacks in federal protections ... cuts in student loans.")

Gephardt points out that the Democrats in late June came up with their own agenda should they retake control of the Congress. Actually, it's a bland document called "Families First," and a clear sign that the congressional Democrats are themselves moving toward the center, a phenomenon not much noticed. (Of course the name "Families First" had been tested in a poll.) Earlier in the year, when the House Democrats pondered their own agenda, there was a strong push by some of them to adopt corporate reform proposals. But even some liberals resisted, in the belief the Party had to be acceptable to a broader swath of Americans—and very little on corporate responsibility ended up in the document. The idea was also to arrive at a plan that the entire House Democratic Caucus, including its more conservative "Blue Dogs" (largely from the South and the Southwest), could agree on.

The final document, which came out under the names of both Gephardt and Senate Minority Leader Tom Daschle, made a number of proposals aimed at the middle class, many of them not new, many having been proposed by Clinton. Unlike Clinton, they proposed requiring health insurance coverage for all children. Clinton had considered proposing this in his convention speech, but decided against it because the administration hadn't figured out how to pay for covering all children. The congressional Democrats were reading the same polling data as the White House: the public was suspicious of big federal programs. Though numerous House Democrats were suspicious and even contemptuous of Clinton's march to the center, they, too, didn't want to be vulnerable to the Republican charge that they were "big-government, tax-and-spend liberals."

But in their leaning on Gingrich as the enemy, continually slamming the Republican Congress, they ran the risk of not appearing to have much positive to say about what they would do if returned to power.

The word "families" is at least as much a buzzword at this Convention as it was in San Diego. Both parties are picking up the same polling information: that middle-class families feel stretched thin, having to work harder (or both spouses having to work) to keep up a sufficient income to send their children to college and to retire with security. These people, married with children and largely living in the suburbs, were the swing voters in this election. To get them back by being culturally conservative and fiscally prudent and at the same time attract women voters by taking initiatives that help the family took quite a juggling act. But Clinton pulled it off. Pollster Stan Greenberg told a group at the Convention that middle-class women are against big government but believe that government has a role in improving people's lives. The "gender gap" was the largest among young women. Greenberg demonstrated through showing a tape with squiggly lines moving up or down as a group of young voters reacted to various statements by turning a dial on "people meters," that the line shot way up when education and minimum wage were mentioned. He said that women were ready to come back to the Democrats because they were appalled by the Republican Congress's cutting funds for education and school lunches and by the government shutdown—which turned out to be a defining event.

Martin Frost, the chairman of the Democratic Congressional Campaign Committee, in a speech to the Convention on Monday afternoon introducing some of the Democratic challengers, said the Democrats were "choosing a new kind of Democrats who will reflect common sense," who are "mainstream Democrats." He repeated "common sense." Frost and Gephardt are trying to push the image of the House Democratic Party toward the center, on the grounds that that will make it more acceptable—and electable.

———

Late Monday afternoon, the Democratic Senatorial Campaign Committee is holding a reception at the Chicago Cultural Center. A placard says that the event is sponsored by the Mortgage Bankers Association of America, the National Association of Realtors, and the National Realty Committee. (In the grand tradition of seeking bipartisan access, the first two groups had also underwritten a National Republican Senatorial Committee brunch in San Diego.) There are huge platters of cheese, pasta served from chafing dishes, a couple of bars, and many lobbyists. I observed one senator up for reelection receiving a check from a lobbyist. The senator, turning red, quickly handed it to his finance manager, who was hovering nearby.

The next morning, at a breakfast in the swank Pump Room in the Omni Ambassador East Hotel, the Senate campaign committee is hawking its candidates to a large roomful of people, many of them lobbyists who were also at yesterday's reception. Among the roughly three hundred people here this morning are a prominent fundraiser from New York, a representative of the Association of Trial Lawyers of America, Washington lobbyists, numerous representatives of business, and some labor people. The placard on the way in thanks contributors who underwrote this event, especially Eastman Kodak. As the people with the checkbooks munch their scrambled eggs, each Senate candidate makes a bald pitch to them. Tom Bruggere, running in Oregon for Mark Hatfield's seat, says that he needs money "to go on television." He goes on, "What I need is before you leave take out your pen and write a check."

Bob Kerrey acts as proud master of ceremonies as he displays his recruits. One of them, Elliott Close, who is running against the nonagenarian Strom Thurmond, says, "My opponent hasn't debated since the 1940s." Houston Gordon, who is running against Fred Thompson, the Tennessee senator well-known from his part-time movie career, says, "I'm not an actor and I won't rent a pickup truck." (Thompson leased a red pickup truck when he ran for the Senate in 1990, playing the part of a good ole boy.) He continues, "I own one." Victor Morales, a Hispanic former high school teacher, who scored an upset in the primary to run against Phil Gramm in Texas and had become the vessel of many liberals' dreams, says, "People ask why I am running. Phil Gramm—do you need another reason?" He tells the assembled donors, "I am going to win. I'd love some of your money to put ads on television."

At a Democratic Congressional Campaign Committee party after the Tuesday night session, the welcoming placard thanked contributors, "especially the Philip Morris Companies and the Public Securities Assn." Given the current furor over smoking, this took a certain intrepidity on the part of the Party.

The Democratic Convention was as synthetic as the Republican one, though the Democrats probably won in the bathos department. It was moving to watch the paralyzed Christopher Reeve on Monday night—laboring to speak from his wheelchair, and he did have a momentary relevance to the Convention when he said, "President Roosevelt taught us that America does not let its needy citizens fend for themselves." And Jim and Sarah Brady, also on Monday night's program, speaking about gun control, brought home once again their pure grit. A policeman who had been shot was also trotted out. But these admirable people were being used, and so was the audience. None of these people had anything to do with the Democratic Party. (Reeve was chosen from a poll by the Democrats of which celebrity speaker people would most like to see.) And the Democrats had their own batch of "ordinary Americans" onstage. The Democrats, like the Republicans, and like the Olympics coverage, were using personal stories to make a point, or hold the audience's interest. Everything had to be "a story." (A leading Democratic politician said to me, "The Republicans put on a show in San Diego, so we're putting on a show." To him, the issue was which was the better show.) The Democrats' Monday night was eerie and unsettling. Both parties were playing cynical games with what have been our few common institutions, and destroying them. In their cynicism they were breeding more cynicism by putting on a "show" and masking reality. How could the public not conclude that politics is phony?

Contrary to the propaganda put out by Party officials, the Chicago Convention speakers couldn't say whatever they pleased. Speeches had to be submitted for scrutiny in advance, and censors working under the podium made sure that the literal Party line was adhered to. They ordered removed from Gephardt's speech a reference to cutting Medicare in order to pay for "tax cuts for the rich." This pairing, heavily employed by House Democrats during the budget fight, was considered by the Convention managers "class warfare," which the Party was now abjuring. Gephardt rebelled by winging the words into his speech. The censors also tried to keep Edward Kennedy from using the word "reactionary" in reference to the Republican Congress. The Kennedy people suggested some euphemisms, which the censors also didn't like. So speechwriter Robert Shrum told the censors that if they didn't like Kennedy's text they should have the President call him. (That ended it.)

Like the Republicans, the Democrats didn't want any real debate at their Convention, fearing that it would make them look fractious. We have reached the point where politicians aren't supposed to be political and the parties aren't to debate issues. Cowering before public opinion, not daring to try to shape it, the parties have given in to what the pollsters tell them the public likes and dislikes. That the conventions have essentially become ratifying events is the handiwork of the parties themselves—and the candidates. The conventions are a reflection of what has gone before. If there had been a significant challenge to Clinton, the Chicago Convention might have been very different, as the losing forces had to be bargained with and placated. The broadcast networks' panic over the declining audiences for the conventions—*less revenue for four nights every four years*—has added to the pressure on the parties to stage entertainment. But the networks' problem has become self-fulfilling. And even if vast masses aren't interested in watching the conventions, that's not a good enough reason for not making them more available to those who are.

On Tuesday, the D.C.C.C. is having a lunch at Cafe Brauer, one of Chicago's most popular restaurants, in Lincoln Park, which also contains Chicago's zoo. The placard for this one says the D.C.C.C. would like to thank its contributors, "especially Ameritech." The lunch is in honor of John Dingell, of Michigan, formerly a mighty power as chairman of the House Commerce Committee, and, should the Democrats retake the House, a giant once more. (Ameritech, a large telecommunications company, has a lot of business before the committee.)

Ameritech has handed out as party favors red-white-and-blue phone cords with its name printed all over them. The large array of investment bankers who also have business before the Commerce Committee, as well as of lobbyists here, bespeaks Dingell's potential. A man from Bechtel, a very large construction company which builds, among other things, power projects, who is here was also at this morning's Pump Room breakfast. Unfortunately, Dingell is on Clinton's train, which is to stop today in his district in Michigan, but other House members have shown up to help fill the gap, and David Bonior, the Democratic whip, pinch-hits for Dingell, so the contributors won't feel shortchanged.

Martin Frost tells the group, "We appreciate those of you who were with us when times weren't so good." And he adds, pausing for significance, "We remember our friends."

On Tuesday night at the Convention, Jesse Jackson and Mario Cuomo do their bit—after some negotiating—to help the White House with its welfare problem. Before the Convention, Panetta and Ickes had several discussions with Jackson, telling him that they really needed his help in trying to calm people down. They argued that even if he thought the President had made the wrong decision on the welfare bill, it was done now, and Clinton could be trusted more than Dole could to try to make the bill better. Jackson himself appeared before some caucuses to help calm things. Ickes also had discussions with Cuomo, who was mainly discontented that, like

Jackson, he wasn't scheduled to speak during prime time—the two hours that the networks grudgingly devoted to covering the Convention. The President may have needed these liberals to speak to the Convention, but the country at large wasn't to know that the Democratic Party still contained such people. They were addressing the activists who either would or wouldn't motivate their followers to vote in November, the people who could stir up or tamp down anger over the welfare bill. "We're mature enough to differ without splitting," Jackson tells the Convention in a speech that's quite helpful to the White House. "If you don't vote, you're irrelevant to the process."

Cuomo's speech has more edge to it. Perhaps with intended irony, he points out that "this is a different party" from the one in 1992. (It is also a party that has left him—once the liberals' great hope—out in the cold.) "It has not been easy for Bill Clinton to get us where we are now," Cuomo says, adding with bite, "and not all of us agreed with every turn that he made." He said that he had argued to the President, the Vice President, and Mrs. Clinton "that the risk to children of his signing that bill was too great," and he adds, needling, "We should all hope and pray that the President is right." And another poke, "We continue to insist as Democrats on all the government we need." Then he does his bit by making the needed point, "Keep your eye on the big idea. The Republicans are the real threat."

The pedestrian nature of the President's acceptance speech, on Thursday night, grew out of his having so many things to accomplish at the same time, and also stemmed from the fact that Dick Morris had had to resign abruptly from the campaign and leave town that morning. The bizarre revelation that Morris was leaving because of a forthcoming disclosure in a supermarket tabloid that he had been consorting for a year with a prostitute in the Jefferson Hotel, close by the White House, hit Chicago like a thunderclap.

In fact, in recent months, Morris had been acting like a man with hubris out of control, and therefore his latest venture wasn't as stunning to those who had been observing him closely as it was to the outside world.

White House people said that Morris did seem to become—in the words of one—"more manic" than usual in the weeks leading up to the Convention. They said that he had overstepped his authority, and taken too much credit for what others had done. He began to shut out the views of even his allies. (In interviews with *Time* for a cover story to appear at the start of the Convention, and in audiences he granted reporters in Chicago, he stressed his brilliant resuscitation of Clinton's fortunes.) A former member of Morris's group said, "All of us whom Dick considered his allies thought his coming-out party was a mistake—that it would diminish his influence, that he was taking a victory lap eighty days too early." As the Convention approached, Morris insisted on clearing speeches that were none of his business, tried to impose his own speech drafts on others—including a reportedly incensed First Lady. Gore, usually a Morris ally, was said to be wearying of him, too. One day, in Gore's office, Morris stood behind Gore's chair and delivered—with Gore in the audience—what he thought should be Gore's speech.

But even a Clinton adviser who almost completely disagreed with Morris said that his departure contributed to the prosaic nature of the President's speech. It also made a difference in its substance.

As Morris was bolting back to Connecticut on the Thursday morning of the Convention, a highly symbolic change was made in Clinton's acceptance speech—one that reflected George Stephanopoulos's now-enhanced authority.

The change came in Clinton's critique of Dole's tax cut. The pre-departure draft, reflecting Morris's centrist strategy, emphasized Dole's tax cut's probable deleterious effect on the deficit. The final draft, reflecting Stephanopoulos's predilection for firing up the Democratic Party base and making a more partisan fight, stressed instead that Dole's proposal would force big cuts in Medicare, Medicaid, education, and the environment. This was the latest manifestation of an argument Morris and Stephanopoulos had been having since mid-1995.

But by the time Morris left, the reelection strategy had been largely set: go to the center on social issues and the size of government but keep the base by talking about Medicare, Medicaid, education, and the environment. Morris's legacy was a cynical strategy that was working. He had had some good ideas and some truly bad ones. (Among the latter, some of his colleagues said, were that Clinton should match Dole's tax cut, and that he should decline the $62 million in federal funds for his campaign, leaving him free to raise and spend as much as he pleased. Other advisers were horrified by the idea—it would look unseemly. Yet as matters turned out, there was little difference between Morris's idea and what Clinton ultimately did—except that Clinton also accepted the federal funds.)

Clinton took literally the suggestions that his speech should point the way toward his second term, and so he gave a long list of things he would do (even if some of them hadn't been thought through), interspersed with his thudding metaphor about "building a bridge to the twenty-first century." Perhaps it wouldn't have been so thudding if it hadn't been so repetitive. Even some of his advisers conceded that specificity didn't necessarily rule out eloquence.

Like speakers who preceded him—in particular Gore and Dodd—Clinton engaged in a little rhetorical device that betrayed his and his advisers' concern about the "character" issue. He praised Dole as a man who loves his country, and having thus set Dole up, Clinton said that he wouldn't make any personal attacks on him. The obvious implication: it wouldn't be cricket to make personal attacks on Clinton.

There was some connective tissue among Clinton's proposals: that his primary emphasis would be on education, and opportunities for the middle class, and he repeated his pledges for "targeted tax cuts" to help people get more education, or buy their first homes. (There was, however, no commitment of large funds for education or a real plan to fix the problem of the declining quality of public education.) Nor was there much that addressed the inner cities, though some advisers had said this was of great interest to him. He talked at length about the need for finding jobs for people coming off welfare, though what he proposed didn't get to the heart of the matter. Nor did his piecemeal expansion of health care to cover people between jobs. (This wasn't a new proposal.) Some of the proposals—such as provide tutors so that every third-grader could read, a polling-inspired goal—hadn't been fleshed out. He didn't talk about curbing the growth of the entitlement programs, of course: acceptance speeches were no place for hard realities, and, anyway, his aides, sounding like Republicans, passed such matters off as the concern of the "elite media." (They suggested that Franklin D. Roosevelt and Abraham Lincoln were also fuzzy in their election campaigns about what they intended to do about big, hard questions.)

Though he was working toward one, Clinton hadn't yet found a governing philosophy that supplanted the New Deal. His agenda was eclectic and experimental, and not easily describable by him. "New Democrat" didn't do it, nor did the words "opportunity" and "responsibility" that were so frequently tossed around at the Convention, and played a prominent role in Clinton's acceptance speech. They are undoubtedly words that poll well, but they come across as just words.

Clinton was already working to undermine Dole's tax cut, by calling it "risky," and by insisting that each of his own "targeted" cuts was paid for. If the tax cut didn't work for Dole, he would be denuded of his main issue, his most important weapon for winning middle-class votes. Clinton was a merciless opponent.

Clinton made only a fleeting reference to wanting a Democratic Congress. But he appeared to have patched things up enough to come out of Chicago with a united Party.

Now the questions were not just whether he would beat Dole, but also what the nature of his victory—assuming he did win—would be, and what effect the Presidential race would have on the struggle for the Congress. Or, which set of alliances—those fighting to hold the House for the Republicans or those struggling to have the Democrats retake it—would do a more effective job of motivating turnout. On that would rest the alignment of political power in America for a long time to come.

Chapter Fourteen

DISCUSSIONS

IN EARLY SEPTEMBER, Tom O'Donnell, Dick Gephardt's chief of staff, was optimistic, but cautiously so, about the Democrats' chances of retaking the House. "If the thing were held today, I think we'd take it back," he told me.

The Democratic Convention, O'Donnell said, had convinced a lot of people that the Democrats were concerned about families, and in at least one poll, in *USA Today*, Clinton did better than the Republicans on that subject. Also, as a result of the Convention he was doing better than before on Medicare.

One factor that made O'Donnell cautious was that previous Presidential candidates—among them Hubert Humphrey and Gerald Ford—had recouped more points than now separated Dole from Clinton (though ultimately losing their races).

At the same time, Maria Cino, the executive director of the House Republican campaign committee, had privately lowered her estimate of how many seats the Republicans would gain, from twenty or thirty to seven. She told me, "As we get closer to the election and we don't see Mr. Dole tightening his margin, we pick up less." But she said she didn't see Republican control of the House in jeopardy. That was shortly to change.

"The question on everybody's minds," a highly influential Republican said to me over lunch in early September, "is when do you throw in the towel on Dole and try to preserve the House and the

Senate." This despair, and consideration of its ruthless consequences, began much earlier than most people understood. "The
conventional wisdom among Republicans," he said, "is that it's
over." He continued, "Republicans have gone from euphoria about
the Convention, which was naive, to whispered words of defeat
among the Republicans' best friends. Now Republicans are saying it
to other Republicans. The next step, they'll say it among Republicans and Democrats. Then they'll run for the door, not say it.

"There have been discussions," he said, among the highest
Republican officials, "as to what's in the best interests of the House,
Senate, and Presidential campaigns. The issue is resource allocation—how much of it is Dole-driven. If we do a direct mail to South
Carolina, do we mention Dole or just the congressional candidates
or just issues? If the spread between Clinton and Dole is fifteen
points, we lose the House and the Senate. And we're now looking at
a twenty-point gap. There's been discussion of this for six months
but now we're down to the short strokes. We have to decide how
much lead time we have, when does the mail go out the door, and
what does it say?"

He explained the cold-eyed view Party officials were taking of
Dole's situation. "There was no real bounce from our Convention,"
he said. "We have not moved off the dime to get people to vote for
us. The thirty-four percent Dole has is made up of Clinton-haters
and hard-core Republicans. The Dole people are still complaining
that the Party is hurting him, but our generic number has moved
up. So I don't know how we're dragging poor Bobby down. Dole has
not become acceptable. At the Convention, people said give him a
chance. It was an opportunity for us for a second look after the
tobacco fiasco, which was the equivalent of Dukakis taking that ride
in a tank, or of Dole saying [in the Vice Presidential debate in 1976]
that World War II was a 'Democrat war.'

"There is an argument that if people believe this is a blowout,
they'll say, 'I want a Republican Congress to offset Clinton.' There
is some research that indicates that's the case, but I don't believe
that. *Turnout* changes with a blowout.

"The R.N.C. has done some sophisticated research. There had been no linkage between the Presidential race and the generic numbers for the House. *Now there is.* That means that Dole is pulling the Party down. We'd been concerned that he was pulling the Party down, but that concern has been private. A big problem is that Clinton is to our right. It shows up in our base not being as motivated as it was before. It's about as motivated as it was in '92 [when George Bush lost to Clinton] and that's very bad for us. Even anger at Clinton is not enough to overcome it. The anger is gone because we have no left to fight. The era of big government is over. The ideological anger is over."

This person expressed his frustration with the Dole campaign's continuing failure to find a theme. Dole was bouncing around on the subjects of his tax cuts, and drugs (allegations of prior drug use by Clinton White House aides, and Clinton's foolishly saying to an MTV audience in 1992 that if he had it to do all over again he would inhale). The use of the subject of drugs was meant to invoke the subjects of moral decay, and of Clinton's character. But Dole couldn't make it work. And in the end there's little the federal government could do about drug use.

"Dole could still win, if they have a strategy," the influential Republican said. "But if they have a strategy they haven't shared it with us. He could win, but the problem is that morale is eroding among Republicans at such a fast pace. In terms of morale, out of ten we're at three and a half."

A House Republican leader talking to me about the House races at about the same time said, "The problem is with Dole. People can't get by his age. They can't get by the harsh look on his face. They turn him off."

At Grover Norquist's Wednesday meeting on September 11th, Norquist expresses unhappiness with how Dole is campaigning. "Dole says, 'I have only three bullets left in my gun.' It's true, but that's not very helpful."

A number of Republican candidates—three House candidates and Sam Brownback, who is running for the Senate in Kansas, and has been supported by Norquist and Ralph Reed—have come to the meeting today to press their case to these conservative activists. Brownback tells the group, as he has been saying in Kansas, "If I lose this race we're going to lose the Senate and Ted Kennedy becomes the chairman of the Labor and Human Resources Committee." The group laughs at the absurdity of such a thought.

Norquist is particularly interested in a House race in Virginia, where the candidate before his group today is running against a Democratic incumbent who votes with the Democratic conservatives. "This is a most important race," he tells the group. (He explained to me later that when such Democrats are in Congress the Democrats can say, " 'See, not all Democrats are liberals.' " He drew an analogy to Charles Stenholm, a conservative Democrat from Texas, and Barney Frank, a very liberal Democrat from Massachusetts. Norquist said, "I'd rather beat Charlie Stenholm than beat Barney Frank.")

An emissary from the Dole campaign, John Taylor, an economics professor at Stanford, has come to brief the group on Dole's tax plan, but he soon runs into trouble when he describes how to talk about how the tax cuts are to be paid for.

Norquist chastises him, saying quietly, but firmly, "We've been trying to avoid the rhetoric of 'pay for tax cuts.' People pay for tax increases. When someone talks about paying for tax cuts it sounds like the speaker is standing in Washington."

Taylor nods, as if accepting the chastisement.

The sentiment in the group, expressed with some heatedness, is that Dole hasn't sufficiently emphasized his tax cut.

Mark Rhoades, who works with Norquist, instructs Taylor, "If you take one idea back from this meeting to the campaign, make it Grover's point that they should emphasize that government spending is too high."

After the meeting, Norquist, still irritated about the Dole emissary's approach told me, "It was outrageous that he took the position that he did. He said people are concerned about how we're going to pay for this. That's the rhetoric of the left. It presumes taxes are revenue coming in. We assume taxes are a cost. The speaker is standing in Washington watching the people's revenue flowing in to him. We want our candidates, our spokesmen, talking about 'us' and 'we,' meaning 'we taxpayers'—and 'them' as government. To say, 'Oh, dear, how can we pay for it' makes us the government. We can say, 'For every dollar we cut taxes we will cut spending even more.' " He added, "The job for those of us who aren't part of the campaign is to go out and change the world in our own way."

On September 14th, the Christian Coalition is holding its annual conference, called "Road to Victory," in the huge ballroom of the Washington Hilton. (Grover Norquist is to appear tomorrow afternoon in a panel discussion of "Eliminating the I.R.S. as We Know It.") Newt Gingrich, appearing before the conference audience on Friday morning and aware that the state of the motivation of these people is a crucial factor in the outcome of the struggle for control of the House, basks in its full-throated reaction to his speech. (Ralph Reed, introducing him, said that when the new Congress convened, "the man who will be standing at the Speaker's rostrum will still be Newt Gingrich"—which brought the crowd to its feet.)

Gingrich comes onstage, illuminated by two spotlights and accompanied by "The Stars and Stripes Forever." The podium is large and modernistic, the stage has pillars on each side and large red-white-and-blue streamers, with two giant projection screens on either side of the stage. The impression given is of grandeur, with great men striding across the stage. The set is meant to strike awe in the audience, and it does. Gingrich tells the nearly five thousand people here, "You have made a difference in America. We together have made a difference in America"—adding, "despite the efforts of the elite media." When he tells them, "You elected a Congress which ended the welfare entitlement," he gets big applause.

Then he performs his two currently favorite shticks. To bring home the import of the tax issue—in a way in which Gingrich wishes Dole would—he holds up two checks. The first says, "Pay to the order of my family," in the amount of $1,272—which he says is the amount a family with a $30,000 a year income would gain from Dole's tax cut. "The other team," he says, "makes you write a check out to the I.R.S." for the amount of $1,272. Gingrich slams "liberal articles" that ask how Dole's tax cut will be paid for, "because the news media cares passionately about government and not at all about families." This draws huge applause. Until he got talked into supporting a large across-the-board tax cut, Dole himself, along with a number of his Republican colleagues, used to insist on that very question. Moreover, the Congress is required *by law* to pay for any tax cuts it enacts.

In Gingrich's other routine, he holds up an ice bucket and explains that the Congress, "under the liberals"—until he took charge—had had two buckets of ice delivered to each congressional office every day. ("I'm not making this up.") Gingrich boasts of getting rid of that practice, saving the American people $400,000 a year. He says, "That's why I'm called an extremist." It isn't, of course, and he knows it. His routine is funny, delivered with good timing and feel for the absurd, but the story trivializes his own efforts to cut the budget and transform government.

He tells the audience that before the Congress adjourns for the year, there'll be a vote to override Clinton's veto of the bill banning partial-birth abortions, and he asks for its help. (The Senate was not expected to override the veto, so the House vote was another opportunity to get members on the record on this controversial issue, another entry for the Christian Coalition voter guides.) He gets tremendous applause. (Later, the House narrowly overrode the President's veto but the Senate, as expected, sustained it.)

Ralph Reed, addressing the group next, gives a surprisingly barbed speech. Alluding to the contretemps about the title of Mrs. Clinton's book, *It Takes a Village*—Dole had mocked it in his acceptance speech and in Chicago both Clintons threw his mockery back at him—Reed says, "We don't say it takes a village to raise a child. We say it takes a family to raise a child." And then, referring to the bill banning same-sex marriages, Reed says, "When *we* talk about the institution of marriage we are talking about a man and a woman." (The Defense of Marriage Act, passed in reaction to a court case pending in Hawaii, was approved by both the House and the Senate by large margins. Clinton signed the bill in the dead of night on September 21st.) And then Reed says: "Neither my speech nor any other speech you'll hear this weekend was written or proof-read by Dick Morris or a call girl." The audience laughs loudly, and Reed is pleased. ("You liked that.")

Then he grows more serious, but continues to knock Clinton. "This election is not about a bridge, it's about character," he says. He says that Clinton was invited to speak to this conference but turned the invitation down—which receives boos. Therefore, Reed argues, "We really have no choice but to evaluate his priorities by his deeds in office." He attacks Joycelyn Elders, Clinton's loose-lipped former Surgeon General, and claims that "because of the efforts of the Christian Coalition, Joycelyn Elders is the former Surgeon General." He gives a graphic description of a partial-birth abortion, and he mocks Clinton's having said he would inhale if he had another chance. Chopping the air with his hand, Reed says that the Christian Coalition isn't going to allow "any more A.C.L.U., Clinton-style judges." He attacks Clinton's record on drug enforcement, and makes a dig at the President for having "discovered tobacco." (This gets instant recognition and laughter from the audience, many of whom are from tobacco-growing states.) And then he says, "Mr. President, we have a message for you. Before you try and tell us to get tobacco out of our house, you need to get illegal drugs out of the White House." This gets a standing ovation—though there has been no evidence of current drug use by current White House employees.

This is a different Ralph Reed from the sophisticated, smooth operator one has seen in other contexts, or the detached, cool analyst. It's also a different Ralph Reed from the one who held the "Faith and Freedom" meeting in Balboa Park in San Diego. This is an old-time, earthy, somewhat demagogic, effective crowd-rouser—and his audience loves him.

He then attacks "left-wing teachers unions" and the media,

and plays on—and encourages—his audience's sense of victimization by the "liberal media" and the Federal Election Commission. "There are some who wish we wouldn't distribute our voter guides this fall," he says. Defiantly, he goes on, "We will not be harassed, we will not be intimidated, and we will not be silenced. We are Americans, too."

And then he gets down to the real business. "The true purpose of this conference . . . is to launch the most ambitious voter education and get-out-the-vote program in the history of American politics. . . . We, together, are going to register a million new voters in a hundred thousand churches," and distribute 17 million congressional scorecards and 45 million voter guides.

"To the pundits and the press we say this: If you think we turned out a large vote in 1994, you ain't seen nothin' yet."

And then he issues a warning to Republicans: "If you want to maintain control of the House and the Senate, and you want to have any chance at all of gaining the White House, you had better not retreat from the pro-life and pro-family stands that made you a majority party in the first place." This seems to come almost as an afterthought, something he must do, and then he ends on a brief, spiritual note.

Reed is smart enough to know that he has many audiences here—the one in the room, the national press, the public, Republican leaders—and some things to accomplish and some to avoid, all at once.

On Saturday, Bob Dole pays a surprise visit to the Christian Coalition conference—but it was a close call.

First, there was a long debate among his advisers over whether he should go. One side argued that for Dole to identify himself with a values-oriented movement, especially the Christian Coalition, would make him look hard and preachy and would have him seem to be lining up, in the words of one opponent of the idea, with "a scary group." Advocates of his attending argued that he still didn't have "the base" lined up, and that it shouldn't be taken for granted.

To those who demanded, Where will they go?—a challenge often asked on both sides in politics—the response was that they just might not be as activist as Dole and the Republican Party needed them to be. This was of course the danger, and it put Dole in a difficult position.

A few days before the conference, Ralph Reed paid a call on Scott Reed to urge that Dole attend it. He had already sent two memos to Scott Reed and also talked to Paul Manafort, the chief strategist of the Dole campaign. "I think you're making a big mistake if you don't come to this event," Ralph Reed told Scott Reed. Scott Reed maintained later that he had already planned for Dole to go, "but I didn't want days of negative ads about it." He also told Ralph Reed that Dole would be talking about partial-birth abortion, which, Scott Reed said in a talk we had later, "is going to win the election for us." It would, he thought, "provide the margin in several Catholic states."

The real point, Ralph Reed told Scott Reed, was that Dole couldn't be in Washington for a day and a half during the Christian Coalition conference and not put in an appearance.

Then, shortly after Dole arrived at the Hilton just before noon on Saturday, an aide informed him that earlier that morning Pat Robertson had told the conference that Dole was so far behind (twenty-three points in one survey) that "there has got to be a miracle from Almighty God to pull it out." Whereupon an angered Dole came close to turning on his heels and leaving. (Dole wasn't a happy man when he returned to the campaign headquarters. Scott Reed was furious, because Robertson knew, when he made the remark, that Dole was coming to the conference.)

Ralph Reed was annoyed by the Dole campaign's efforts to keep Dole's imminent appearance at the conference under wraps. He wanted it to get major coverage; Scott Reed wanted just the opposite.

Addressing the Christian Coalition audience, Dole cracked, "I was just driving by and saw all the cars." (Ralph Reed thought that that was much too casual a remark.)

And Dole pledged, "When I get the partial-birth abortion bill I'll sign it. I won't veto it, I'll sign it." This is, of course, the safest pro-life position to take, the one on which there was the most consensus. He received cheers and more enthusiasm from the audience than it actually felt for him, but not as much enthusiasm as it has shown other speakers.

The following Monday, Ralph Reed saw in *The Hotline* tracking poll that the Presidential race had closed to eight points. The next day, he sent a memo to Scott Reed saying that Dole was getting the better of Clinton on morality, crime, partial-birth abortion, and drugs, and that he should keep it up. He recommended that Dole appear at an evangelical college in the South or a battleground Midwestern state. He specifically recommended Wheaton College in Illinois, Hillsdale College in Michigan, and several other schools. He then called Manafort, who seemed enthusiastic. But nothing happened.

At this point, Dole was actually doing less well with evangelicals than Bush had done. And Clinton was doing better than Dole with Southern white women. Stan Greenberg and Celinda Lake's polling for EMILY's List also indicated that "there aren't any angry white men," Greenberg said. (The new cliché for the election was "soccer moms": middle-class suburban women who feel stressed by their family and income-earning responsibilities. The "soccer moms" were the "angry white men" of 1996. It seems that politics cannot exist without a cliché.) In fact, according to Greenberg, when people were asked which party "shares your values," Clinton came out thirteen points ahead of Dole. (With Morris out of the White House, Greenberg was now doing more polling directly for the President.) And Dole was losing ground on the question, Which party did you trust to handle taxes and the budget? He still led Clinton on this by three points, which wasn't very much, and was starkly different from the way the parties had been viewed on this question for decades.

And the one factor the Clinton camp set the most store by, the economy, was holding up, the recovery continuing. (A *New York Times*/CBS poll indicated that a majority of registered voters was giving Clinton credit for the relatively good economic times.)

Stan Greenberg actually agreed with those Dole advisers, or would-be advisers, who felt that Dole would be doing better if he had remained concentrated on taxes and drugs, and also if he had talked simply about cutting taxes rather than about cutting taxes and also balancing the budget. But it's not at all clear that he could have gotten away with that. Dole's tax cut wasn't working for him as an issue because the public was now far more sophisticated about the deficit—a major political development—and also because much of the public was now skeptical that Dole, or any politician, would deliver on such a promise.

Dole seemed at times almost to be trying to help Clinton. To the dismay of his staff, he said he opposed the Family and Medical Leave Act, which in the Republicans' as well as the Democrats' polls was wildly popular. Moreover, as the Clinton camp well understood, having to take unpaid leave for family emergencies was more likely to affect the woman's income. (Toward the end of September, Clinton signed a bill requiring health insurance plans to cover at least forty-eight hours' hospitalization for mothers who have just given birth.)

Dole was having a hard time finding a subject that he felt comfortable with and that worked. Both he and the House Republicans were in trouble on education, which was turning out to be a major issue of the election, and one of great importance to the middle class. Dole's attack on the teachers unions backfired, as did his support for eliminating the Department of Education. Democrats, from Clinton to House members, hammered Republican House members for voting to cut education funding and to eliminate the Department. The Republican attack on a "bureaucracy" was interpreted as an attack on its mission. (Actually, Republicans weren't trying to cut education funds by very much, but the issue was too good for the Democrats to pass up.) The AFL-CIO made it the subject of one of its ads. The education issue was a large factor in the continuing "gender gap" between Clinton and Dole.

So, though both sides were reading similar polls, Dole and the Republicans, without a credible tax cut, and on the wrong side of the education issue, were hobbled in their attempts to appeal to the middle class. (The Republicans were, however, getting credit for the welfare bill.) Then Dole went at Clinton's character indirectly—he was reluctant to take it straight on, mainly because it might reinforce the impression of him as mean and nasty—through the drugs issue, but that wasn't strong enough to help him much.

In an historic shift in American politics, the three great "wedge" issues that Republicans had been using against Democrats—welfare, crime, spending—had been neutralized or taken over by Clinton. All three issues were to some degree or another about race. Breaking free of these issues was what the "New Democrat" movement, which Clinton had spearheaded, was all about.

Another Republican leader, referring to the themeless and, he felt, isolated Dole campaign, and its effect on the House races, said: "Together, our team is stronger than theirs—but. Our team is the governors, all Members of Congress, all Senators, the chairman of the R.N.C., and our coalition. Yes, the AFL-CIO has a lot of money, but if you asked, Would you rather have the AFL's money or the Christian Coalition voter guides, that's a tough call. They also have the trial lawyers and the teachers unions. If you take our coalition—the Christian Coalition, Grover's group, the N.R.A., the N.F.I.B., talk radio, which I consider part of our coalition—we have much more resources than they have, much more reach than they have. In the ability to generate votes and win people over I'd take our team any day. But if we don't have a coherent message, a sense of shared mission, it doesn't work."

The relentlessly cheerful Bill Paxon by mid-September was still predicting that the Republicans would pick up twenty House seats. In the course of our phone conversation, Paxon told me he had to ring off because Ralph Reed was waiting to see him. Then Paxon tried to pass it off as a once-a-year-or-so friendly visit. In fact, Reed told me later, he talked to Paxon during the election "a couple of times a month."

Ralph Reed also kept in touch with several of the consultants who worked with the Republican leadership and on congressional campaigns. His pollster, Vern Kennedy, also polled for Republican Jeff Sessions's campaign for the Alabama Senate seat. Others Reed kept in touch with were Frank Luntz, the thirty-three-year-old Republican pollster, and Joe Gaylord, the political consultant and close adviser to Newt Gingrich.

Clinton wasn't quite home free. The polls consistently showed that people had doubts about Clinton's character and truthfulness, but that they largely discounted that because other issues were overriding. Also, they had heard charges about his character for a long time. Still, Whitewater was pending and new developments could occur at any time—and it couldn't be dismissed that the public's patience with this aspect of him could wear out. Peter Hart, the Democratic pollster, called Clinton's character issue "the long fuse."

According to a close aide, Clinton worried about Iraq, because Saddam Hussein was so unpredictable. (A retaliatory strike by the United States in early September to punish Saddam for an incursion into the north had had ambiguous results.) "We could have done without Iraq," a Clinton adviser said to me.

By mid-September, Clinton, finally confident of reelection but fighting overconfidence on both his part and his staff's—he had a thing about overconfidence—was growing increasingly interested in seeing the Democrats retake the Congress. A Clinton aide said, "Clinton was interested in getting a Democratic Congress, because of investigations, but he couldn't say, 'Give me a Democratic Congress.'" The one-word reason his advisers gave privately was "Whitewater." This was code for hearings not just on Whitewater but also the bevy of Clinton scandals, past and perhaps future. And if the independent counsel, Kenneth Starr, brought damaging charges, a Clinton adviser said, it would be more comfortable to have a Democratic Congress.

Moreover, as Clinton aides pointed out, historically a second-term President's party usually suffered losses in the midterm election. So Clinton wanted all the help he could get in the first two years of his next term, both to get things done within that period and to ward off trouble. The sense was that if reelected, Clinton would have a brief time to accomplish things. But the most negative reaction to Clinton's acceptance speech, according to Stan Greenberg's dial system, came when Clinton said, ever so briefly, that he wanted a Democratic Congress. "We're more likely to get it the less he talks about it," an adviser said.

A clear public sign of his interest was a two-day trip, September 18–19, to Washington State, which he was certain to carry, where he made appearances with Randy Tate's opponent, Adam Smith, and two other Democratic challengers for House seats. Unlike 1994, Democratic candidates now want to appear with Clinton. Smith actually changed his mind on this more recently, having said in July, "If he wants to campaign in my district, he should campaign for himself. I wouldn't feel comfortable standing on a platform next to him—with him saying he likes me."

Since early September, the Democratic congressional leaders and the heads of the two Democratic congressional election committees had been pressing White House officials for more Presidential effort in House and Senate races, and for a meeting with the President to discuss this. Leon Panetta and Harold Ickes were strongly for giving some resources to the House and Senate committees. Bob Kerrey, chairman of the Senate Democratic campaign committee, argued that the Republican Senate candidates were very conservative, and that their election would reinforce a rightward trend among Senate Republicans.

Given Whitewater and other possible investigations, not to mention the general harassment potential of such a conservative Republican Senate, I asked Bob Kerrey whether he had drawn the picture for the President of the consequences for him.

"I didn't have to," Kerrey replied.

On September 17th, after a briefing of the bipartisan congressional leaders on Iraq, the President met with the Democratic leaders and told them he'd give them some funds right away. Each congressional campaign committee got a million dollars from the Democratic National Committee—a pittance when compared to the hundreds of millions that would be spent on the Clinton campaign. (This was less money than was given to the congressional campaigns in 1994, but several White House people—especially the President—remained annoyed that congressional Democrats had blamed Clinton for their loss in that election.) At about the same time it was also agreed that there would be three "unity" fundraisers—in New York, Los Angeles, and Washington—at which the President would appear, with the proceeds divided three ways among the House and Senate Democratic campaign committees and the D.N.C. (A congressional Democrat said that he realized he might have Kenneth Starr to thank.)

On September 28th, though he was in no danger of losing Massachusetts, Clinton made an appearance with John Tierney, Peter Torkildsen's opponent.

But there were still limits on how far the President and his political advisers were willing to go in helping the House and Senate candidates. "We haven't won this election yet," Doug Sosnik, the White House political director, told me on October 1st. "We still have to get two hundred and seventy electoral votes. Though the press has decided we've won, the public hasn't." He added, "We're trying to strike a balance between where we are in our race and helping the congressional Democrats. We don't want to be blindsided."

On Wednesday, September 18th, Grover Norquist's group is meeting in a basement room in the Capitol because Gingrich is to appear. A large crowd has turned out to hear him. Another parade of candidates make their case. While the group awaits Gingrich, Peter Roff, of GOPAC, relays some alarming news. Yesterday, in Washington State's "jungle" primary, in which candidates from both parties appear on a single list, Randy Tate trailed his opponent, Adam Smith, by two percentage points. (The gap narrowed somewhat after absentee ballots were counted.) "We need to pay attention," Roff says. "This is problematic." He points out that two other House freshmen from Washington State, Rick White and Linda Smith, also had close calls. "We have our work cut out in Washington State," Roff says.

A staff member of the House Budget Committee reports on where things stand in the negotiations between the Republicans and the White House on final appropriations bills. "There is probably agreement on all sides that we do not want a government shutdown," he tells the group. "We lost that battle." He adds, "We're willing to spend a few million dollars as an 'exit fee' for getting out of town."

A representative from one of the groups complains that in their urgency to go home and campaign, the Republicans are giving in too much to the administration on spending bills. "It's getting expensive," he says. "Some of us would rather have you stay another few weeks so that it costs less." The Budget staff member replies, "The feeling is that the longer we stay in session the higher the risk we'll lose."

Gingrich arrives a half-hour late. He's wearing a navy blue suit, a bright blue shirt, and a patterned tie. He gives the group his analysis of how Republicans should conduct their campaigns. He goes through the routines about the two checks and the ice bucket, and says that the message should be that Republicans stand for lower taxes, pinching pennies, and against drugs. He recommends that Republicans say, "Everybody who thinks there's no waste in Washington, vote Democrat and then pay your taxes. And everybody who thinks there's waste in Washington, vote Republican and then spend your tax cut. . . . Vote Democrat, but then don't complain when you run out of money, when your taxes are increased, and your kid becomes a drug addict." His audience chuckles.

Gingrich tells the group that House Republicans are looking strong. "We let them beat us up for a very long time. We are now on the way back," he says. Expressing confidence that the Republicans will make gains in November, he says, "I believe that we're between plus six and plus thirty." (His real belief, according to close associates, is toward the lower end of that range.)

After Gingrich concludes his remarks, Norquist gives him one of A.T.R.'s "Friend of the Taxpayer" awards. And Norquist announces that later that day, seventy-five members of Congress are to be photographed receiving the award from him. (The picture, accompanied by a press release, would be sent to newspapers in their districts.) The group applauds as Gingrich accepts the award; a photographer records the scene.

The Republican House members' strategy by mid-September for dealing with their liabilities—Dole and their own previous performance—was to pass more bills and then get out of town as soon as possible. A House Republican leader said, "To show a continuing record of accomplishment is going to be the meat of our campaign this fall." He also said, "Newt keeps adding to the list but I keep ignoring him." He added, "Obviously, there has been an effort to not nationalize the election, unlike 1994."

The Republicans' continuing effort to pass legislation caused continuing friction with the Dole campaign. By mid-September, Scott Reed, Dole's campaign manager, considered himself "at war" with the Republican congressional leaders over their desire to pass the bill to stem illegal immigration. "Every time they send Clinton a bill to sign it helps him," Reed told me. "The worst week we had was the week after our Convention. Clinton signed three bills at the White House, and he moved up six to eight points. That was bad."

So, when Senator Alan Simpson, Republican of Wyoming and chief sponsor of the immigration bill, and Lamar Smith, Republican of Texas and the bill's chief sponsor in the House, called Reed for a meeting in earlyish September, Reed told them he was busy and they should come to the Dole headquarters, near Union Station. Dole was trying to block passage of the bill by supporting a provision denying public education for children of illegal aliens. Clinton had said he would veto any bill that contained this provision, and a sizable number of senators from both parties had said they would filibuster the bill if the provision was in it. In the meeting, Simpson told Reed that he was wrong to try to stop the bill, that he should be an American, should be for the immigration bill. And then Simpson, a six-foot-seven man with a towering temper, told Reed, "This is the most incompetently run campaign in American history."

Reed, who it turned out also had a temper, shouted at the distinguished senator, "Fuck off. I'm not a statesman. I'm not a legislator. I'm a campaign manager and it doesn't help Bob Dole if you continue to send Clinton bills to sign."

Despite Dole's objections, and Gingrich's support of him on this issue, the congressional Republicans decided to drop the offending provision. An immigration bill was passed and sent to the White House, where the President signed it on September 30th.

Marc Nuttle, in Washington toward the end of September for one of his reconnaissance missions, looks weary and worried. He has just seen the tracking poll numbers of the Dole campaign. He's also talked to people this morning at the Republican National Committee, the National Republican Congressional Committee, and the National Republican Senatorial Committee. "The tracking numbers inside the Dole campaign are not good," Nuttle says. "They had been holding at a gap between Clinton and Dole of nine percent of likely voters, but that number's gone to fifteen, and we're behind in a lot of states where we should be ahead or dead even." (A Republican official later confirmed Nuttle's figure.) "They've been tracking on ads," Nuttle says, "and none of the Dole ads have traction. The drug ads, only a little bit." He says, "There's no real coalition campaign, no coordination with outside groups. Therefore they live or die by their TV theme."

The National Federation of Independent Business, Nuttle says, is watching about 250 congressional races. "The N.F.I.B. is the only group to have directors in fifty states. A lot of groups call us for regional analyses." Nuttle says that if the election had been held a few days ago, before Dole's number took its most recent dip, the Republicans would have lost seven House seats but maintained control of the House, and would have gained one Senate seat.

He tells me that he doesn't agree with the N.R.C.C. that the Republicans will gain seven House seats. "They're counting some I'm not yet," he says.

He adds that he continues to advise some of the 35,000 state-based special interest groups and he advises his larger clients on how to be in touch with them. "I want to get them in the business of electing men and women who believe in free enterprise," Nuttle says. "I give them criteria for deciding what's at stake. I send them packets of information."

The N.F.I.B., Nuttle says, is now helping 250 Members of Congress "in some way." Only about 100 to 125 members are receiving the maximum contribution, Nuttle says. The top 100, Nuttle says, get the maximum contribution, and a mailing to the membership in their district, and might get an N.F.I.B.-sponsored event in their district.

"It's not like there's a wave coming across the ocean that will sweep one party in, as happened in '94. In '96, it's bits and pieces that you don't know how they're going to add up," Nuttle says. "The image is of a bunch of corks bobbing in the water: someone takes a paddle and hits the water. Some go under, some don't. It's the chaos theory versus the wave theory."

Not long before the 104th Congress adjourned to go home and campaign, I checked in again with my three Republican candidates.

Peter Torkildsen is hopeful that the yawning gap of twenty points or more between Clinton and Dole in Massachusetts won't have a direct effect on his own race. He thinks that the tight race for the Senate between incumbent Senator John Kerry and Governor William Weld will brake the pressure from the top of the ticket on congressional seats. He also hopes that the Senate race will increase turnout, with a large proportion of ticket-splitters. "George Bush got thirty-two percent of the vote in 1992," Torkildsen says. "There wasn't a strong base. I'm positive Bob Dole will do better than that, but I can't say by how much."

Torkildsen is preparing to go to his district to make an announcement that he assumes will be welcomed by his constituents: a federal grant of $1.1 million for a new fish and wildlife visitors' center. Earlier, Torkildsen had already flown up to his district to announce at the G.E. plant in Lynn an additional million dollars in contracts for an engine used in helicopters. He hopes soon to be able to announce a new water and sewer grant, and also a highway grant.

Every week in September and October, and sometimes three times a week, the National Republican Congressional Committee held an "incumbent retention" meeting where incumbents made a pitch to a board of Republican members for the full $60,000 the N.R.C.C. could give them. By making the candidates make their case, the committee got a better sense of how the campaigns were doing and what they were spending money on. Torkildsen had received the $60,000 in "coordinated expenditures" that the National Republican Congressional Committee could give to the candidates.

In his campaign, Torkildsen is stressing independence; his theme is "Leadership, Independence, Integrity." He frequently points to his participation in bipartisan efforts to get legislation passed. "I'm willing to work with people in the other party," he says, "but a lot of people understand that, given my voting record all along."

Randy Tate professes nonchalance about his coming in behind his opponent in the primary. "Our focus has always been November 5th," Tate says. "That's a calculation we made early on." Tate tells me he had recently appeared before the "incumbent retention" meeting. "I said, 'I'd like your sixty grand, and any other money you might have.' "

Both he and Torkildsen are hoping that the N.R.C.C. will establish an "independent expenditures" unit, allowed under the recent

Supreme Court decision, to give them more funds. The N.R.C.C., in fact, came close to doing so, but decided it didn't need to because it could get more mileage out of spending corporate contributions—soft money—on its "issue advocacy" ads. The "independent expenditures" unit would have had to spend "hard money," which is more difficult to raise. (Both the Senate Democratic and Republican campaign committees did set up "independent expenditures" units.) In either case, a campaign committee's spending soft money or making "independent expenditures" in order to fund national ads made a mockery of the campaign finance laws.

Tate's nervousness about his situation comes through, however, when he speaks of his anxiety to get home and "doorbell"—his term for making calls on as many of his constituents as he can—and also raise money. "I'm going door-to-door every day I'm home," Tate says.

Tate tells me that in a meeting last night of the House Republican Conference he said that while there were still important things to do in the final spending resolution, "if you only get ninety percent of what you want it's ninety percent more than what you had." Tate told the group, "Each day that we're here will be one less day I'm knocking door-to-door, one less day I'm talking to voters. Let's not get hung up on issues around the margin. If the public sees us staying around here and bickering, we'll be worse off." Tate tells me, "I got a round of applause."

Greg Ganske, sitting on a leather couch in his office, looking wan, has come back to Washington in order to cast some votes at the end of the session. He contracted encephalitis while he was in Peru at the end of the summer operating on disfigured children, and is still very weak. He had been seriously ill and was hospitalized for a week after his return to Des Moines. (His progress to and from the House floor is very slow, and the effort makes him very tired.)

One thing Ganske wants to accomplish before this session of Congress ends is a ban on physicians' taking out patents on certain procedures and then charging royalties. He is also working on legislation to bar HMOs from including in their contracts "gag" clauses that prohibit doctors from telling patients about procedures the HMOs wouldn't pay for. (Both measures were supported by the Clinton administration. The patents measure passed, the gag clause prohibition did not.)

"I've been off the campaign trail for a month," Ganske says, "but people have helped."

Ganske tells me that not much is being made in his district of the Gingrich issue. "It wouldn't be smart to do that," he says, "because I've been independent."

Chapter Fifteen
SHOOTING PARTY

HER FEET PLANTED firmly in the correct position—right foot to the rear—Tanya Metaksa peers through her yellow sunglasses, carefully levels her shotgun, and fires at the small round black disk that is rolling away from her. She misses. "Oh, man!" she exclaims.

On a beautiful Saturday afternoon, a clear, crisp early fall day, the leaves beginning to turn, Metaksa has come to the Lappawinzo Fish and Game Association, in Pennsylvania's Lehigh Valley, in response to a plea from the local National Rifle Association organizer, Scott Delaney, who has told her that he thinks the incumbent Democratic House member, Paul McHale, is vulnerable. The House Democratic campaign committee recently discovered the same thing. McHale, a sophomore, hadn't been on anybody's initial list of endangered members, but his is one of the many House races that suddenly tightened this fall. McHale's poll number is below fifty percent, which is considered a bad sign for an incumbent. But the Republican congressional committee has its doubts, and hasn't given McHale's challenger, Bob Kilbanks, a member of the Christian Coalition who defeated a more establishment candidate in the primary, any support yet. (It later gave him $30,000; its priority all along was to take care of the incumbents first.)

Metaksa has just flown in, overnight, from Kansas. "This is my fifth candidate in three days," she told me. Since Thursday, she has been in Missouri and Kansas, to help Republican candidates for the House, and Sam Brownback, the House freshman who is running for Bob Dole's Senate seat.

Metaksa says that she might not go to Washington State to help Randy Tate after all. "We may use our money differently," she says, adding that Washington State is still a priority for the N.R.A., in part because of issues in the state legislature. In fact, the N.R.A. is going through something of a crisis. It has developed financial problems and recently laid off dozens of workers. Some attribute the problem to its large new headquarters building in Virginia. There are fierce power struggles among its leaders. Its membership has been dropping. Some observers attribute this to the N.R.A.'s becoming less a recreational outfit and more a militant political one. Metaksa says that the problem stems from the fact that "all cause groups, left and right, depend on who's attacking them," adding, "Our people feel they were successful in '94 and their problems are over."

The race in the Lehigh Valley has turned into a semi-major one. Tipper Gore came to the area yesterday to campaign with McHale, and House Majority Leader Dick Armey has been here to support Kilbanks. Tom DeLay will be here next week.

Scott Delaney, the local N.R.A. organizer, a beefy, bearded, intense man in his thirties, says that "this is hunting and gun country," with over 10,000 N.R.A. members. The event at this club today is clay shooting. Shooters follow a course of varying difficulty that has been laid out among the trees and streams of this area, taking aim at black (rabbits) or orange (birds) clay disks that are hurled from manual traps at varying speed and heights. Metaksa, wearing cream-colored slacks and sweater, white sneakers, a white cap, and a web jacket embroidered with her name and an insignia that says "Charlton Heston Celebrity Shoot," was treated like a celebrity herself when she turned up earlier in the bar-and-grill room of the clubhouse, a simple, low-slung, dark-brick building. Delaney tells me that there are about twenty-five such clubs in the area, and "we make sure we cover them all," bringing candidates out for a day of shooting and meeting the club members.

Over a lunch of grilled chicken sandwiches, Delaney lists a number of "anti-hunting bills" pending in the Congress and says, shaking his head, "I can't believe that these things are happening in the United States of America." Delaney is upset with McHale for voting for the assault weapons ban. Metaksa tells the people at our table that the N.R.A. was successful in stopping funding for the National Center for Injury Prevention and Control (part of the Centers for Disease Control and Prevention, in Atlanta) to do research on gun injuries, and also got through the Congress a prohibition on gun-control advocacy by the agency. Delaney is pleased that the N.R.A. has put a crimp into such government "anti-gun propaganda." The N.R.A. also got an item into the final appropriations bill that allows licensed gun dealers to trade interstate on the spot, whereas before the guns had to be shipped. So, while because of its ultimate failure to get the assault weapons ban repealed many observers wrote off the N.R.A. as an effective force, it was still able to exert its influence on less publicized issues.

Metaksa knows that the N.R.A. has a political problem. When I asked her for her view of why many Members of Congress see the N.R.A. as a political liability, she replied, "Voting with the N.R.A. gets them negative editorials in their newspapers and some don't want that kind of heat."

Bob Kilbanks, the challenger, joins us at lunch. He's wearing light-blue jeans and a navy sweater. A pleasant-looking man with straight, dark-blond hair, and clear, vacant, blue eyes, Kilbanks shakes hands with the hunters in the room. He complains that there has been little evidence in this area of the Dole campaign—no signs, no bumper stickers. Asked if he wants Gingrich to come to the area, he hesitates and then says, "I don't know that that would be particularly helpful." He adds, with sarcasm, "My opponent attacks me as a 'Gingrich Republican.' "

A very young reporter from Channel 69, a local independent station, carrying his own camera, interviews Metaksa and Kilbanks outside the clubhouse. Metaksa says, "We're here to support Bob Kilbanks because Bob Kilbanks understands that freedom matters most. He understands the Second Amendment and the freedom to keep and bear arms."

Kilbanks says that he is "honored" that Metaksa has come to help him.

The young man forgot to turn on the microphone so they have to do the whole thing all over again. And he has trouble with Metaksa's name. She's used to this, so, smiling, she helps him out: "M-E-T, A-K for AK, S-A for semi-automatic."

On the shooting course, Metaksa is carrying an intricately engraved Browning 12-gauge double-barreled shotgun. In her group of five shooters are Scott Delaney and his grandfather, and Ray Nemeth, a craggily handsome antique- and modern-gun dealer, who graciously explains the ins and outs of the course as we proceed. Also along is Collins Spencer, a black legislative affairs specialist for the N.R.A. who is responsible for the Northeast, and who has driven up from Washington.

Having carefully positioned herself at another shooting station (there are ten altogether), Metaksa shouts in her strong voice, "Pull it!" and the trapper, hidden somewhere in the woods, sends an orange disk flying through the air, fast and low, making it hard to hit. She misses the single bird but then hits two birds sent whizzing by as a "nested pair."

Metaksa joins the group's joking. She says that she's more used to shooting a 28-gauge—she has a dozen guns—which she prefers because it's smaller and has less recoil. ("I don't like pain.") But she says she doesn't like to carry her gun through airports around the country. ("It's such a hassle.") "The thing about shooting," she says, "is that it's unisex. You don't need a lot of heft, you don't need a lot of brawn. It's concentration." She adds, "I shoot against myself. I'm very competitive."

She tells me that she does a lot of shooting at benefits put on by "Hunters for the Hungry." The shooters give away the meat, and people pay to shoot with a governor, which provides the money to process the meat.

As she approaches the last shooting station, seeing the difficulty of the shot, Metaksa says again, dragging it out longer, "Ohhh, maaaann."

But it turns out that she has won the contest within her group, racking up thirty points to the second-place finisher's twenty-five.

Some volunteers have laid on a spaghetti dinner in the Lappawinzo club's dining room, fitted out with long wooden tables. Metaksa has removed her cream sweater and slipped on a red jacket over a cream silk shirt and a string of pearls. She has the logistics of dressing for these days figured out. She works the room as people eat their spaghetti. About sixty-five people are here, most of them middle-aged or older and all dressed very casually.

Scott Delaney starts speaking at 5:40. He thanks the people who provided the spaghetti and praises Ray Nemeth "for his staunch support of the Second Amendment." Delaney tells them, "We have two days to register the rest of our voters," and that "the next thing you need to do is get bumper stickers on your car. This is a grassroots campaign. A bumper sticker is worth a lot of money in advertising." (Delaney's car's bumper stickers, other than those for Kilbanks, say, "Criminals Prefer Unarmed Victims," and "The Second Amendment Ain't About Duck Hunting.")

Delaney calls on Ray Nemeth to speak. In 1994, Nemeth founded an organization called the American Freedom Association, "to preserve the Constitution and the Bill of Rights." It runs ads and informs members about pending legislation concerning firearms. Nemeth, wearing a plaid wool shirt and aviator glasses, explains that he first got involved in the political process in 1994, "to neutralize Bill Clinton's legislative agenda." Nemeth says that "gun bills were flying through the Congress right and left. It was a very dangerous time." Nemeth refers to "legislation that has been put through that has taken away our Bill of Rights." Nemeth adds, "The threat is no less real than it was in 1994. If we lose the House of Representatives, you're going to see anti-gun legislation like you've never seen."

It's clear from the audience reactions that these people believe fervently in their interpretation of the Second Amendment, on which they are constantly reinforced by the N.R.A. It's also clear that if there were no Second Amendment they would be just as fervent about what they see as federal encroachment on their rights. They believe, and they are encouraged to believe, that they are being singled out. The N.R.A. reinforces them in the belief that they, rather than criminals, are being picked on. But of course the numerous federal, state, and local criminal laws are aimed at criminals—as are the gun-control laws. Ray Nemeth would probably be considered by the world at large a "gun nut," but he is a perfectly normal and pleasant man who feels strongly on this issue, and it all makes sense to him.

Introducing Metaksa, Delaney, talking about what the N.R.A. stands for, chokes up as he reads its charter when he reaches the point where it says it "supports the Constitution." His voice cracking, Delaney can hardly continue.

"N.R.A. is a risk-taking cause," Metaksa tells the group, "the cause of safety, responsibility, and freedom." She goes on, her strong voice filling the room and the audience paying rapt attention. She is low-key but firm. "The cause is under attack," and she adds that had the N.R.A. not gotten involved in the 1994 elections, "the Second Amendment wouldn't make it into the twenty-first century."

She tells them, "My husband, George, and I have been involved in the N.R.A. for most of our lives." She proudly quotes Clinton as having told the Cleveland *Plain Dealer*—"One of the few times he's told the truth," she cracks—" 'The N.R.A. is the reason the Republicans control the House.' " And then she tells them, "I have a pretty good idea about what makes *us* tick. . . . N.R.A. members and gun owners think that freedom matters to most people, but we are the people to whom freedom matters most."

Chapter Sixteen

DOORBELLING

SEATAC, WASHINGTON, OCTOBER 11TH. Now that the 104th Congress has adjourned, the endangered Republicans (and everyone else) can campaign full-time. Randy Tate, whose district includes this town between Seattle, to the north, and Tacoma, to the south, is giving it his all.

In order to liberate themselves, the House Republicans made numerous concessions to Clinton, especially on spending bills. They were worried that the administration might be trying to maneuver them into shutting down the government again, and that was out of the question. It reached the point where, as Eddie Gillespie, the Republican spokesman and strategist, put it, "If Clinton had wanted six billion dollars in unmarked bills stuck under an orange cone outside the White House, he'd have had it. They just want to get out of town." In fact, the Congress essentially acceded to Clinton's requests for more spending on education and the environment, and gave him another six billion dollars besides. This came on top of giving him a welfare bill, an immigration bill, a minimum wage increase, and an expansion of health insurance.

"It was devastating," Scott Reed, Dole's campaign manager, said later. "We were devastated that our 'friends' on the Hill had done this." He said that in May, he, Haley Barbour, and Gingrich had agreed on Congress's adjourning as early as possible in the fall—but, he added, "not that Congress would get out of town and give Clinton everything he wanted." He and Dole, who was then in

Florida, discussed over the phone what they could do, but, Reed said, "It was too late. There was nothing we could do. That's when we started on Clinton's credibility. That was the only thing left to do."

So, despite the misgivings on the part of Dole and his advisers about what it might do to Dole's standing, he started taking Clinton's character on directly. Clinton's "word is no good," Dole said. One problem was that Dole and his campaign kept talking aloud about whether he would take on Clinton's character, thus making it clear that this was just another tactical decision— calculated outrage. Dole even asked audiences whether he should "get tougher" on Clinton. But getting tougher on Clinton, some of Dole's advisers understood, even if it worked, would solve only part of Dole's problems. "It might pull Clinton down," one said, "but the real problem is how to get Dole's numbers up."

At the same time, Dole started calling Clinton a "liberal" ("liberal, liberal, liberal"). But such were the precautions that Clinton had taken that, Scott Reed recalled, "it was tough to paint him as a liberal."

(Just before Congress adjourned on October 4th, the House Ethics Committee, which had been considering the case for twenty months, raised four new charges against Gingrich, including the quite dangerous question of whether he had misled the committee.)

This week, secretly, a small group of Republican leaders finally made the decision that had been building for months. Following the first Presidential debate last Sunday, October 6th, these leaders, more worried than ever about holding the House, quietly reached the conclusion that it was time to definitively break with Dole, and concentrate their efforts on trying to hold the Congress. Dole hadn't done well enough in the debate to change the dynamics of the race. (A couple of weeks earlier, at a dinner in Newt Gingrich's "Dinosaur Room"—so named for its glassed display of a *Tyrannosaurus rex* skull—attended by a number of people from around the country, plus Joe Gaylord, Don Fierce, and Grover Norquist—the state of the House campaigns was reviewed and it was decided the time was near when a contingency plan should be made to break free of Dole.) The Republican leaders' decision to abandon Dole was tightly held, with only a few people—Haley Barbour, Gingrich, Gaylord, Fierce, Bill Paxon, and Eddie Gillespie—knowing about it. Bob Dole and Scott Reed weren't told.

Haley Barbour had already secretly commissioned a poll which asked: "If the election were held tomorrow, how would you vote for President and for Congress?" and then, "If the election were held tomorrow and Bill Clinton was going to be elected, would you vote for a Democratic Congress to implement his policies or would you vote for a Republican for Congress so as not to give Clinton a blank check?" A Republican official told me, "There was a thirteen-point swing between the first question and the second." The largest swing, he said, was by self-identified moderates and women. Then the Republicans tested the same questions in a focus group, and got a similar result.

The idea was to figure out how to break free of Dole without completely jettisoning him, since that could hurt the congressional effort as well as Dole—but making such a distinction would turn out to be difficult.

State parties in states from which the Dole campaign has effectively pulled out (Missouri and Illinois among them) were shifting resources to the House and Senate campaigns. Haley Barbour and Gingrich pressured the Dole campaign heavily to stay in California—Scott Reed had wanted to pull out—because of the large number of congressional seats at stake there. With no Presidential presence there, even a weak one, it would be harder to get people out on Election Night.

In the debate last Sunday, Clinton followed the strategy of staying "Presidential," not responding to Dole's barbs, and stressing the good economic condition the country was in. Dole did display his wit, but was still trying to tell the country who he was and assert what he wasn't, stressing that he was compassionate. It was a little late for that. To show that he wasn't too old and out-of-it, at the end he gave out his campaign's web site address, stumblingly—and incorrectly.

Republicans felt that Jack Kemp had let down the side in his debate with Gore on Wednesday, October 9th, by being both repetitive (about his hobbyhorse, supply-side economics) and unprepared. (The far more disciplined Gore was, of course, prepared down to his toes, and knowledgeable about a wide range of issues.) But none of this should have been a surprise about Kemp. Dole wasn't surprised. He told his advisers, "We knew exactly what we were getting with him."

On Wednesday of this week, there was an emergency meeting following Grover Norquist's regular weekly session, to assess the situation. A small group, which included Heidi Stirrup, of the Christian Coalition, and Joe Phillips, of the N.R.A., had asked Norquist if they could meet in his offices after the regular meeting. At noon, the meeting-after-the-meeting began in a smaller conference room, and focused on the congressional races. Norquist, Stirrup, and Phillips were joined by a representative of the House Republican campaign committee and a couple of other activists. The purpose was to determine how motivated the groups on the Republican side were. A former head of the Christian Coalition Washington office worried that new R.N.C. ads about union bosses might stir up labor union members against the Republicans, just as attacks on the Christian Coalition in 1994 had gotten its members exercised. Phillips said that the Democratic Convention, with all its emphasis on gun control, had aroused N.R.A. members. Norquist himself said that his Americans for Tax Reform was far more active now than in 1994. But there were reasons to worry.

On Thursday, October 3rd, Don Fierce, the Republican consultant, called Ralph Reed and said to him, "Let me tell you what I've seen out there. I don't see our Christians activated."

Ralph Reed replied, "We're going through the motions. I don't know how to motivate them."

On Capitol Hill, Tom O'Donnell, Dick Gephardt's chief of staff, was growing impatient with the White House. He was dissatisfied with the "unity" dinners that shared the proceeds among the three Democratic committees. "I'm not big on unity," he grumbled to me in early October. "I'm for disunity. I'm not big on events that raise money for a race that's over."

He not only didn't want to share the wealth with the Democratic National Committee for a Presidential race he considered won, but also was wrangling with the White House over Clinton's schedule and priorities. ("We have friends down there to whom we can speak frankly.") O'Donnell said, "I don't want a forty-nine-state strategy pursued. I don't care if he wins Florida. I care if he spends money for ads in the Wisconsins and the Washingtons and the Californias of this world. I tell them, 'Forget winning forty-nine states, even forty-four states, and reallocate your money into states that'll help us." His friends at the White House had told him to wait until after the debate. A decision was still pending.

"It's not going to make an awful lot of difference if he wins forty-seven states or forty-eight states," O'Donnell said. "History will record a lot of difference if he has a Democratic Congress or a Republican Congress." He added, "We're getting closer to the goal and more races are in play and we need more help." Both sides in the struggle for the House were contending with the fact that there was an unusually large number of races up in the air at this point in the election.

In response to the importuning of some of the worried members, including Tate, and deep concern on the part of leading Republicans that the Republican House candidates weren't doing well enough—there was a dip of about seven points in the Republicans' support in the generic polls—the Republican National Committee and the National Republican Congressional Committee recently decided to put up another round of ads in about twenty districts. The R.N.C. and the N.R.C.C. would supply two ads attacking "union bosses." Tate had sought out Bill Paxon, the head of the N.R.C.C., on the House floor and said that the Republicans had to do something about the AFL-CIO ads. "I can't fight my challenger *and* the AFL-CIO," Tate said. "I need air cover." Paxon assured Tate that his committee would respond.

"There was sheer panic out there," Maria Cino, the executive director of the House Republican campaign committee, told me later. In fact, Tate's campaign has thus far refrained from running the "union bosses" ads because of the large proportion of union members in his district, and because the first one referred to such bosses "in Washington." (They did use the ads, adjusted, later.)

The first ad, which was run early in October, had a splotchy picture of AFL-CIO president John Sweeney and said, "The big labor bosses in Washington are spending big money spreading big lies to buy their control of Congress." The second, which followed a little over a week later, showed fat, cigar-smoking men at a table, passing around big piles of cash, and said, "The big labor bosses in Washington, D.C., have a big scheme to buy the Congress." In both cases, the ads showed Democratic challengers on whose behalf the union ads had been made. They were paid for through a combination of hard and soft money from the R.N.C. and the N.R.C.C., funneled through the states (which could use a higher percentage of soft money on ads than the national committees could), since the Republicans decided that they could call them "issue advocacy" ads, just as the AFL-CIO did theirs. A Republican official said to me, "It's a joke—and the AFL-CIO has proved it to be a joke. We're just playing by the same rules."

Washington State has become the epicenter of the fight over control of the House. The humiliation of 1994 was the greatest here—it had the highest proportion of members of a House delegation change hands (six out of nine). Democrats are hoping to regain three and perhaps even four of those seats. Clinton is leading in the state by double digits, and the Republicans' situation has been made even more difficult by the fact that Ellen Craswell, a Christian fundamentalist who has no governing experience and says that she would govern according to the Bible, won the Republican gubernatorial primary. (The Christian Coalition has effectively taken over the Washington State Republican Party.)

Randy Tate's House seat is at the epicenter of the epicenter. National groups have descended on this race, as have their state affiliates. While Tate has the support of national conservative groups, in particular the Christian Coalition and other members of Grover Norquist's coalition, Adam Smith, his opponent, is receiving help not only from the national AFL-CIO and its state affiliate, but also the trial lawyers, the National Abortion Rights Action League (NARAL)—there is a strong pro-choice element in Tate's district— the National Education Association and its state affiliate, and national and local environmentalist groups. These organizations have been working together within the state. (In late October, the League of Conservation Voters was to name Tate one of its "Dirty Dozen.")

Labor's effort in this heavily unionized state began in the spring of 1995. Finding it difficult to get workers—who might be holding down two jobs, and have their household work to do as well—to come to meetings, the state AFL-CIO political director decided instead to train shop stewards, the people who were on the job with the other workers every day. The stewards also became conduits for encouraging workers to make phone calls (on an 800 line) to Washington to protest certain Republican-backed legislation. Labor also set out to "reconnect" with its members in Washington State through a recent "union household walk"—going to union households to offer to help workers register, and encourage them to be permanent absentee voters, because once they're on the absentee list they'll receive a ballot every election time. This would help busy workers vote. (The state labor council is planning to send out a very large number of pieces of mail.) In a new twist, it's also planning to send union organizers to over 100 work sites, covering over 80,000 workers, during the shift changes, to give them a labor flyer and encourage them to vote and to help get other people to the polls.

John Sweeney is coming to Tate's district next week, and Steve Rosenthal is planning to come soon, "to look around."

At lunchtime at the Holiday Inn in SeaTac, Tate and Smith are to hold the fourth of their debates. People associate Seattle with such yuppie enterprises as Microsoft and Starbucks (which originated in Seattle), but this area south of Seattle is heavily populated by blue-collar workers, most of them employed by Boeing (about forty percent of the district); the rest of the population consists of retirees and people who commute to work in Seattle. It has no major city, and a lot of strip malls. The district is home to a lot of 1994's "angry white males"—angry about NAFTA and about the inclusion of additional gun control in the crime bill. The district runs along Puget Sound and there is a strong streak of environmentalism in the area—many residents are union members who are environmentalists who like to hunt and therefore oppose gun control. The voters here are less easily classified than the usual categorizations would suggest.

In their first two debates, the focus was on Tate's record, but in the most recent one Tate went on the offensive, attacking Smith as a liberal who had voted in the state legislature for a big tax increase and for a sweeping health care plan similar to the one the Clintons had proposed.

The two men have striking similarities. Both are intense; they are nearly the same age (Smith is thirty-one, Tate will soon turn thirty-one); and both went into politics, in the state legislature, directly out of college, or, in Smith's case, law school. Both come from modest backgrounds: Tate grew up in a trailer park, which his father managed, and Smith is the first member of his family to have gone to college. Smith is slim, with dark hair, a thin face, and piercing eyes, and is as obviously ambitious as Tate. ("I was born to take on Randy Tate," he told me.)

During the lunch preceding the debate, a man who runs a hair-cutting shop says that he hasn't decided between the two candidates yet. "The Democrats are too much tax-and-spend, but Tate voted with Newt Grinch"—he smiles at his coinage of the name—"to cut Medicaid, Medicare, and tried to cut back on environmental regulations. I want to leave a good future for my grandchildren." He continues, "And they shut down the government for twenty-one days. People didn't get paychecks. There was no reason for this."

A large black woman, an organizer with the Washington Federation of State Employees, a branch of the American Federation of State, County, and Municipal Employees, second in size here only to the Machinists union, says, "We endorsed Smith early. Just about every union in the state has endorsed Smith, but because I live in his district it's very important to me that he win." She adds, "I think Newt has hurt the whole Party. We have Republicans supporting Adam. I'm shocked by that," she says in mock horror. "You feel the energy, because we've been hurting since '94," she says. "It's hurting labor people and homeless people. It's a crisis, so people are mobilizing."

But one of the biggest issues here is whether the local airport should be expanded to have a third runway, which has met with a lot of local opposition because of the additional noise and congestion it would bring, and because it would hurt property values. (And the Republican congressional campaign committee *had* urged its candidates to stress local issues.) The big question is which of the two candidates is more against the third runway.

Tate and Smith stand at podiums on a stage, red and white balloons behind them. Both are very earnest. Smith starts by asserting that he would be a "less partisan" voice in Washington (partisanship is out this year). And he stresses campaign finance reform, saying he wants to limit soft money and "the influence of outside money in the district." Smith seems to be trying to have it both ways—benefiting from the help of outside groups and deploring the phenomenon. This sets him apart a bit from the labor ads, some of which have been criticized in the newspapers as unfair. (But, Smith told me later, he considers campaign finance reform one of his strongest issues.) He also needles Tate about being such a prodigious fundraiser. Smith says that people say " 'it's perfectly all right if the business community puts a lot of money into ads . . . on behalf of Congressman Tate, but unions need to be stopped.' "

Tate, surprisingly, given the impact the issue has had, says that he wants to abolish the Department of Education, but he mitigates that somewhat by saying that as a result "you will be able to bring more money back to the local level." This is, of course, a false trade-off, since abolishing the Department wouldn't yield up so much money. They argue over enforcing anti-drug laws; Tate says there should be the death penalty for people who deal in certain quantities of drugs. Smith, "to show how liberal I am," he says with sarcasm, points out the drug-enforcement laws he's supported. They debate Medicare (whether slowing the rate of growth was a cut), crime, and the environment. Tate points out that his father will go on Medicare on November 1st, and says that obviously he wouldn't do anything that would hurt his father. (Ganske has an ad to this same effect.) Trying to draw a bright line, Tate says, "There is a clear point between me and my opponent: I want to reduce taxes and he wants to raise them." (Tate is also running a dark, grainy ad against Smith, showing a door opening and a figure slipping in, and saying, misleadingly, on the basis of a vote in the legislature, "Adam Smith doesn't support your right to defend yourself in your own home.")

Two of the more striking aspects of this debate are that there is very little mention of the social issues, and the name "Dole" was never uttered.

But the debate was essentially over the record of the Republican Congress, and, in fact, the role of government—which programs should be cut or preserved. The Gingrich Congress forced that issue. But Smith stays on the safest territory: Medicare, school lunches, Head Start. He is willing to say that the Department of Education is "too bureaucratic." So the debate doesn't stay on a high plane for very long. Smith doesn't want to be seen as excessively pro-government. Smith's basic argument is that Tate is a Gingrich sycophant, and Tate is calling Smith a tax-and-spend liberal. He uses the word "liberal" several times. Tate also argues that he is being picked on, especially by the AFL-CIO, and he has a point. But there are lots of groups in this fight, on both sides.

Smith no longer disdains appearing with Clinton, and was plenty glad to be able to appear with him recently before a larger crowd than he could ever gather for himself. But, he told me after the debate, he tries not to answer the question of what he thinks about Clinton's record. Smith calls himself a New Democrat, but says he avoids linking himself to Clinton electorally: "It's more the perception if I say, 'I think Bill Clinton is a great President, send me there to help him.' " He turned down an offer of a visit by George Stephanopoulos and asked that the Democratic National Committee send him a check instead. The disadvantage of making a partisan appeal works from the bottom up as well as the top down. Like Clinton, Smith is running as a hollow man, but Clinton does it better.

After the debate, a man with long hair, dressed in jeans and a Budweiser T-shirt and wearing a blue cap with a Tate button on it, approaches Tate to tell him, "I don't think our military should serve under the U.N. I think we should phase out the U.N." He is also under the impression that Goals 2000, the education program that encourages states to meet certain national education standards, "comes down through the U.N.," adding, "A lot of our programs come down through the U.N." Tate nods sympathetically but noncommittally.

On Saturday morning, Tate and his father, whom everyone calls Bob, are out in Bob's red Ford Explorer for a day of "doorbelling." (A large green-and-white "TATE" sign is atop the car.) Bob Tate is wearing jeans and a blue shirt; his son the congressman is dressed in black corduroys and a blue shirt and Rockport shoes. Bob Tate is a legislative district leader and was a Robertson supporter in 1988. (Robertson won the state caucus in Washington.) Randy Tate, also a Robertson supporter, was an alternate delegate at the 1988 Republican Convention. A major Democrat in the state says,

"Randy was *the* hotshot young Christian. He used to talk about it a lot, but not now.")

As we proceed to the first neighborhood they plan to hit, Randy Tate tells me, "I think we're up, but think it's going to be decided by half a point. It's an up-for-grabs race." He expresses exasperation at Haley Barbour's having held out money for running ads until late in the campaign. "It's about time," he says. "They should have spent the money earlier."

Randy Tate carries a "walking list" drawn up by his campaign, precinct by precinct. "This is a pretty Democratic area," he tells me, "but the precincts we're hitting today are swing precincts. You just don't want to lose big in some of these. We need to at least stay close."

At their first stop on a residential street, Bob and Randy divvy up the houses they'll go to. At Randy's first one, a modest gray shingle home with a truck and lumber outside, no one is home, so Randy writes a note on a flyer he hands out on these house calls ("I'm sorry I missed you")—"so people know I've been here"—and sticks it inside the door. He tells me, "They had a yard sign here last year." (The flyer has an attractive photograph of Tate, his wife, and their daughter, and compares his positions with Smith's on five tax questions.)

At the next house, a woman comes to the door. "Hello, Mrs. Platt," Randy says brightly, "I'm Randy Tate. I'm running for Congress. Would it be O.K. for me to put my yard sign here?" Mrs. Platt agrees. Randy marks his list "Y."

The next stop is at a yellow shingle house. "Hello, Mr. Gorrie. My name is Randy Tate. I thought I'd come around and say hello and give you my leaflet. It shows where I stand on some of the crime issues, providing a third runway to SeaTac." Mr. Gorrie says, "I've been following you. I'm one of yours," and he agrees to let a yard sign be put in front of his house.

Knocking on the door of the next house, Randy says, "My knuckles will get callused over the course of the campaign."

At another house, Randy tells an elderly lady, "They're really gunning for me on television."

The lady replies, "Oh, they are. That makes me so mad."

"They've spent millions of dollars trying to attack me on Medicare and all this other stuff. It's just a bunch of baloney."

The lady agrees to let him put up a yard sign and tells him, "Hope you win!"

This is no ideological zealot coming to their door, but a friendly young man making folksy conversation. This was one of the few "conversations" where an issue was even mentioned. It's a human, not a political, exchange. Tate thinks that many of these people will vote for him because he was nice enough to drop by. (Adam Smith is said to be much stiffer in his house calls, on which he is striving valiantly but with difficulty to keep up with Tate. During the congressional session, Tate came back home every weekend, often flying through the night.)

Randy then meets up with Bob, who says they should put up the yard signs now. So Randy takes one from the car and holds it while Bob takes a crowbar and drives the sign into the ground. Randy explains, "Crowbars are a necessity because of the rocky ground." Then father and son go back to the other house that has agreed to a sign and Randy suggests putting it along the fence close to the house. If they're any distance from the house, he explains, kids come and take them away. Randy says, "It's this kind of thing that makes a difference in a close race. A yard sign is the last thing people see on their way to vote."

At the next house, where no one is home, Randy says, "Even if you don't hit every house, people talk among themselves." He adds, "One night, I hit thirteen houses straight where no one was home."

Bob returns to say that he has been turned down about a yard sign.

On the next street, Randy assigns Bob four houses and takes five for himself. At the first house, a small dog is barking. Randy says he's only been bitten once. He adds, "I always rattle the fence to see if there's a dog."

Next house. "Hello, Mr. Wilcox, I'm Randy Tate." Mr. Wilcox says, "I know. You gave me your first button." Randy feigns recollection of the moment. "I'm all for you," Wilcox says, and the usual *pas de deux* about the yard sign takes place, and Wilcox of course says, "Yeah, go ahead." "Hey," Randy says, cheered by this positive encounter, "we need your help on Election Day."

"Bunch of damn Democrats around this neighborhood," Wilcox says.

When Randy and Bob meet up, Randy says, "You get any?"

"Only got one," Bob says.

Randy says, smiling, "That all you could do?"

Randy tells me, "I find this a great stress reducer."

At the next stop, a bearded man in a plaid shirt comes to the door. After Tate introduces himself, the man says, "I know, you're running for Congress. How's it going?"

"It's going great," Randy says, and he asks, "Have you made up your mind on this race yet?"

"I've already voted," the man replies, evidently confusing the primary with the general election. (Washington State has a very liberal absentee voting system, but the absentee ballots haven't been distributed yet.)

"I hope you'll consider us." This time, Randy doesn't ask about a yard sign.

The man says, "I haven't met your opponent yet."

As we walk away from the house, Randy shrugs.

Another stop, this time a young man comes to the door.

"Sorry to interrupt the Notre Dame game. I'm Randy Tate."

"Oh, hi."

Randy says he's running for Congress, mentions his brochure, and asks if he can put up a yard sign. ("Do you go for signs?")

"I don't live here. My mom does, but I don't know if that's what she'd want."

"Okay, no problem," Randy says, rather weakly. "If she does, have her call us."

At another house, where a man has come to the door in a warm-up suit, and tells Randy he'll vote for him, Randy asks him if he's a square dancer. The man is, and is delighted that his congressman is so well-informed. Afterward, I asked Tate how on earth he knew that the man was a square dancer.

He replied, "I always look around for clues as to what they're interested in. That guy had a square-dance bumper sticker on his car."

I leave them shortly before three o'clock. The Tates, father and son, will go on knocking on doors and pounding yard signs into the ground until dark.

Chapter Seventeen

CLOUDS

By MID-OCTOBER, the Presidential contest had taken an unexpected new turn that was to have a profound effect on the struggle for control of the House of Representatives, and, if he won, the President's second term.

The disclosure after disclosure that appeared in the press, beginning with a story in the *Wall Street Journal* on October 8th, about questionable if not illegal fundraising by the Democratic National Committee, and the President's obsessive efforts to raise money for his reelection, added a new category to the questions about Clinton, and changed the dynamics of the Presidential race. Clinton's having been an adulterer had been taken into account in the 1992 election; Whitewater in its various ramifications was complex and seemed largely in the past (despite the ongoing investigations). Polls indicated that people were prepared to vote for Clinton despite misgivings about his character (and because his opponent wasn't an acceptable alternative). Now, the new money scandals brought sleaze right into the Oval Office.

A motley collection of characters trooped across the stage: Indonesian businessmen and their American-based outriders; a former low-level White House aide handing out a business card indicating that he still worked there and giving a White House phone number, while he trolled for business and contributions in Taiwan; the U.S. representative to Taiwan, an Arkansan, charged with pressuring Taiwanese businessmen to contribute to Clinton's reelection (he denied this); Arkansans cashing in on their connections to Clinton by setting up "trading companies"; phantom donors. Presumably illegal contributions—from foreign sources—kept turning up. The kind of sudden fame that can come to someone who pops up in the midst of a scandal was now happening to a large new cast of characters.

One of the most precious commodities in America, if not the world—the President's time—was parceled out to White House meetings with prospective or recent large donors, and people they brought along. In a new twist, some donors purchased access not only for themselves but also for foreign businessmen and -women and others who otherwise wouldn't be allowed anywhere near the President. The story soon broadened to include questionable contributions to the Clintons' legal defense fund, which at least had returned these contributions earlier—before they became known to the press. Much of that money came in suspicious form through another character to enter the story, Charles Trie, who had once run a Chinese restaurant the Clintons had frequented in Little Rock, and was now a businessman who, like some others who had known the Clintons, did deals of some sort—in Trie's case, most of them with connections to mainland China. (Mrs. Clinton said at first that she didn't remember Trie.)

It was through Trie, who also contributed to and raised money for the Democratic National Committee, that a Chinese arms merchant attended one of Clinton's numerous coffees with donors—seventy-one over a year and a half, according to news accounts, sometimes two a week, sometimes two a day. (Clinton did say later that meeting with the Chinese arms manufacturer was "clearly inappropriate.") Gore and Mrs. Clinton hosted other coffees. There were also, of course, frequent dinners with donors, and other enticements, such as state dinners and overnight stays at the White House. Other unsavories purchased access for themselves: Jorge Cabrera, a businessman who had been convicted of tax evasion (and later was also convicted for drug smuggling), and gave the D.N.C. $20,000, was invited to a small fundraising dinner hosted by Gore and also to a White House Christmas party—and pictures of him with a smiling Mrs. Clinton and with Vice President Gore now appeared in the papers and on television screens. Gore got caught in the muck by appearing in April at a fundraiser at a Buddhist temple in California, where money was supposedly raised from penitents who had taken a vow of poverty. The confession of one nun that someone unknown to her had handed her $5,000 in cash to donate—a clear illegality—made it impossible to explain the event away. Gore at first insisted that he didn't know it was a fundraiser, but a piece in the *Boston Globe* in early January suggested that he did, and Gore then acknowledged that he knew that it was a political event put on by the D.N.C.'s Asian-American Leadership Council, to which one pays $2,500 to belong—but still said that he hadn't known it was a fundraiser. (It later emerged that the National Security Council staff had warned Gore's staff against his going, because of the temple's ties to Taiwan.) A White House aide told me that such groups as the Asian-American Council had been given what are called "donor fulfillment events" all year long. This made the story a doubly bad one for Gore. He and Clinton have had a remarkably close working relationship, but the money scandals could threaten Gore's Presidential ambitions and sour the relationship.

Much of this mess came about because of the President's obsessive concern about having enough funds for the election—not letting the Republicans, who would raise more money, get too far in front. A White House aide told me, "The bottom line is this: we had to raise a hundred and thirty million not to get too outspent. We were outspent two hundred million as it was." Clinton himself sometimes attended fundraisers several times a week. And the pressure was felt down the line. A leading Democrat said, "There was unbelievable pressure to raise two million dollars a week to keep the ads up—incredible pressure to raise money. They went and aggressively fundraised." He continued, "The fundraising in this election was unlike what had ever gone on before."

The Clinton White House's handling of the scandal bespoke the worry there—almost in direct proportion to the indignant insistence that nothing new had happened. In some instances its handling of the scandal made matters worse. White House officials' insistence that policy wasn't discussed at meetings of the President and one of the story's principals, James Riady, the Indonesian businessman and old friend from the days Riady spent working at a bank in Little Rock, had to be reversed later. Then some White House aides continued to insist that the discussions between the President and Riady, about U.S. policy toward Indonesia and China (where the Riadys had big banking and business interests), were simply the kind of social chitchat that goes on all the time. Donations that had been heatedly defended—such as the $450,000 given to the Democratic National Committee by an Indonesian landscaper and his wife (who was connected to the Riadys), both of them legal aliens (who are allowed to contribute, while foreign nationals are not), most of it after they went back to Indonesia—turned out to be illegal or just too embarrassing, and were returned.

The role of the Riadys' former employee, John Huang, the energetic fundraiser for the D.N.C., kept taking on new proportions. Huang had represented the Riadys' conglomerate, the Lippo Group, in the United States and then served in the Commerce Department (Huang had been given nearly $800,000 in severance pay by the Lippo Group when he went into the government). One of the conversations between Clinton and Riady, with Huang present, turned out to include a discussion of whether Huang should move from Commerce to the D.N.C. The admitted number of visits Huang and Riady made to the White House, released by the President's spokesmen, kept changing. (The Riadys had also hired Webster Hubbell—the former Justice Department official and Hillary Clinton law partner who had gone to jail on charges of defrauding clients and law partners—for at least $100,000, before his jail sentence began. Republicans said darkly that this must have been hush money to keep Hubbell from telling the independent counsel what he knew about Whitewater.)

Top Republican figures, elated by this new development, helped spread the story. They worked with David Bossie, a longtime

Whitewater conspiracist and press agent for the issue—he had fed stories about it to several media outlets. Bossie had now joined the staff of the House Oversight Committee, headed by Dan Burton, of Indiana, who was looking toward conducting hearings. Burton, an erratic fellow, once enacted a mock death scene in his own backyard to "prove" his theory that former White House Counsel Vincent Foster, whose 1993 death had been officially ruled a suicide, had been murdered elsewhere and then his body was moved to the Virginia park where it was found. Burton met Bossie over the Foster case. When a second major newspaper picked up the Huang story, a Republican operative told me, "We knew we were off to the races." (During a period when Huang was missing, and under court order to appear, the Republicans made an ad about 'Where is Mr. Huang?' but he showed up the day the ad was to be run.) It was the Huang-Lippo-Hubbell connection that had caught Bossie's attention.

Though no link between money thus raised and administration policy decisions had been proven by the time of the election, the whole thing was distasteful at best, and there remained a number of questions about Huang's activities. Some policy decisions—such as suspending a study of Indonesia's treatment of the people of East Timor, which it had taken over in 1976—did parallel what the Riadys would have wanted. Quid pro quos are hard to prove, especially when it comes to a governmental decision, which can have many authors. But it would be wiser for a President to at least not accept questionable quids.

White House aides' red-faced sputtering that Bob Dole had been particularly amenable to the needs of Dwayne Andreas, the head of Archer Daniels Midland, who was actually a bipartisan big-time donor, and that what Clinton and his fundraisers had done was no different, was beside the point. (They often brought up the fact that the former chairman of Dole's presidential campaign finance committee, Simon Fireman, had recently been fined one million dollars and put under house arrest for making illegal contributions to the Dole campaign.) And whatever happened on the Republican side appeared to be nothing on the scale of the Democrats' questionable and perhaps even illegal fundraising. And Bob Dole wasn't sitting in the Oval Office.

There was no known precedent for a President having gone to such lengths to woo and show his gratitude to donors. Clinton wasn't the first President to allow access to himself to be sold, but never, it seemed, had this been done on such a grand, or stomach-turning, scale.

This was a difference in degree that became a difference in kind.

The broader scandal, of course, of which this was just a part, was the amount of "soft money" that was being raised and spent by both parties—well beyond anything that had gone before. Suddenly, this phenomenon, too, was receiving substantial press attention. The oceans of soft money drowned the Presidential campaign finance laws. According to the reports to the Federal Election Commission through the reporting period that ended October 16th (the last report before the election), both parties had raised nearly three times as much soft money—$95.4 million by the Democrats and $111.6 million by the Republicans—as they had in the 1992 election.

And the whole thing wrought a change in the atmospherics of the election. It added to the yecch factor about Clinton—the willingness to stomach only so much unpleasantness about him. It affected the mood of the public. And it was to affect the outcome of the election.

Clinton, as he campaigned, adamantly refused to address the subject, and the press covering him was kept at a safe distance. The White House later spun the story that its "response system" had broken down in dealing with the money scandal, but that wasn't quite what happened. The White House response, according to a well-placed official, was guided by "a sense we had been well-served in the campaign by not answering a lot of these things." He continued, "We had lived for a year with the mantra 'Public character trumps private virtue.' I think that led us to not deal with it. The strategy we had lived with was not having the President talk about these things. That strategy had worked for a year. The President said very little about Whitewater or the F.B.I. files and then he would push off on his issues of the V-chip and college education. Day by day, crisis by crisis, that had been the strategy and it served us very well. It was a stock play. We ran it again."

Bob Dole had some fun with the money issue, but much of it was in Dole-speak which left his listeners baffled. ("Here is a President who often talks about a bridge to the future. More often it seems it's a bridge to wealthy political donors. It goes through a Laundromat first, then takes a left at the Democratic National Committee and then rolls all the way down to the Oval Office.")

Dole finally gave a tough, reasoned speech on Clinton's character in San Diego, on the day before the second Presidential debate, to be held there. The idea was to plant thoughts for questions that would be asked by the citizen panel in the second debate. It was a smart and strong speech, separating the subjects of private and public behavior, and focusing on the latter. But, to the shock and horror of the Dole campaign, the gambit didn't work. None of the citizen panelists asked about the character issue, or the money scandal. At the same time, the Dole campaign was also upset with Jack Kemp for not taking Clinton on directly on ethics, but that wasn't Kemp's style. Mrs. Dole even enlisted Vin Weber, a top Dole adviser and good friend of Kemp, to fly out to join him and try to talk him into attacking Clinton. This didn't work, either.

As a defense against the charge that Clinton was avoiding the subject, his aides said after the debate that Clinton would have talked about the campaign finance scandal if Dole had brought it up—but Dole, fearing "meanness," didn't. This of course didn't rule out Clinton's addressing it.

Actually, an internal debate was going on, on Clinton's plane and back at the White House, over, as one top Clinton adviser put it, "whether you give sustenance to those charges by dealing with them, or whether it would be better to stick with the themes the President had already been using." The pollster Mark Penn, who was on the President's plane in the closing days of the election, was of the view that the President should stick with the themes that had been working. Another official said to me later, "We were trying to win an election, not an argument." But even Clinton eventually came to wonder whether he had made the right decision.

Dole kept up his attack on Clinton's character for several days after the debate, and—predictably—this backfired.

On October 22nd, Ralph Reed has come to Washington to make a speech at the National Press Club. In his speech, he talked of the "deep sense of moral and spiritual unease that accompanies this 'epic age.' " Judged by "the moral fiber of our people, the integrity of our leaders, and in how we treat the least and most innocent and vulnerable among us," Reed said, "we are in great danger." He took on the Clinton administration on several counts: the "issues of faith and family"; partial-birth abortion; the "war on crime and drugs." He mocked "the current administration's answer to this social contagion"—"midnight basketball, school uniforms, and teen curfews," and asked how teenagers could both play midnight basketball and obey a curfew.

Reed's "news peg," however, was a mischievous reference to the news reports the previous week about Gore's having attended the fundraiser at the Buddhist temple, and an announcement that the Christian Coalition would that day file a formal complaint with the Federal Election Commission about "these illegal acts by the D.N.C."

When I asked Reed in a talk we had afterward if he had intended to make the F.E.C. complaint the news about his speech, he laughed and replied, "The best defense is a good offense." He said he'd been "amazed" that no one had filed a complaint about this "blatant violation of the law."

When we talked about the Christian Coalition's efforts for the election, now just two weeks away, he said, "We've got more volunteers involved this fall than we've ever had before. In the past we've had to hire workers to get voter guides out in those states where we didn't have a stronger grassroots network, and now we've not had to do that because our grassroots network is so much stronger."

He said that his own people weren't very demotivated by Dole's lagging campaign, because "our people were never for Dole to begin with." Reed added, "Dole was somebody they felt they could live with, but he was not their first love. They've never put all their marbles in the Dole basket, so Dole going down has not hosed them down in the same way that it might have others. I think people are clearly disappointed and there's a lot of frustration out there about the fact that the campaign is not working hard enough on the moral and social issues."

As for his efforts in the House races, Reed said, "We obviously know where the opportunity races are, we know where the marginal seats are—everybody knows what they are. There's about forty of them, and there are about twenty-five of them that will decide the whole kit and caboodle, unless there's a total blowout, and we're active in every one of those districts." He listed some of the districts he had been especially active in, including those of Helen Chenoweth of Idaho (who was on the far right and had defended the militias after Oklahoma City) and J.D. Hayworth of Arizona, a former sportscaster and one of the more obstreperous freshmen. (Reed's efforts for Hayworth in 1994 were cited in the F.E.C. suit against the Christian Coalition.) Reed said, "I was just in J.D.'s district two weeks ago, and gave a speech, and raised money for voter guides, and got our people whipped up, and that's what we're trying to do." He was going shortly to New Hampshire, where Bob Smith, the incumbent Republican senator, was in a very tight race.

Reed had three purposes when he went into a state or district where there was a hotly contested race. First, he would make his presence known, by holding a press conference. He wouldn't say, for example, "Vote against Paul Wellstone" (he had recently been in Minnesota), because that might cause more legal problems for his organization, but he would point out that the liberal Senator Wellstone had voted to sustain the President's veto on the partial-birth abortion ban, and that the issue would be in the voter guide. This was a very fine distinction. The second point of going into a district or state was to raise money, and the third was to energize his troops and tell them to work—he banged the table with his hand as he told me this—harder than they ever had, "because we've got control of Congress on the line."

Reed told me that now that the Senate race between Jesse Helms and Harvey Gantt in North Carolina was tightening, the Christian Coalition was going into the state. "But if it didn't tighten, we might not have gone in," Reed said, adding, "We can turn on a dime. If a race starts to get outside the margin of error, we may or may not go in, 'cause we're no different from anybody else, there's no point in wasting your donors' money." Reed had given up on the race against Vic Fazio (the Democratic leader from California whom Reed had intended to at least shake up), because Fazio's opponent had run an ad that morphed Fazio's face into that of Richard Allen Davis, the murderer of twelve-year-old Polly Klaas. (In its own lapse of taste, the Clinton campaign made an ad using Polly Klaas's father.)

Reed pointed out that the Christian Coalition did support the occasional conservative Democrat but in the end, in order to have the right committee chairmen and a pro-life Congress, that meant a Republican Congress.

Reed said that he had given up on trying to get the Dole-Kemp ticket to talk more about moral values. After the Vice Presidential debate (when Kemp failed to raise any of the social issues), Reed said, "I just decided I had to quit worrying about them, I had to focus entirely on getting our vote out, and I just couldn't worry anymore about whether they were going to get their message out. I became convinced, beyond a shadow of a doubt, that it was not going to happen. No matter what I said or did, and no matter what anybody else said or did."

The next day, October 23rd, it's standing room only at Grover Norquist's Wednesday group meeting. The election is just under two weeks away, and the group is quite keyed up. Norquist begins, "We have all sorts of excitement today."

The first, he says, is an "ethics chart" drawn up by the Landmark Legal Foundation, a conservative public interest law firm. The large chart is a mass of colored circles, lines, curlicues, showing the supposed links among administration officials, and former administration officials, to ethics charges (or suppositions) against them. The document is a work of both research and imagination. "It looks like the Clinton health care plan," Norquist remarks.

Norquist says, "Let's say Clinton gets through the election, and then pardons everybody."

The Landmark Legal Foundation man, Mark Levin, goes through what he thinks are the Clintons' greatest vulnerabilities, and detailed discussion ensues.

Pressed by Norquist to predict what will happen, Levin says, "We view this as probably one of the two most corrupt administrations in history." He adds, "Landmark doesn't take a political position on one side or another." He goes on, speaking of Clinton, "If he's going to pardon them and take the heat, he's better off pardoning before any indictments, saying, 'I have a mandate. I'm not going to put up with this anymore.' "

Norquist asks if Clinton could fire the independent counsel, Kenneth Starr.

"That would be very dangerous," Levin replies, and he points out that there are rumors in the press that the White House wants to force out Attorney General Janet Reno for having expanded the independent counsel's inquiry to include the firing of the travel office workers, and the F.B.I. files.

They talked of Clinton's "obvious dangle of a pardon to a convicted felon." (Clinton was refusing to rule out a pardon to anyone convicted on Whitewater; at the same time, Susan McDougal, who had been convicted, was choosing to remain incarcerated rather than reply to certain questions from Starr.)

Someone asks whether anyone in the House has suggested that Clinton should be impeached. Levin replies that he doesn't know about that. Norquist says, "It would be important for a member to say that if he obstructs justice through pardons we should impeach."

Another man says, "We need to make it clear what the parameters are," and another says, "I don't think it's helpful to talk about impeachment now. It would seem we are asking for a Republican Congress in order to impeach him." Peter Ferrara, chief counsel and economist for Americans for Tax Reform, who is working on a paper on the pardon, says that if Clinton abused the pardon power, "We could say, 'This is a criminal conspiracy to take over the government.'" Levin says, "I don't think we should take impeachment lightly. I don't think the American people will tolerate a President pardoning himself."

The group next took up the House races. Ed Brookover, the political director of the National Republican Congressional Committee, has come to brief them. Brookover tells them that there's a "ton" of poll data showing that "the election is moving our way." Echoing Marc Nuttle's analysis, Brookover says, "There is no big wave on the congressional level, but a series of firefights, some of them started by the unions."

The week before, the group heard from a representative of the Republican Senate campaign committee, who showed ads and gave them a situation report on Senate races. Eddie Gillespie, of the Republican National Committee, was also there. He handed out an R.N.C. leaflet that warned that a Democratic Congress would be very liberal.

Looking for tacks to take to hold the House, some Republican officials and their allies sought to frighten people about the consequences if the Democrats retook the House, by citing some liberals who would be committee chairmen. They pushed this point with business groups and friendly columnists. The list did contain some horrors from business's point of view—the domineering John Dingell, of Michigan, would return as chairman of the Commerce Committee; the pro-regulatory Henry Waxman, of California, would recapture chairmanship of the Health and Environment Subcommittee. They also played to racism and anti-liberalism by pointing out that John Conyers, of Michigan, would become chairman of the Judiciary Committee and Charles Rangel, of New York (Harlem), would take over the Ways and Means Committee.

Gillespie had told the group last week that a hundred corporate PACs still had $100,000 each that they were ready to spend.

Now Brookover, of the House election committee, tells Norquist's group, "We have ten million saved, and we are outspending the labor unions in every district where we think it's close in the last month." He says that the unions "made a big mistake" by starting their ads so early, because they have had negligible cumulative effect. "They didn't get bang for bucks," Brookover says.

He brings up the Randy Tate race—the group cheers at the sound of Tate's name—and says that a Seattle television station has Tate ahead by fifteen points. A young woman from DeLay's office says that she is taking vacation time to go out to help Randy Tate, because "I'm worried." Brookover says he's "very comfortable" about the get-out-the-vote efforts in almost all the states, and adds, "We're also counting on you guys, too. Keep up your work."

Brookover also says that it is likely that Democratic Representative William Orton, of Utah, who comes from a marginally Republican district, will go down to defeat. Referring to an act by Clinton on September 18th, in a picturesque ceremony at the Grand Canyon, declaring 1.7 million acres of land in Utah as federal property, to be set aside as a national monument, Brookover says, "When the President gave away Utah, we said, 'That election's over.'" (The set-aside came about, a prominent Democrat says, because Al Gore was embarrassed that the Sierra Club, which was pushing for this project, hadn't yet endorsed the Clinton-Gore ticket. It did endorse the ticket three days after the President acted.) Orton, Brookover said, "fools a few voters out there, but in the end, he's for Dick Gephardt and Dave Bonior, not Newt Gingrich and Dick Armey."

He continued, "We think we have to keep up the contrast campaign [the political industry's term for attack ads] to the end. If you see anyone go positive, call us up."

Someone asks about the Dole campaign, evoking laughter from the group. "It just doesn't matter," someone says.

Brookover shows them some ads, including the one, in black and white, morphing California congressman Vic Fazio into Polly Klaas's murderer. It's greeted with cheers and applause.

Norquist asks, "If we pick up seats in the House, and we pick up seats in the Senate, how's the left going to explain that?" Peter Roff of GOPAC says, "They will talk about Clinton, they will ignore" their losses. Someone else says, "*We* should talk about Clinton. Clinton will have won by moving to the right."

A representative of Jonas Savimbi's group, UNITA, is here. Norquist, the longtime admirer of Savimbi, asks the representative whether Clinton is going to "give away" Angola—by failing to pressure the government to hold elections, with UNITA participating. The problem, Norquist says, is that "nascent roots of democracy there are being smothered by the fuzzy foreign policy of the Clinton administration." (The Clinton administration had recently renewed economic sanctions against UNITA.)

As the meeting is about to end, an aide brings Norquist a message. Norquist says, "Breaking news: Judge Royce C. Lamberth has just ordered U.S. marshals to compel testimony from John Huang."

Des Moines, October 25th. The race between Greg Ganske and Connie McBurney, his Democratic opponent, is considered very close. Ganske is ahead in his own polling, but his numbers, as well as the Democrats', show the race narrowing. Moreover, this is a heavily unionized district, for most of its recent history represented by a Democrat—that's the main reason Ganske was put high on the "vulnerable" lists—and labor is mobilizing for an unprecedented effort to get out the union members' votes on Election Day. Dole has effectively pulled out of Iowa. Besides, Tom Harkin, the liberal Democratic senator from Iowa, is running well ahead of his opponent. The air war is heavy, with both sides clogging the television channels with back-to-back ads morning and evening. In his own advertising Ganske has hit hard at McBurney, a former weather announcer on a local television station here, as lacking the experience or the knowledge to serve in the Congress. Other Ganske ads, some of which he writes and pays for himself, show him to be the warm family man. He has just had one made starring his wife, Corrine, who is also a doctor, talking about his compassion, and which also included a shot of the family.

McBurney has two kinds of ads: one set attacks the "Ganske-Gingrich agenda"; the other portrays her in a positive light, stressing her wide range of interests and activities.

The Democrats are rather defensive about McBurney, who won the primary over a more established party figure. Her defenders say that she isn't simply a featherhead weather lady, and her literature talks of her volunteer work in local causes, and her job at a children's hospital as a child advocate. A forecaster in Iowa, one Democrat explained, becomes a major figure because the weather affects so many people's livelihoods. There is of course some hypocrisy in Ganske's argument about McBurney's inexperience, since he had had no political experience before he ran for Congress in 1994. But his ads questioning her depth have had an impact—partly because her own performance gives them credence. Attractive and poised, with shoulder-length brown hair, McBurney doesn't look like your stereotypical weather lady, but she also doesn't seem prepared for this race.

In a debate with Ganske last night at KCCI-TV, her former television station, McBurney's response on what to do about Medicare—Ganske had gone on the offensive by prodding her to say what she would do—suggested she wasn't ready for this. She said that she would open it up to competitive bidding and cut waste, fraud, and abuse—"and then let's see where we are."

A Ganske ad about Medicare, which runs frequently, says that he had voted to "save" it (coincidentally or not, this follows Gingrich's advice), and voted to increase spending for it by sixty-three percent. Then it says that McBurney's position on Medicare is unknown: "We're still waiting, Connie."

Ganske came off in the debate as the more knowledgeable. For each of McBurney's now-familiar—from the Democrats—charges, Ganske had an explanation, even if it wasn't really an answer. He had insisted on this or that amendment; another bill had mitigated the effects of the first one. He made much of the stream of legislation passed by the Republican Congress in the last few months.

A competitive man—he had been a high school wrestler—Ganske needled McBurney with condescending comments like "Mrs. McBurney has her facts wrong."

McBurney had studied her brief on other issues—targeted tax credits, Ganske's votes—but she seemed uncertain. Still, she had ample material to suggest that Ganske had marched with Gingrich on key issues. (Once again, there was little attention in the debate to social issues, in this case only the subject of school prayer, introduced into the debate by a member of the viewing audience, which was invited to phone in questions. Neither Dole nor Clinton was mentioned.)

After the debate, McBurney's managers hurried her off the set before reporters could reach her to ask any questions. She has generally been unavailable to reporters covering the campaign. (Following the debate Ganske told a cameraman who expressed some indignation about the labor ads, "If there is any Republican freshman who has not been a Gingrich clone, it's me.")

The number of national figures who have come or will come into the district bespeaks the importance placed on this race. Former Vice President Dan Quayle, who has been very active in this year's elections, has been here to help Ganske, as have John Kasich, the Ohio congressman and chairman of the Budget Committee, a rising Party figure, and Susan Molinari. Hillary Clinton came here for McBurney last weekend, and Tipper Gore and Donna Shalala are scheduled to appear for her.

Another big factor here—much talked about privately—is Ganske's illness, which is widely believed to be working in his favor. It's hard to paint as "mean" a man who has gone to Peru to operate on disfigured children. And Ganske is still unwell—he tires easily, and he often has to sit down during his appearances. (At his request, the rivals were seated during last night's debate.) Each audience is reminded of his sacrifice as he mentions his continuing health problems. A focus group study done for McBurney showed that the one thing best known about Ganske, despite the AFL-CIO barrage against him, is his illness. A Democrat advising McBurney told me, "Gingrich is not as much a factor as I would like."

This morning, Ganske is appearing at a Rotary Club breakfast. He looks particularly tired, and detaches the microphone from the podium and moves to sit in a chair. "As you know, I had an illness," he tells the audience, adding, "Some mornings are better than others, and this is not one of my better mornings."

In his talk, he portrays himself as a moderate man who has fought hard for his state. And he does something unusual in this election: he lays out the facts about the budget and explains why entitlement programs have to be tackled, discretionary programs having already been sharply cut. Most politicians, including the President and Bob Dole, prefer to ignore this issue.

He also complains about the "Medigogue" and "misinformation in this campaign." In answer to a question about the ads against him, Ganske says, "This has been a rather stressful campaign, both from a personal viewpoint and with the illness." In a conversation later, Ganske complained about the AFL-CIO ads. The ads have become a crutch for Republicans, a way of dispensing with charges against them by attacking the ad blitz itself. The ads did break new ground in "issue advocacy," but the whining about them was excessive. The Republicans had always had a financial advantage over the Democrats and still did; business was spending a good deal more than labor. In any event, for the struggling incumbents, it was far preferable to complain about the union ads than to consider their own inadequacies.

Ganske tells the Rotarians that the ads are "clearly an attempt by organized labor to target a number of districts around the country and to buy back Congress"—this is true enough—and he adds, "You will by far and away see the most liberal group of committee chairmen that we've seen in Congress for a long, long time."

He points out that he had voted for the Kennedy-Kassebaum health care bill, the Safe Drinking Water Act (passed in 1996 to overcome strong criticism of the bill passed by the House in 1995 that virtually eviscerated the federal Clean Water Act), and rules banning House members from accepting gifts from other than friends—in this spirit, Ganske turns back a bag of coffee beans he is proffered by the Rotarians—and reforming the lobbying laws.

Ganske, like a lot of politicians this year, is facing a great deal of cynicism and apathy on the part of the voters, and he does his bit to temper it. After listing the legislation the Republican Congress passed in the last few months, he says, "So you should be hopeful. There is hope for change."

Stressing his major theme, he tells the Rotarians, "I will stay an independent voice for you." He relays once more that he "challenged the leadership" on the tax issue and on the treatment of rural areas under Medicare. "I will go to the mat, so to speak, for you," he says, "and I will also keep my promises for you."

Over coffee afterward, Ganske tells me that he's seeing "less activity" from groups that were quite active on his behalf in 1994—the Christian Coalition, the N.R.A. (Ganske voted to maintain the assault weapons ban). "I had a sense of more enthusiasm in 1994," he says. The question in Iowa, as elsewhere, is whether groups who expect the person at the top of the ticket to lose will be sufficiently motivated to organize and vote.

"What we have tried to do all along," Ganske says, "is point out my independence." He goes on, "We will finish with a closing spot that stresses my independence—of the leadership of both parties, the special interests." And, he says, he'll also emphasize that "I will keep my promises," adding, "Because I really think people think politicians will say anything to get elected. We keep getting back from our tracking polls, when people are asked why would you vote for him, they say, 'One thing about him, he does keep his promises.' "

Chapter Eighteen

DOWNDRAFT

IN THE FINAL WEEKS of the election, the race for the House grew very tight. In mid-October, Joe Gaylord, the consultant who advised Gingrich, counted district by district and informed him that the result would be a net gain or loss of six seats for the Republicans. At just about the same time, Matt Angle, executive director of the Democratic Congressional Campaign Committee, predicted a net gain or loss of five seats for the Democrats.

The Clinton White House, in a meeting of the President and his political advisers on the night of Friday, October 18th, decided to give the Democratic candidates for the House and Senate more help. The two congressional campaign committees had already been given a second million dollars in soft money from the Democratic National Committee. They now wanted, they said, another five to ten million dollars. That afternoon, Bob Kerrey, Tom O'Donnell, and officials of the House and Senate campaign committees met with Doug Sosnik, the White House political director, to argue that the committees should be given more money and that spending on media ads should be reallocated to places with close Senate or House races, such as Washington State, Iowa, Ohio, and Wisconsin. By then, Dole had announced that he would spend a lot of time in California, which gave them a peg for asking that more also be spent on media in California. They argued, "You don't need to win forty-nine states. Take forty-four and help us in these media markets."

Sosnik told them that they could argue all they wanted that the

President shouldn't continue to make a major effort in Florida instead of spending more time in states where there were more congressional seats at stake, but they would lose the argument—that the possibility of Clinton being the Democratic Presidential candidate carrying Florida for the first time since 1976 was too important electorally for the long run. A Clinton victory in Florida, which has twenty-five electoral votes, Sosnik said, would have a substantial impact on Electoral College math. California (where Clinton was leading), Texas, and Florida had been a critical factor in the long-standing supposed "Republican lock" on the Electoral College. Besides, Sosnik said, the Clinton-Gore campaign had already spent a lot of money and candidate time in Florida, and the investment couldn't be thrown away.

(In a meeting in the residence a couple of weeks earlier, Sosnik had urged that the Clinton campaign be more aggressive about trying to win the House and Senate, and was shouted down. Others said the Presidential race was still "too fluid.")

In the meeting on October 18th, Senator Christopher Dodd, general chairman of the Democratic National Committee, argued that it made sense to reallocate some funds from the Presidential campaign to the contests for control of the House and Senate—especially the House. The one person in the meeting at the White House who was skeptical about transferring the funds was Gore. He argued that the President should stay on his own course, that it wasn't good for Clinton to be appearing on television with a congressional candidate. Others in the meeting inferred that Gore wasn't eager to do things that would help make Dick Gephardt the Speaker of the House.

But another influence on the decision was the numerous Members of Congress who called the President on Air Force One and begged him for help. By now, the President had in effect become his own political director.

An adviser who was in the political meetings said to me later that if Dick Morris had still been there he'd have probably opposed transferring resources, including the President's time, to the congressional campaigns. He had taken that position before—the discussions had actually begun in the spring—arguing that if people believed that Clinton was trying to help the Democrats win the Congress, it would hurt both Clinton and the Democrats. This objection also fit Morris's "triangulation" theory: that Clinton should distinguish his differences with both the congressional Democrats and Republicans. Though some of Morris's advice remained a force in the White House even after he had gone, its strength had waned by the time the election neared.

The upshot of the Friday night meeting in the residence was that the President's time was reallocated so that he would spend more time in states he had already sewn up; ads would continue to be run in states that had in effect been won and states where the Clinton-Gore campaign had stopped advertising some time ago, for one reason or another. This amounted to a reallocation of two to three million dollars' worth of advertising. As for direct transfers of funds, it was agreed that the D.N.C., already in debt, would join the Senate campaign committee in taking out a loan. Officials of the Democratic Congressional Campaign Committee, also in debt, decided that they didn't want to take on any more.

Clinton's was a cold-blooded decision that a Democratic Congress would be more convenient—for him—by far than a Republican one. He wasn't deciding to help his buddies on the Hill, because he didn't have buddies on the Hill.

Acting on their decision in early October to break with Dole, on Monday, October 28th, the Republicans brought out an ad warning voters not to give Clinton "a blank check." It was as close as the Republicans could come to not garroting Dole publicly. In the ad, a fortune-teller looked into a crystal ball, and a voice-over asked, "What would happen if the Democrats controlled Congress and the White House?" and then it showed headlines about such things as Clinton tax proposals and the Clintons' health care plan. The characters who had played the "union bosses" reappeared in this ad as "the liberal special interests." And the ad named, for each district in which it was run, the Democratic challengers on whose behalf these special interests had spent a specific amount of money. It closed with the voice-over asking, "Who's going to represent us?" (The ad was actually run a few days earlier than planned as a result of Scott Reed's not-long-secret trip to Dallas on October 23rd to try to talk Ross Perot into quitting the race—an obviously desperate, and predictably futile, mission, and one that came as a surprise to Haley Barbour. Scott Reed said later, "I went to Dallas because we were losing the race.")

At that point, private data on both sides indicated that the Republicans could lose the House. Dole was continuing to sink, and Clinton to rise. Republican strategists, including Joe Gaylord, worked up a worst-case analysis that showed the Republicans losing a net nineteen House seats—thereby losing the House.

Eddie Gillespie tried valiantly to make the case to the press that the "crystal ball" ad was consistent with the Dole campaign, because it said that Clinton is a liberal. In a conversation with me, he said, "We don't specifically say, 'Forget about Dole.' When you have eighty-four percent of the people saying in public polls that Clinton is going to win, you don't need to make that point for them." He conceded, "We're threading a needle," and added, "It's the only thing we have left."

Also in late October, in an effort to reach conservative voters who said they were going to vote for Clinton, the R.N.C. bought a large amount of time on Christian radio—which its officials figured wouldn't be picked up by the Washington press. The ad warned that Hillary Clinton might take over implementation of the welfare program (both Clintons had hinted at this), reminded people of the Clintons' health care plan and the uproar over gays in the military, and said that if the Democrats retook the Congress, "Teddy Kennedy will be running the place." (Conservatives always referred to him as "Teddy.") It also mentioned partial-birth abortion and possible higher co-payments for Medicare (which the Republicans, not the Democrats, had proposed). In a more unusual turn, Clinton, too, ran an ad on Christian radio, which emphasized the exceptions he would make, if given the opportunity, to allowing partial-birth abortions (as opposed to the more restrictive ban he had vetoed) and his signing the prohibition on same-sex marriages.

At the same time that the "crystal ball" ad was released, the National Republican Congressional Committee gave its candidates the signal to cut loose from Dole. Nothing like this is ever officially said. The signal went from operatives through the Republican pollsters, many of whom had several House clients (for whom in effect they acted as general consultants), who were told that it was all right for their candidates to openly break with Dole—or that no one would object if they did. Silence was assent. Field representatives of the Republican National Committee were also told that the "blank check" message worked—a clear signal to pass that word on to the campaigns.

Dole, indignant that the American people didn't seem to be very indignant over the new Clinton scandals, now traveled the land as a Savonarola, crying, bitterly, "Wake up, America!" (Some Republicans referred to this as "Dole's 'Fuck You, America!' Tour.") It was a sad sight.

The Sixth District of Massachusetts, which starts north of Boston and runs up to the New Hampshire border, contains thirty-six cities and towns with such historically resonant names as Peabody, Newburyport, Gloucester, Salem. This morning, Peter Torkildsen, the incumbent Republican sophomore, is bowling at a senior citizens event at the Sunnyside Bowladrome, joshing with the elderly people with whom he is bowling, making fun of his own more misses than hits. He started the day at 5:20 A.M. with a visit to Lucent Technologies. His race against John Tierney, whom he narrowly defeated two years ago, is considered close. This race, like the Senate race here between Republican Governor William Weld and the incumbent, John Kerry, also considered quite close, has attracted national attention.

Tierney is probably the only candidate in the nation who has cut an ad with Hillary Clinton endorsing him, but a recent *Boston Globe* poll showed that Mrs. Clinton is the most popular public figure in Massachusetts. Besides Mrs. Clinton, John Kenneth Galbraith has come into the district for Tierney, as have Robert Reich, George Stephanopoulos, former Texas Governor Ann Richards, and Sarah Brady. Gore is coming here soon. Most of the people who have been here for Torkildsen have been Republican congressional figures, including the unlikely Dick Armey, an unyielding conservative. Jack Kemp was here last week. Dole hasn't been here since the pre-primary period, but there's no point in Dole's fighting for Massachusetts, and that suits Torkildsen fine.

Torkildsen is defending himself as having one of the lowest voting scores in support of the Republican leadership. (According to *Congressional Quarterly*, he had the fifth-lowest record of support of the leadership.) He points out that he voted against the Medicare bill. But Republican moderation didn't guarantee safety. A vulnerable Republican is a target, whatever the voting record. Tierney and the groups opposing Torkildsen, which include the AFL-CIO, point out that Torkildsen did vote for the final budget reconciliation bill, which included the Medicare bill. In debates, Tierney also points out that if reelected, Torkildsen would vote for Newt Gingrich as Speaker. (The AFL-CIO's Steve Rosenthal makes the same point in explaining the AFL-CIO opposition to Torkildsen.)

In their debate last night in the Bedford Town Hall, Tierney, a slim, youthful forty-five-year-old with a long, heart-shaped Irish face, a full head of brown hair, and a slight smirk, attacked Torkildsen several times as a disciple of Gingrich. ("Peter Torkildsen campaigns like a Democrat but he votes like a Gingrich Republican.") Torkildsen, pleasant, polite, and slightly vague, stressed his "independence," and pointed out that he had voted to increase the minimum wage and the college loan program. Like Ganske, Torkildsen points out that he voted for the Safe Drinking Water Act. But, unlike Ganske, he voted against anti-environmental riders on appropriations bills. He attacked Tierney as a liberal and his description was accurate. Tierney, who supports a health care plan more comprehensive even than the one originally proposed by the Clintons, is a true liberal, and out-and-out campaigns as one, in a year when many Democrats are running as centrists. (One of his advisers says that he is probably more liberal than his constituency.) He has quite strong union support in his district.

Now, this morning, in his Jeep Cherokee on the way to the next stop, Torkildsen says that his polling percentage two years ago at this point was lower than it is now, "So I'm cautiously optimistic." He adds, "I am most appreciative that Bill Weld is running for the Senate. He'll generate turnout. If the Presidency were the only race generating turnout there would be reason for serious concern."

At a seniors center in Gloucester, a fishing city, Torkildsen earnestly goes from table to table, talking to people who in some cases are more interested in continuing their card game. A young woman who volunteers at the center tells him they need a low-income seniors living facility and he gives her his card, on which he's written the contact in his office. Vito Cuomo, the executive director of the Gloucester fisheries, a heavyset man, arrives at the seniors center and tells the group, "Every time I've called Peter Torkildsen he's been there for me. The man works his butt off. He's been there for the city of Gloucester. He's a good man."

Back in the car, Torkildsen calls his campaign manager, who tells him that in their tracking poll he's now at fifty-one percent, with Tierney at twenty-eight percent. ("That's very good news for me.") But, Torkildsen relays, their poll also shows Weld losing ground against Kerry—the Torkildsen campaign always includes the Senate race in its polls. "Having to deal with the Newt problem has been easier because of my voting record," Torkildsen says. He points out that he voted against putting school lunches into block grants to the states, for funding for the National Endowment for the Humanities and the National Endowment for the Arts. (Tierney accused him last night of "cherry picking" for votes against the Republican leadership.) "I say every chance I have that I voted to restore funding to end the shutdown," Torkildsen says. But Torkildsen doesn't do as much explaining and apologizing as

Ganske does, in part because he doesn't have to. And he's not defiant, like Tate.

At a Rotary Club lunch in Swampscott, in a restaurant overlooking the gray Atlantic on a gray day, Torkildsen recites to his audience the Congress's accomplishments, and his own in bringing bacon to the district. (When we arrived, Torkildsen asked an aide to park closer to the highway, so that people could see his big sign atop the car.) Torkildsen cites getting more money for the defense budget than Clinton wanted, which will bring in more funding for weapons produced at the General Electric plant in Lynn. He talks of his support for education, opposing cuts other Republicans wanted to make, and of his efforts toward the creation of the Essex Heritage District and his getting additional funding for the Salem Visitors Center.

"Every issue that I've voted on in Washington," Torkildsen says, earnestly, "I've always looked at on its own merits. Sometimes I've been criticized for not voting with Republicans enough, sometimes I've been criticized for voting with the Republicans too often."

He takes questions.

"You're a nice guy," a man in the audience says. "You couldn't even use Newt's name when you were talking about some people. How does the public, who like you and respect you, deal with the fact that you work for some mean-spirited people, and you have fealty and obligation to support them on close votes?"

Torkildsen responds, "I have an obligation to do what's best for my constituents. . . . I do not feel the pressure down in Washington, D.C., because I'm a Republican from Massachusetts. When I tell somebody, 'I have to disagree with you on this,' normally the response is, 'You're from Massachusetts, we really couldn't expect you to vote on this.' . . . I don't doubt at all the Speaker is very unpopular. That doesn't mean that I have to support him over my district. My district always comes first."

The man persists: "Why don't you just get a better Speaker?" Torkildsen flushes and smiles at his own predicament.

At something of a loss for words, Torkildsen says, lamely, "We'll see."

A few days before the election it became known that the Republican National Committee had given Grover Norquist's Americans for Tax Reform $2 million in soft money—the number later grew to $4.6 million. Apparently in order to keep this expenditure "independent," Haley Barbour told the press he didn't know how it would be spent, and Norquist told the press he had made "no specific commitment" to R.N.C. officials on how he would spend it. Norquist told me that the money was to be used for mailing 17 million pieces of literature and making 4 million phone calls, through a telemarketing company. Norquist, whose A.T.R. is a 501(c)(4) organization under the tax laws—nonpartisan, nonprofit, but with contributions nondeductible—had an ostensibly nonpartisan message in these mailings and phone calls: that neither the Republican nor Democratic Medicare plans proposed to cut Medicare. Norquist told me that the purpose was "to offset the AFL-CIO ads." He said, "It's a bipartisan message, but since the Democrats were attacking the Republicans it redounded to the benefit of the Republicans."

On the day before the election, Norquist said to me, "This is the Battle of the Bulge." And, upping the ante a bit, he said, "If the Democrats don't take complete control of the government—the Congress and the Presidency—they are a spent force. The left is slowly losing. If they don't take complete charge they can't change the rules. Under no change in the rules, we win slowly. If we win the Presidency and both chambers we change the rules." (He talked about ways the unions and the trial lawyers could be weakened through changing the rules.)

On the Sunday before the election, the Christian Coalition distributed 45 million voter guides, according to Ralph Reed. It maintained "enhanced phone banks" in several races. Though Reed refused to release a list of the races in which the Christian Coalition made an "enhanced effort," he said that they were made in every major contested House race and in the states of Alabama, Arkansas, Georgia, Kansas, and Louisiana, where picking up open Senate seats was possible. Even before the election, People for the

American Way, a liberal group that has been following the Christian Coalition for years, released a study in which it charged that the 1996 guides showed "a pattern of deceit and distortion." It said, for example, that candidates were asked if they favored repealing the ban on semiautomatic weapons, but in the guides the term was shortened to "firearms," which suggested that people who opposed the repeal opposed the legalization of even hunting rifles. The People for the American Way paper said, as it had in an earlier study of the voter guides, that the questions were used selectively— "adding questions when it helps their favored candidate and not including questions when there is no political advantage to be gained." For example, it said, the Iowa Senate voter guide left out the question, included in other guides, of whether the candidates favored the Balanced Budget Amendment, apparently because the Democratic incumbent, Tom Harkin, did.

The guides on the Presidential race listed various numbers of issues on which Clinton and Dole differed, but the lists varied, depending on the state. They included the Balanced Budget Amendment, the fifteen percent tax cut, banning partial-birth abortions, "homosexuals in the military," and Food and Drug Administration regulation of tobacco. (The tobacco issue wasn't included in voter guides for states where the product wasn't grown—such as Iowa and Massachusetts.)

In the final days of the campaign, the campaign finance scandal stories concerning the Democratic National Committee and Clinton's own activities kept coming, and their effect was spilling over into the contest for the House. Clinton, one of the great blame-shifters of our time, was angry at the perpetrators—apparently overlooking the fact that they included himself. He also was angry at the press (who he had felt from the beginning of his Presidency had been trying to do him in). A couple of the news stories caused particular problems. One was that the Democratic National Committee had decided not to file the quarterly report to the Federal Election Commission that was due just before the election. Legally, it could avoid the report, but politically, the decision was a disaster. It was reversed the next day. The other revealed that thirty-one Democratic donors had listed the D.N.C. headquarters as their home address. (Eddie Gillespie commented to the press: "Either they've turned the D.N.C. into a condominium or there's been a violation of federal election law.")

For Dole, the more time he spent in California the more his level of support there declined. In the end, he became like the Flying Dutchman, who had to keep moving. His final fly-around, lasting ninety-six hours, had touches of both desperation and nobility. His determination and spunk became the story about him, rather than the fact that he was going to lose. And it probably inspirited Republicans more than a sad petering out of his campaign would have.

The dispiriting effect of the money scandals on the Democrats was apparent. The generic polling on which party people would vote for for the House had been putting the Democrats ahead in early October, but the margin narrowed as the month went on, with the Republicans leading toward the end in some polls. And about ten days before the election Clinton's number was beginning to drop, and Ross Perot, running as a third-party candidate but largely irrelevant until now, as he attacked Clinton sharply on the campaign finance shenanigans was beginning to pick up support. Clinton's own polls showed that undecideds were going to Perot.

On the Sunday before the election, an anguished Matt Angle, the executive director of the Democratic Congressional Campaign Committee, said to me, "There's no question that there's been a loss of momentum here. The wind's not blowing our way. The air has gone out of the Presidential race. The sense of anger against the Republicans is gone. Two weeks ago, we'd have won the House. I underestimated the effect of the fundraising issue. It changed the subject in a way that didn't help Democrats. It's taken the edge off. In some Southern states, where the President was making inroads and we hoped to pick up seats, the President is cratering. It's amazing how quickly the President has dropped in the last ten days.

From October 20th to yesterday, he's lost twelve points in key parts of Texas. It's pretty close to a free fall. The congressional candidates are holding up well, but there's a question of how much of this they can sustain. As for turnout, there's no air in the tires, on both sides. Nobody knows about those Washington State races. They're all close. It's a very volatile electorate out there. The public will push on and off candidates more than I've ever seen. The President's campaign flattening doesn't help. A national story that demoralizes one side or the other really hurts. It makes your base unhappy. They need to be talking their candidate up to their colleagues at the office."

It was as if the gods had stepped in to punish Clinton for his arrogance and insouciance when it came to fundraising. He had surrendered what moral authority he had left. It was still clear that he would win the Presidency, but his victory wouldn't be pretty, and it now appeared that, after all, he might have a Republican Congress to torment him.

A senior Democratic official said later, of the campaign finance scandal, "It hurt. It froze us in place for a while."

A White House official said, "It did take some of the steam out of the whole thing. It was a campaign that never captured the imagination of the public or the elite press or the working press, and this was just one more element of giving people reason not to get excited about the campaign."

In the last days of the campaign, the mood in the President's entourage was not a happy one. Clinton had badly wanted to win by fifty-one percent, so that he could say he had a mandate (as he could not with forty-three percent of the vote in 1992), and now that goal seemed to be eluding him.

"It had a depressive effect," a member of that entourage said. "You went around to the rallies in the last two weeks and the enthusiasm and excitement weren't there. It cast a pall on the campaign. The crowds were a little off. The President and the Vice President were hiding from the press to avoid questions. You didn't have the excitement of a crowd with a President who is getting reelected." He added that without the funding issue (to which he attached the unfortunate but widely used sobriquet "Indogate"), "Perot would have stayed dead. Some of the late-breaking votes would have gone to Dole, and Clinton would have had fifty-one percent.

"It had a definite psychological impact on us: deflating, depressing. It should have been a happy time but it wasn't. Indogate took all the joy out of it. Nobody thought we'd lose—but it was becoming a joyless victory."

On Election Eve, Clinton flew into Iowa, because the Senate race, in which Democratic incumbent, Tom Harkin, had been well ahead, had tightened, and also to lift the spirits of the base there.

Dole stopped in Des Moines on Monday night during his fly-around, and went to a bowling alley with Greg Ganske.

Chapter Nineteen

DECISIONS

ON ELECTION NIGHT, Grover Norquist is in Atlanta to be with Newt Gingrich. Ralph Reed is at the Mayflower Hotel, in Washington, preparing for various media interviews around town and a press conference tomorrow.

Marc Nuttle is at the National Federation of Independent Business's office in Washington, gleaning from the N.F.I.B.'s state directors and Republican sources what's happening in the various states. He's worried about the level of enthusiasm of the interest groups on the Republican side. Late this afternoon, he predicted that the Republicans will have a net loss of House seats but will hold the House because they have better candidates (this goes back to the Democrats' recruiting problems). Beginning his spin on the results, Nuttle said, "If the Republicans pick up one seat in the House or Senate, labor will have some explaining to do."

The race between Clinton and Dole is effectively over early, as Clinton carries Florida by 7:00 P.M. E.S.T. and Ohio by 7:30 P.M. (Clinton's investment in Florida paid off.) The networks have announced that the Democrats have picked up a Senate seat in New Hampshire, where the challenger, Dick Swett, has defeated incumbent Republican Bob Smith. The Democrats appear to be doing very well in New England, which Clinton is sweeping.

At the AFL-CIO headquarters on 16th Street, a large group has gathered in the ground-floor lobby, watching television monitors and helping themselves to food from large buffet tables. Steve Rosenthal, along with John Sweeney and a couple of other union officials, is in the "boiler room" set up down the hallway to watch the returns come in and get reports from their field coordinators. "I've been waiting for this night for two years," he told me earlier. Now, as the returns come in from New England and other early-reporting states, Rosenthal is happy.

At the N.R.A. headquarters on Capitol Hill, a deluxe suite of offices over Bullfeathers restaurant and bar, Tanya Metaksa and three aides are crowded into a small, hot room, watching the returns and working at computers. Each time one of the N.R.A.'s favored candidates wins, a release is typed up and zapped out. Metaksa is glum. It appears that not only have the Democrats picked up a Senate seat in New Hampshire, but they've also won in Senate races in New Jersey and Georgia. Upon hearing some clapping from the larger room where most of the people are gathered, Metaksa wonders who's finding anything to cheer about. Tom Wyld, her press aide, rushes in and says "Brownback"—meaning that Sam Brownback has won the race for one of the Senate seats in Kansas. Metaksa shoots her left fist out, and shouts "*YES!*"

Bill Paxon and Maria Cino are in their N.R.C.C. offices on the second floor of the Republican National Committee's building, a block up First Street from the N.R.A.'s headquarters. Paxon, his shoes off, feet propped up on a table, is less cheery than usual. Now he learns that with a small portion of the vote in in Michigan, Dick Chrysler, an endangered freshman, is ahead by two percentage points, but Paxon and the aides with him decide not to count on that. (Chrysler ultimately lost.)

Maria Cino, working in another room with two aides, is calling field representatives. (All of these people have to be making calls to the field because the networks don't devote much coverage to House races.) She's concerned that the Republicans appear to have lost an open seat in New Jersey, and that Gary Franks, a black Republican from Connecticut, is in trouble. (Franks, one of the few

New England Republicans to have Gingrich come to his district this fall, did lose.) It looks like North Carolina freshman Fred Heineman, who had long been considered endangered, is losing. (He ultimately lost in a rematch with the Democrat he defeated two years ago.) Cino's worried about Nancy Johnson, of Connecticut, chair of the House Ethics Committee, who had come under attack at home for not pursuing the probe of Gingrich vigorously enough. (Johnson won narrowly.)

Cino, who maintains great calm, says at 9:30 P.M., "The reality is some races where we thought we were doing better we're not, and some where we didn't expect to win we're doing well. But it's too early. In 1994 we declared we'd won the House around now. This year it's going to be 3:00 A.M." (She was being optimistic.) An aide tells her that CBS is withdrawing its declaration of Bob Smith's defeat in New Hampshire.

Bill Paxon is now even more serious. He's discouraged about losing Franks and the New Jersey open seat. An aide tells him that two Pennsylvania Republicans are in trouble. (Both won very narrowly.) "That's not go-od," Paxon replies in a singsong manner. An aide tells him that incumbent Daniel Frisa, of New York, is losing. This wasn't unexpected, since his challenger was Carolyn McCarthy, whose husband had been shot to death during a madman's shooting spree on a Long Island Railroad commuter train in 1993, and who switched parties and ran a pro–gun control campaign. (Even after the murders, Frisa voted to repeal the assault weapons ban, and he had been trailing badly for weeks.) "I don't remember it being this long last time," Paxon tells me. "I think it's going to be a little tighter than I expected. It's going to be a nail-biting night. We ain't sleeping tonight." A lobbyist from the Realtors and the C.E.O. of the Home Builders have come by to see him.

A little further up First Street, at the Capitol Hill Club, where about six hundred contributors to the N.R.C.C. and Party workers have gathered, David Rehr is also less upbeat than usual. "It's decidedly mixed," he says. (A poster outside the party room says that this event was underwritten by Ameritech, the National Association of Home Builders. the National Retail Federation, and the National Association of Chain Drug Stores.) Wayne LaPierre, executive vice president of the N.R.A., is here. Some people from the Christian Coalition have stopped by.

At 10:00 P.M., the polls have closed in Iowa, and Clinton has carried it. But the House results are still slow in coming in.

At the Renaissance Hotel, in downtown Washington, where officials of the R.N.C. are monitoring events and where Dole will make his concession speech, Eddie Gillespie and a colleague are in room 226, Gillespie drinking a beer and smoking a cigar. At 10:25 P.M. Gillespie says that Peter Torkildsen appears to be losing, but he's not sure how many precincts have been counted. Clinton is carrying Massachusetts by a wide margin. Kerry has defeated Weld for the Senate seat. Peter Blute, the only other Republican in the Massachusetts delegation, has been defeated. In the Senate races, Jesse Helms has once again defeated Harvey Gantt.

Working the phones in his shirtsleeves, Gillespie says, "I just don't think we can call the House until 4:00 A.M. I just didn't expect so many tight races."

He tells a reporter on the phone, "It does appear that the principles of lower taxes and a balanced budget are going to carry the night." He's spinning. In the same phone call, he refers to the legislation passed by the Congress in the previous few months and says, "I think the American people have said that if the President and the Congress are willing to work together for commonsense legislation, they're happy with that." (Gillespie's spin-talk is more portentous than he is.)

A reporter calls Gillespie to tell him that the Dole campaign has put out a concession statement even though the polls haven't closed on the West Coast. And that then the Dole people put out a statement taking back the earlier statement. The reporter wants a comment from Gillespie. Gillespie's response is a long peal of laughter.

In another room at the Renaissance, Don Fierce has gathered

with some other Republican operatives, at Haley Barbour's request, when the evening started out so badly for the Republicans, to "figure out what the hell we were going to say the next day." (The Republican candidate for governor of Indiana, who the Republican surveys had said was ahead by ten points, was losing. There was the series of defeats in the Northeast. "We thought, 'My God, we could lose everything,' " Fierce said later.)

At 11:15 P.M., Maria Cino says wearily over the phone, "We're either breaking even or gaining one seat."

In Atlanta, Gingrich and the group around him started to worry.

At 11:30, Dole makes his actual concession speech. He thanks Haley Barbour, but it doesn't seem heartfelt. He says, twice, "We're going to keep the Senate. We're going to keep the House." Dole says, "Tomorrow will be the first time in my life I don't have anything to do." The loss of a race for the Presidency, even if expected, is often a bewildering experience for the candidate. He has been working so intensely, and been so focused on the race, so totally consumed by it, that he can be quite disoriented when it's over. This would be even more the case with Dole, not a man of wide interests. He had spent thirty-five years in Washington and had given up his Senate seat. He has been surrounded by people but is essentially a solitary man. But the final days of his campaign have at least given him a more upbeat ending.

Clinton's victory is less than he had hoped for. (The final count was Clinton 49.2 percent, Dole 40.8, Perot 8.5.)

Clinton's acceptance show at the state capitol in Little Rock is oddly magisterial—too magisterial even for a President, especially on election night. Clinton has been successful of late at appearing more Presidential than he did in his first two years, but this Mussoliniesque scene suggests that he still doesn't have a real feel for it. The Clintons and the Gores walk out of the capitol building on a red carpet, onto an outdoor stage, to a fanfare. Clinton looks solemn, deliberately solemn.

While Gore gives a long, leaden speech—more suited to a Convention nominating address—about Clinton's achievements, Clinton stands stiff and still.

Then Clinton gives a long speech. It's odd that neither of these two smart men has a sense of occasion tonight. An election victory is time for celebrating—briefly. It's late, and there are more returns to be announced.

It's clear that Clinton and Gore want to start the second term with dignity and a sense of purpose, but their timing is off. (Because Clinton's victory speech went on so long, Ralph Reed's scheduled interview on ABC has been dropped.) Clinton thanks everybody, including the Secret Service (of whom Mrs. Clinton has been suspicious, and who know a lot). He proclaims, in what is clearly meant to be his theme, and his governing philosophy, for the second term, "The vital American center is alive and well." (Aides said later that he had lifted the term "vital center" from a recent *New York Times* editorial.) He now has to demonstrate that the center can be "vital," and not just a safe political refuge. But he has set a direction, even if that direction is circumstantial. Clinton has no mandate for large government programs. Still, he recites a long list of things he wants to do in the second term—improve education, raise the lot of the underclass, strengthen families, clean up the environment, work against drug use by youths, pass campaign finance reform. He says that the outcomes of the House and Senate races aren't yet known, but both chambers are likely to be closely divided, and "it is time to put country ahead of party." As Dick Morris had urged, he will be above party, working from what Morris once described to me as a "synthesis" of the country's views. This doesn't call for much daring, or even leadership.

"When we are divided," Clinton says, "we defeat ourselves." This is a bit of preemption, laying the groundwork for the Republicans getting the blame if the next term is marked by partisanship. The Republicans have a dual imperative, which will make matters complex for them. On the one hand, they need to show that they can get things done, as the public demands; on the other, they wish to "destroy" Clinton. (I have heard this word used.)

Clinton goes through a bit of melodrama about "when I was

born in a summer storm to a widowed mother," and finally concludes. Aaron Copland's "Fanfare for the Common Man" is played, a piece of music that doesn't suggest commonality. The fireworks that follow the speeches are another touch of grandeur.

As of 1:00 A.M., Randy Tate is trailing, and in Massachusetts, John Tierney is running ahead of Peter Torkildsen.

Matt Angle, of the Democratic Congressional Campaign Committee, says by phone, "As of now, we're not beating as many of them as we thought, and they're not beating as many of ours as they thought. We did well in the Northeast and then it stalled out." He says that it appears that Greg Ganske is winning.

Gingrich gives a little speech for the television cameras, saying, "If we retain control, which now looks likely, it will be the first time in sixty-eight years." Though Gingrich looks cheerful, he has had a tense night, and he still isn't sure how it will come out.

Bob Kilbanks, on whose behalf Tanya Metaksa went to the Lehigh Valley, has lost badly to the Democratic incumbent, Paul McHale. Kilbanks was a fringe figure who remained a fringe figure. William Orton, the Democrat from a marginally Republican district in Utah, where Clinton assigned more land as a national monument, has been defeated. Clinton's action is believed by both sides to have made the difference.

Very early in the morning comes the astonishing news that Bob Dornan, the hotheaded Republican from California, is only very slightly ahead. His opponent, a Hispanic woman, ran a strong campaign against him. When Dornan thought he'd won, he said he'd introduce a resolution of impeachment against Clinton. (Dornan was ultimately defeated.)

By mid-morning Wednesday, the Republicans were down nine seats in the House. They'd held on, but with no triumph. It had got down to survival.

"We were hoping to pick up more seats," Grover Norquist admitted later, when I asked him how things had gone in Atlanta with Gingrich. "We weren't dancing."

The three candidates I was following met varying fates: one has lost, one has won, and one is in a recount.

Greg Ganske has won, 52–47. He had wriggled out sufficiently from the Gingrich problem, and had a weak opponent. And even Republican officials said that his illness had worked in his favor. (Ganske was the fifth-largest spender on House races—$12,337,935, including more than $550,000 of his own money. Ganske raised two and a half times as much as McBurney.) There are no reliable figures for all "issue advocacy" spending, since it doesn't have to be reported to the F.E.C.

Torkildsen is considered down, but at about 4:00 A.M. he decided to demand a recount. Even some of his own people don't think he has a chance to win that (he is behind by about 200 votes), but a combination of peevishness, of wanting to show his own people that he would give it his all, and of having nothing else to do, led Torkildsen to keep the race up in the air for a while. (A call to Tierney's campaign office this morning was answered with, "Good morning, Congressman John Tierney's office.")

Randy Tate is one of three Washington State Republicans who by this morning have been declared to have been defeated. Adam Smith has beaten Tate handily, 51–46. The Democrats are very pleased and Republicans very down-at-the-mouth about the overall result in Washington State. (The other two House races ultimately turned around, becoming Republican victories. Ellen Craswell, the Bible-citing candidate for governor, has lost, as expected, to Gary Locke, King County executive, who will be the first Chinese-American governor.) Tate, the top-rated target, from an evenly divided district, was up against forces that were too strong for him, even with his allies' help, and his embrace of Gingrich hadn't helped.

Tate received slightly less than twice as much in PAC contributions as Smith did. Overall, Tate raised more than twice as much money as Smith.

"In the case of Randy Tate," Matt Angle, of the D.C.C.C., said, "You had a fatally injured incumbent and a good candidate on our side. We ran a better campaign and a better candidate. We targeted better, identifying voters whom you can convince. Tate didn't decide early enough whether to hug or stiff-arm Newt, and he started out hugging."

Of other members in tight races, J.D. Hayworth, the obstreperous Republican freshman, won, as did Helen Chenoweth. Andrea Seastrand, the California conservative freshman whom the Christian Coalition tried to help and the environmental groups had targeted, lost to Walter Capps, a professor of religious studies at the University of California at Santa Barbara. (Capps's daughter, Laura, worked in the White House for George Stephanopoulos, who made three trips to help him. The President showed up in Capps's Santa Barbara district in the closing days, making a last-minute speech on campaign finance reform and praising Laura Capps highly.) Once Clinton heard that Bob Dornan was in a tight race in his Orange County district, a formerly safe conservative bastion in which Clinton had done well in 1992, Clinton went there, too; hoping to defeat the man who said on the House floor that during the Vietnam War, "Clinton gave aid and comfort to the enemy."

Torkildsen lost the recount, as expected—by a wider margin than on Election Night. That left the House Massachusetts delegation without its two Republicans. The Democratic tide in Massachusetts was simply too strong. (Clinton carried it by thirty-four points.) Besides, Torkildsen's district was essentially Democratic, and he had won the first time against a Democrat who had been indicted. Torkildsen's attempts at moderation turned out to be a wishy-washiness that neither caused the Democrats and the liberal groups to give him a pass, nor stirred up a passionate desire on the part of the groups on the right to save him. Given all this, the mere 371 votes that separated him and Tierney was an accomplishment of sorts for Torkildsen.

Though Torkildsen said he didn't take PAC money, the contributions to him by individuals were nearly three times the amount donated to Tierney. In all, Torkildsen raised about $250,000 more than Tierney did. But Tierney had intense support from labor and other liberal groups.

After the recounts, and some runoff elections in Texas, the final result was that the Republicans had a net loss of nine House seats but retained control of the House narrowly, leaving them a margin of only ten votes, the smallest margin since 1952.

Though the Democrats nearly shut out the Republicans in the Northeast, Republicans continued to make gains in the South.

In the Senate, the Republicans gained two seats. The impact would be greater than this number would suggest, because ideologically the new Republican senators moved the Senate further to the right.

After a long night (Maria Cino didn't get to bed until ten o'clock Wednesday night), which came on top of efforts of at least two years, people were exhausted and, despite their obviously prepared spin—prepared days if not weeks earlier—were still sorting out what had happened. In many cases the spin needed some adjusting, as matters didn't turn out as hoped on either side.

Now would come the time for claims, and counterclaims, and the search for honest conclusions. Some of the conclusions are surprising.

Chapter Twenty

WHAT HAPPENED?

THE REPUBLICANS, in holding control of the House, may have tacked down, but not nailed down, the realignment they were seeking.

It is a virtual certainty that Clinton's stall, over the campaign financing scandal, at the end of the campaign cost the Democrats the House. In close races, it's impossible to say what single factor, or group, made *the* difference in the outcome, and many of the House races were quite close. Twenty-six Republicans were elected with fifty-one percent of the vote or less. The total difference between the votes received by Republican and Democratic House candidates was approximately 250,000, out of approximately 87 million votes, or three-tenths of a percent. The result was 48.8 percent for the Republicans to 48.5 percent for the Democrats (with minor parties making up the rest).

It's clear that toward the end the finance issue took the dynamism out of the Democrats' and their allies' effort to regain the House, and cost Clinton the fifty-one percent margin that he desperately wanted. The private musings of the President himself, and the testimony of even close Clinton aides supports this conclusion.

Clinton, who denied in a post-election interview with *The New York Times* that the campaign finance issue was a factor in how the contest for the House came out ("I'm absolutely certain it didn't have anything to do with winning the House back"), has, in talks with his advisers, questioned his own election-end strategy on the issue. In mid-January a Clinton aide told me, "The question the

President asks now is should we have done television to respond to that in the last moments, because he feels we paid a price for that at the end of the election." Clinton believes, the aide said, that the campaign finance issue did affect turnout in a number of races, and "that a strong response would have helped more than it hurt." This is a rather large admission.

This aide was one of several in the White House who felt, as the D.C.C.C. official, Matt Angle, did on the closing weekend, that the campaign financing scandal had taken "the air out" of the Democratic side in the closing days.

Another White House aide said, of the campaign finance issue, "It definitely hurt. There's no question about that. Our own research showed it drove voters to Perot. But for that issue, Perot would have stayed dead. Otherwise, some of the votes would have gone to Dole because of the money issue. There's no evidence it cost us a single state, but it almost certainly put him below fifty percent."

Still another aide said, "We peaked at the end of October, the week of the 20th." (This was just about two weeks before the election.)

Doug Sosnik, the White House political director, told a reporter just before the election, "God intended for this election to be held October 29, not November 5."

Not all the President's aides were in agreement, of course. One insisted that the result in the House was caused by the fact that the Democrats hadn't recruited candidates of high enough quality, and by the fact that the Democrats had little positive to say. "To simply attack Gingrich wasn't enough," this person said.

Whether or not this aide was trying to deflect blame from the President, it is the case that many Democratic House candidates didn't give a sufficiently explicit explanation of what they would do if they were reelected. Attacking their opponents for lining up with Gingrich *wasn't* enough. A political adviser to the President said, "I think this campaign was an end of an era in politics. Campaigns have to have a positive view of the future."

Yet despite these liabilities the Democrats appeared to be on their way to winning the House until the campaign finance scandal broke. Clinton, in the *Times* interview, blamed the last-minute infusion of money by the Republicans (on ads, mailings, etc.) for the loss of the House. Some other Democrats also mentioned the large sums that the Republicans threw into the race at the end, through their own spending and the money turned over to others as a factor in the Republicans holding the House. The Republicans did outspend the Democrats substantially at the end; the Democrats had used up so much money on assuring Clinton's victory that they had less left at the end to spend on the Democratic Congress. The Republican National Committee had deliberately held back some of its funds until the end, in part because the key strategists had to see what the message would be—which also involved the question of whether Dole would take hold. But hoarding money to spend at the end isn't a novel tactic, and the Democrats shouldn't have been as taken aback as they later professed to be. In fact, no one mentioned it at the time.

But none of the others I talked to about what happened at the end thought that the Republican money was as important as the Democrats' financing scandals. Mark Gersh, of the National Committee for an Effective Congress, says, of the Republicans, "If they'd had the money and not John Huang, they would have lost."

Don Fierce, the Republican strategist, said, "The most wonderful thing that happened to us was the Huang story. We had run out of things to say."

Some people argued that the Republicans held the House while Clinton held the Presidency because people deliberately split their tickets in order to ensure a balance of power, but there's strong reason to be suspicious of that. It's a too intellectual concept of human behavior. People vote for a person out of like or dislike; they aren't likely to vote for someone they don't like in order to achieve a balance of power. (The rightward ideology of so many House Republicans made this even less likely. People certainly weren't likely to vote for Clinton and, say, Helen Chenoweth.) Following the 1996 election, Andrew Kohut, the esteemed pollster and director of the Pew Research Center, pointed out that the answer in the polls about ticket-splitting—as in most polling—is very affected by the question. Kohut said, "We found very few people in our post-election surveys who said they voted for their congressional representative because they wanted to put a check on Clinton's power. But if you ask people if they think there's a virtue in having the Congress controlled by one power and the White House by the other, particularly when they have a very mixed view of both parties and their political leaders, they say yes—but very few vote that way." Besides, four out of five voters supported the same party in the Presidential and congressional contests; less than one in ten voted for a Democratic President and a Republican House member.

"After we stalled out," Matt Angle, of the D.C.C.C., said, "it was hand-to-hand combat in about fifty districts."

A prominent Democratic consultant said, "Our campaign didn't have a lot of energy at the national level. Absent a campaign with edge, there wasn't enough energy to stop the energy of the money scandal. You could see it everywhere. Clinton could have easily won this election by fifteen points. It cost the House."

There is a good bit of empirical evidence that supports the view that the campaign finance issue cost the Democrats the House. Exit polls showed that the eighty-three percent of the voters who decided whom to vote for before the last week of the election favored the Democrats by four percent, while those who decided in the last week favored the Republicans by fourteen percent. This was a dramatic break with the normal pattern: when a party is losing ground, as the House Republicans were before the end of October, it usually loses by a wider margin toward the end, as the undecided voters go with the trend. (This is what happened to the Democrats in 1994.)

In a historical irony, people took out their anger over the money scandal more on the Democrats running for Congress than on Clinton himself: they favored Clinton over Dole (by a wide margin) and associated the scandal, which occurred in fundraising for and by the Democratic National Committee, with the Democratic Party. Stan Greenberg and Celinda Lake, who polled for EMILY's List, found a *fifteen percent* drop in the Democratic Party's standing on ethics in the period between mid-October and Election Day. The money scandal was one too many for a lot of people.

Most of the shift was among the more traditional women: married women (22 points), low-wage workers (29 points), and homemakers (18 points). The campaign finance issue had its greatest impact on voters in the rural Midwest, the South, and the Rocky Mountain states—where traditional women are a higher proportion of the population than elsewhere.

Clinton's own standing dropped from 51.5 to 49 percent in the last two weeks, and a drop of that size has an impact down the line. (The first figure is the average of polls done for the Democratic National Committee for October up to two weeks before the election and the second is the average of the public polls a few days before the election.) Since nine out of ten Clinton voters also voted for Democrats for Congress, the loss by Clinton of over two percentage points cost Democratic candidates, who but for Clinton's drop in support would have received the majority of the votes cast for Congress overall. Some of this drop is believed to have been caused by people simply deciding, out of disgust, to not vote. (The turnout, at 49 percent, was the lowest since 1924.) Mark Gersh says, referring to the twenty-six seats won by Republicans by fifty-one percent or less, "The races you narrowly win you wouldn't have won without events toward the end." Greenberg's and Lake's work found a significant drop-off in people who, two weeks before the election, answered positively—by seventy-five percent—the question, Does the campaign make you want to go vote? On election night and for a few days afterward, the percent of *those same people* had dropped to sixty-nine percent. Greenberg says, "The election clearly fizzled, and very likely had an impact on the turnout."

There was another important change from the past in the way the 1996 House elections broke. A political maxim has it that late-deciders go against incumbents—they are familiar with the incumbents and if they are still up in the air toward the end it is probably because they have serious doubts about them. But in the case of the House races, a higher than usual proportion of the late-deciders—eleven percent of the voters decided in the last three days—went to Republican incumbents.

The Republicans won most of the competitive open seats—they took ten formerly Democratic seats and the Democrats took four formerly Republican seats. Since the voters are likely to know less about the candidates for open seats, those contests are more likely to be affected by national trends. Candid Democrats find it highly discomfiting—and Grover Norquist finds it highly reassuring—that the Democrats have lost a net twenty-five open seats in the last three congressional elections.

Of the seventy freshman Republicans who faced reelection, the Democrats succeeded in defeating only twelve—they had hoped, of course, for a higher number. The average support for the freshmen from marginal districts had dropped by five percentage points since 1994, but that was one or two points short of enough to defeat more of them.

It wasn't only Democrats who were of the view that the campaign finance issue had cost them the House—even though it was in the Republicans' interest to say that their victory in the House reflected a long-term trend, that it was not the result of a fluky issue coming in at the end. On the day *before* the election, David Rehr, of the National Beer Wholesalers Association, told me, "Ten days ago, the Republicans probably would have lost the House and maybe the Senate, too. It was really bad. Dole kept collapsing and Clinton was really rolling. Then there were the crystal ball ad, and the Clinton money stories."

If the Democrats would have won the House but for the campaign finance scandals, what does that say about the relative power of the contending forces, especially those on the right? After all, in 1994, a significant ingredient in the Republican victory was the default on the left, the people who simply stayed home because they were angry at Clinton or didn't think it mattered. Now the liberal groups were better organized. "Their base turned out better than ours," Don Fierce said.

Ralph Reed said after the election, "We fought each other to a draw." He cited the fact that the liberal groups "weren't out there in '94." But a senior Republican figure said that the Christian Coalition had "half to two-thirds the energy it had in 1994." The de-energizing of the Republican groups by the Dole campaign took its toll. Ralph Reed felt that the Dole campaign had taken its base for granted and paid a big price for that.

It's possible, based on what happened in 1996, that the public has moved away from the social issues—such as abortion, school prayer, and the like. When I suggested this to a Republican strategist, he replied quickly, "That's what scares me." Other issues may prove elusive as well. Don Fierce said, "If Clinton gets a balanced budget, what do we talk about? Our Party can't sit there in the mind-set of fighting the New Deal when the Democrats have agreed it's over."

If the public has moved away from the social issues, to other values issues that affect their daily lives, and if economic issues are of greater political import than social issues—something that Ralph Reed understands—where does this leave the groups that organized around the social issues in the early 1980s?

It leaves them struggling, as are both major Parties, for a new definition, even new coalitions. Bob Dole was awkward and ultimately unsuccessful in his attempts to hold the groups on the right and win the independent center, but no Republican candidate will find this easy. Ronald Reagan was an exception in many ways. And Bill Clinton's 1996 campaign may well have been *sui generis*.

A Republican strategist said something surprising in a post-election conversation. He said that "the problem for the Republican Party is much greater than for the Democratic Party. In an election, people want to vote Democratic because there's a little more compassion on the Democratic side. When they voted Republican, it was because the Democrats had gone too far."

In the aftermath of the election, each group of course claimed victory. Some of them achieved this by retroactively lowering their goals.

"We feel like we did our job," Ralph Reed said in a conversation shortly after the election. But he was clearly disappointed that the Republicans hadn't won as many open seats as he had expected.

"Overall, we feel we achieved two things that are historic," Reed said. He was referring to the fact that the Republicans now had the first Republican Speaker who would serve more than one term since 1928, and that for the first time in the history of his movement it had made gains down the ballot or held its own without the Presidential balloting going its way. Reed said, "In 1980 we had a very popular Presidential candidate and then a very popular President. In 1994 all we had to do was swim backstroke with the tide. This time we were swimming against the tide."

Reed pointed out that a number of Republicans who won open seats in the House and Senate "represent a shift to the right," and that "there are four additional reliable pro-life votes in the Senate." He argued that his grassroots movement had defeated the money and media that the AFL-CIO poured into the race.

Reed felt that the social issues hadn't been very prominent in the election because the candidates knew that the Christian Coalition was waging those issues through the voter guides and scorecards and its get-out-the-vote drives. Two Senate candidates had told him that people knew where they were on the social issues and that they had to reach out to the middle by talking about education and crime.

"In a narrow and parochial way, we're in a stronger position because we've completed the institutionalization of our movement," Reed said. "People could argue after '94 that that was a fluke, or that the Christian Coalition was a fly-by-night phenomenon. Now they can't.

"We're in a stronger position than in '94 because after that election we had to wait until after the Hundred Days [while the House voted on the Contract], and then until after the shutdowns to have our issues voted on—we had to take a number, in effect."

But then Reed looked at the 1996 election in a different and more surprising light. He said, "But if you move beyond the narrow confines, we've all lost ground." When I asked him why, he replied, "Because the conventional wisdom is that Gingrich and his gang overreached and have to be more moderated. Cutting against that grain will be difficult."

He said, "It's going to be a matter of working smarter, not harder, not make the same mistake that Clinton made in '93 and the Republicans in Congress made in '95. We'll have to pick our shots more carefully. At this point, I think it'll be partial-birth abortion."

When I talked to Reed a few weeks later, he was further along on his congressional agenda. Besides another vote on partial-birth abortion, he would make the Balanced Budget Amendment a big priority, and push for something in the area of religious freedom— probably school prayer. He said, "That will allow us to get on record votes on issues that will be very effective in our voter guides and scorecards."

Though the AFL-CIO didn't meet its primary goal of taking the House back for the Democrats—and immediately began to say that that hadn't been its goal—and though the spinners on the right said that union members hadn't gotten their money's worth, labor could legitimately claim some achievements. The chief one was that it came back as a considerable political force. According to Steve Rosenthal, the political director of the AFL-CIO, the labor federation spent the extra $35 million on "issue advocacy" it had announced that it would: $25 million on television and radio ads, and the rest on efforts on the ground to organize and conduct get-out-the-vote drives. (The AFL-CIO's own PAC, the Committee on Political Education, spent another $1.2 million, and the labor affiliates $49 million more through their own PACs.)

Labor did increase its turnout over both 1992 and 1994—almost ten percentage points over 1994. Of its forty-five top-tier Republican targets in the House, it succeeded in defeating eighteen, or forty percent—a respectable showing, especially, as Rosenthal pointed out, when one considers that, according to the Center for Responsive Politics, labor was outspent by business six-to-one overall. (This includes the $35 million labor spent on "issue advocacy.") Rosenthal also argued that the House Republicans' deliberate self-moderation, and passing bills, in the last few months of the Congress had helped them. (The research by Stan Greenberg and Celinda Lake bore this out.)

And in the end, a significantly lower percentage of union households voted Republican than in 1994. The percentage went from forty in 1994 to thirty-five in 1996. "That may not seem such a big deal," Rosenthal said, "but that's over a million votes."

Labor argued that it had also met its goal of, as Rosenthal put it, "making the issues of importance to workers the center of the debate." Labor—with major help from Bill Clinton—did achieve the goal of placing economic issues, rather than the social issues, at the heart of the election agenda. "We came a long way," Rosenthal said, "and we still have a way to go."

Whether another such round of heavy attacks on members' votes—even whether the same kinds of targets would be provided in future elections—would be even as successful as it was in 1996, were questions that remained for the future.

It has become fashionable, especially since the election, to write off the N.R.A. as a spent force, and though it may not strike terror in politicians as much as it used to, and it didn't win all the races it went into, it still can be a force in politics and can affect legislation—even if it loses the big ones. Tanya Metaksa likes to talk in terms of the "ten thousand" races the N.R.A. went into at the federal, state, and local levels, presumably because that produces a high percentage—a claimed eighty-four—of victories and shows the N.R.A.'s reach. But, whatever its specific impact as compared to that of others on the same side, the N.R.A. was on the winning side of seventy-seven percent of the two hundred and eighty House races it entered, and sixty-three percent of the twenty-seven Senate races. It actually picked up additional supporters in the Senate. It claims that nearly half of its supporters who lost their House seats were replaced by people of like views on gun legislation. (The races at the state and local levels are of importance to the N.R.A. because that is where the fights take place on whether people can carry concealed weapons.) The N.R.A. claims that ninety-two percent of the congressmen who voted to repeal the assault weapons ban and ran for reelection won. (Another way to look at this was that all but four of the twenty-three incumbents who lost had voted to repeal the ban.) The N.R.A. spent more money on "independent expenditures" in 1996—including one for Randy Tate—than it did on regular contributions, most of it for radio ads in congressional races. (It made no television ads.)

Metaksa realized even before the election that "there's a dampening effect for our folks from the top of the ticket."

Grover Norquist pointed out that while the Dole campaign seemed pleased that the N.R.A. wasn't backing Dole, since 1980 no Republican has won without its support: it supported Reagan in 1980 and 1984 and Bush in 1988 but not in 1992.

The N.F.I.B., which spent $878,174 on two hundred and forty-five House races (and $193,947 on the Senate), plus $125,000 on "issue ads," took flat-out credit for the outcome in the House. Jeff Butzke, the political director, said the day after the election, "I think if it weren't for our program Dick Gephardt would be taking over the House." He argued that the organization made a crucial difference in twenty to twenty-five seats.

Marc Nuttle, back in Oklahoma a few days later, said that the N.F.I.B. endorsements probably had more impact than contributions and other forms of help. (Nuttle's predictions about the outcome had been more on target than most.) He said, "The N.F.I.B. endorsement makes them part of that community. It's a direct impact that grows slowly, as opposed to a big media buy." He made a higher claim than Butzke: that the N.F.I.B. had made a crucial difference in "probably seventy-five to a hundred" races. I asked him about the role of the 35,000 state interest groups that he had been telling me all year he was working with and would be a big factor in the election.

"Not really that many got engaged," Nuttle said. "The ones who did something at the Convention or in the campaign were five thousand or less." He continued, "We called and mailed, and the N.F.I.B. did a telecast to their members, and I talked to the groups—but I didn't get a good response."

David Rehr was candid, as usual. After claiming that "in terms of where we put our money we won eighty-five percent of the House races," he added, "Our biggest goal was to keep the Congress a pro–small business Congress, and that was achieved, but by a narrower margin than we'd hoped." He said, "Most of our strongly committed friends were reelected—Randy Tate was an exception— but I'd be happier if we'd won more seats. Based on the opportunity, there were potentially more gains to be made, but you could see them slipping away."

EMILY's List had two principal goals: to elect more pro-choice women to Congress, and to get more women—in particular non-college-educated women—to participate than had in 1994. (They accounted for almost half the voters who had participated in 1992 but stayed home in 1994.) After the election the EMILY's List press release said that 1996 saw "the second largest increase in history" for pro-choice women elected to Congress—the actual number was nine (the highest year was 1992, with twenty-one victories). It also claimed that women had provided the margin of victory for Clinton's reelection, which was the case. (Clinton won the women's vote over Dole by seventeen percentage points—the largest "gender gap" since 1980.) Non–college educated women voted for Clinton in a landslide. Their turnout was higher than in 1994, but still not as high as it had been in 1992. But the survey research for EMILY's List showed that Clinton and the Democrats were heavily favored by those who had voted in 1992, dropped out in 1994, and still didn't vote in 1996. If they had turned out, Clinton's—and the House Democrats'—margins might well have been different. (About half the "angry white males" of 1994 came back to the Democratic fold in 1996, voting for Democrats for Congress.)

But men played a major role in helping the Republicans keep control of the Congress. Greenberg says, "The Republicans wouldn't have been in the game without the men. It's the men who make them competitive as a national party." A combination of usually Republican men and traditional women—including the now-famous "soccer moms" (suburban women with children, and therefore the more traditional voter)—who were offended by the finance scandals and switched to the Republicans, caused the Republicans to keep control of the Congress. In the Presidential race, the "soccer moms" went for Clinton. Congressional Republicans had done a better job of reaching independent women voters than the Democrats, convincing fourteen percent of them to change their opinion from negative to positive, according to the Greenberg-Lake research, on whether the Republican Congress had succeeded. (This was at the same time that women were moving away from the Democrats in droves on the issues of "ethics and honesty.")

Grover Norquist emphasized how pleased he was that the Republicans maintained control of the House—and that was valid in the sense that the opposite outcome would have been a major blow to his movement. "They threw everything at us and we stopped them," he said. "This is the decisive election for the next twenty years." (Norquist was excited—"ecstatic," he said—that three states had passed his anti-tax initiatives.) The number of governorships held by the two parties didn't change, while in the 1995–96 election cycle Republicans lost a net fifty-three seats in state legislatures, with a net loss of control of five state legislatures.

"What we just went through," Norquist said, "was the last Nixon Republican who was clueless about how to build a coalition. Wedge issues are intensity issues—prayer in school and so on. Dole was pre–alternative media; he didn't call up Rush Limbaugh or Michael Reagan or Gordon Liddy.

"The next generation of candidates will be more coalition-savvy."

Norquist was optimistic that the prospects for Republicans' holding the Congress in the future were good. He argued that if the Democrats didn't take the House in 1998—and it seemed unlikely that they would—about twenty-five Democrats would retire. "Keeping the House this year was the triumph," Norquist said, "because they had to take the House to change the rules to keep from losing strength. When they couldn't take the House and the Senate, they couldn't change the rules. They couldn't change the campaign finance laws to kneecap Republican donors and raise union dues and go back to financing the big-city machines, which we've begun to defund. They would take over our committees and increase franked mail and try to make themselves invulnerable. The secular trend continues: today there are more self-employed people and small business owners than there are labor union members. The secular trend is every year more people are self-employed. That tends to make them Republicans.

"Therefore the long-term trend is toward the Republican Party. There will be more Republicans in five years and fewer Democrats than there are today. That's a general trend. That's a problem for the left.

"So now the goal is to figure out how to cut the budget so that the Democratic Party is weaker in two years and four years."

Norquist added, "And they're [the Republicans] going to unleash committee chairmen to issue subpoenas and do other things we've been asking for. It's not going to be pretty."

The Republicans figure on picking up more seats in 1998 because they expect more Democratic retirements by then and they are going by the historically bad results for an incumbent President midway through a second term. If so, the realignment would go forward and become stronger. Democrats argue that Republicans are talking numbers out of context: that the Democratic pickup of House seats in 1974 followed Watergate; that the Republican pickup in 1966 was a correction of the 1964 landslide and also a result of Vietnam; that the Republican setback in 1958 followed a recession and the scandal (tiny, it now seems) that forced Sherman Adams to resign as Eisenhower's chief of staff (over a vicuna coat, an oriental rug, and free hotel rooms). The assumption behind this argument, of course, is that there would be no major problems or scandals in Clinton's second term. Also, the Democrats argue, the 1990 redistricting created so many districts in which neither side has an advantage that the House races will be increasingly nationalized.

The amounts of money raised and spent on the 1996 election broke all precedents. The two parties, including their congressional committees, raised a total of $990.6 million, according to final Federal Election Committee figures. But the amounts in themselves are only an indicator—of the pressure that the politicians and the parties are under to raise the money. The Clinton scandals begin to suggest the lengths that political figures will go to to obtain the funds.

The F.E.C. figures show that, counting the Presidential and Congressional committees, the Republicans raised $138.2 million in soft money, while the Democrats raised $123.9 in soft money. But these were only the direct contributions to the national committees, which have to be reported; the information on how much soft money was raised indirectly through and for the state parties isn't available. In hard money, the Republicans raised $416.5 million and the Democrats raised $221.6 million. Overall, the Republicans outraised the Democrats by forty-three percent. For the House and Senate elections, the Republicans outraised and outspent the Democrats by more than two to one. (The House Republican campaign committee raised $92.8 million in hard and soft money, or more than twice what its Democratic counterpart raised—$38.96 million. The National Republican Senatorial Committee raised $93.9 million in hard and soft money, while its Democratic counterpart raised $44.97 million.) The amount of soft money raised and spent by both parties was three times the amount spent four years ago. About eleven times as much labor PAC money went to Democrats as to Republicans, and two and a half times as much corporate money went to Republicans as to Democrats; but because there was so much more corporate PAC money ($50 million) versus labor PAC money ($26 million), the amounts received by both parties from PACs were roughly equal. Since the amounts spent on "issue advocacy"—by labor, by the business coalition, by environmental groups, pro- and anti-choice groups—don't have to be reported, there's no way to know precisely what they amounted to. But experts estimate that a total of about $50 to $75 million was spent on "issue" ads by outside groups.

The fact that the turnout percentage was the lowest in over seventy years suggests that the voters found a lot not to like about how our politics works now. Both Presidential candidates had large flaws, and this clearly affected races down the line. Yet there were real issues between the parties.

As the parties now seek their new definition, the groups that back them may have to retool as well. Repeat performances of 1996 may not suffice. The same political stratagems don't always work twice, not to mention three times.

If the political system is capable of getting hold of the campaign finance disaster and truly fixing it, the ground rules will have changed.

The struggle over the alignment of power will go on. The Republicans have the advantage, and many advantages, but they don't yet have a lasting hold on political power in America.

Chapter Twenty-One

EPILOGUE

Clinton's transition soon—perhaps inevitably—became choppy. The odd thing about it was that some of the lessons of the post–1992 election transition hadn't been learned. Deadlines were set publicly—the President will name a Secretary of State this week—and then not met. The transition had actually been worked on since September by a small group that included Erskine Bowles, the North Carolina businessman whom Clinton was wooing to be the new chief of staff; the attorney and close Clinton friend Vernon Jordan; and Mickey Kantor, the outgoing Commerce Secretary and former trade representative who was also close to Clinton. Leon Panetta, the outgoing chief of staff, was heavily involved. But the effort, eventually and inevitably, ran into Clinton's indecisiveness—particularly on personnel decisions. And though Clinton and his aides didn't talk publicly about "diversity," it remained a goal, and led to awkwardness toward the end. On the day after the election, at a rally on the South Lawn of the White House, the President—in contrast to his pledge four years earlier to name a Cabinet that "looks like America"—said he wanted to "get the best people to create that vital center." He added that he would "cast a wide net." There was open talk about seeking people from business, but that never happened, and from Republican ranks, which ended in the appointment of former Senator William Cohen, of Maine, as Defense Secretary. It took Clinton quite a while to choose a Secretary of State as different candidates came to the fore. He did consider former Senate Majority Leader

George Mitchell, but then, at the urging of Vice President Gore, Richard Holbrooke, the former Bosnia negotiator, had a brief moment as a strong contender. Former Senator Sam Nunn, of Georgia, was another strong contender, and had a typically lengthy, late-night interview with Clinton. Madeleine Albright, his ultimate choice, was in the running all the while, and in addition to her credentials as a foreign policy analyst for the Democrats over the years and as Ambassador to the United Nations, she had the backing of women's groups, who pressured the White House for more high-level appointments of women. Albright was the one candidate who could do Clinton some immediate political good, and the longer the vacuum went on, the stronger her position became. The brilliant, self-promoting (even as these things go) Holbrooke was, as one White House aide put it, "the long ball"—favored by Gore—but in the end Clinton went the safer route. (Subsequently, Albright vetoed Holbrooke for the U.N. job because of his aggressiveness.) Mitchell was a serious contender, and was thought to have the job the Friday after the election, but lost out as the situation unraveled and the President took a somewhat postponed trip to Australia and Manila. Senate Republicans, still burning from what they saw as Mitchell's partisan leadership, objected. (They had also told Richard Lugar he couldn't take the job because that would open a Senate seat in Indiana, and the governor was a Democrat. They didn't mind Cohen's taking Defense, since he had already left the Senate.)

Anthony Lake had earned a fair amount of enmity over his four years as National Security Adviser—most especially from Secretary of State Warren Christopher and his closest allies, but elsewhere in the government as well—because of his rivalrous and secretive ways. The National Security Adviser is supposed to make the foreign policy team work together. So the President made Lake's deputy, Sandy Berger, with whom he was more comfortable anyway, National Security Adviser, and Lake was named to head the C.I.A. as a consolation.

A striking aspect of the transition was the large number of people who told the President that they would leave if they didn't get a better job—five White House aides, by one count—and of

Cabinet officers who announced their own decisions to leave even though they had been asked not to before the President made a decision about successors. Clinton may be a "screamer," but he doesn't seem to strike fear, or even awe, in his subordinates. One cannot imagine aides of, say, Lyndon Johnson behaving this way. (George Stephanopoulos deliberately let it be known before the election that he was leaving, lest anyone conclude his departure was involuntary, or motivated by disappointment.)

Attorney General Janet Reno was left dangling for a while, but most of Clinton's advisers felt he had no choice but to reappoint her as Attorney General if she wanted to stay—which she made clear publicly that she did. To fire her at a time when she was deciding on Republican requests for an independent counsel on the money scandal would have been unseemly. (She declined to appoint an independent counsel at this point, but did launch an investigation.) White House aides—and the President—had felt for some time that she wasn't "part of the team," and her idiosyncratic ways made her a loner. (Reno had appointed four independent counsels—but the Whitewater counsel was requested by the Clintons themselves. Reno kept expanding his assignment.)

Gore took a particular interest in two appointments. One was of Andrew Cuomo—who is part of the Gore network in and out of government—as Secretary of Housing and Urban Development. The other was of William Daley, brother and son of Chicago mayors, who was named Commerce Secretary. Clinton had angered the Daleys by passing over Bill Daley in the first transition, even though he had been led to believe he would be given a Cabinet post. Gore wanted to make sure that the Daleys weren't unhappy as the year 2000 approached.

Outgoing HUD Secretary Henry Cisneros, who also played a major role in the transition, insisted that Clinton wasn't appointing enough Hispanics to high places. Clinton had appointed two Hispanics: Bill Richardson, a House member from New Mexico, had been named to the U.N. (but he's only half-Hispanic and many Hispanics didn't count him as one of theirs), and Aida Alvarez was being named head of the Small Business Administration. So Clinton astonished many in Washington, including people in the White House, by installing Federico Peña, his outgoing Transportation Secretary, who was virtually on his way back home, as Secretary of Energy. Peña's departure had been encouraged by the Clinton people. Peña's premature and incorrect statement that ValuJet, the budget airline whose plane crashed in the Everglades in May, 1996, was safe was an embarrassment to the administration. But Clinton phoned him at midnight one night—and announced his appointment the next day. (Hazel O'Leary, whom Peña would replace at Energy, was also considered an embarrassment—because of her extensive travel and other ill-considered actions—and she took the hint and resigned before the President had a replacement.)

The President did learn from prior experience to concentrate on the White House staff first. He and Mrs. Clinton had both said that choosing the staff six days before the first Inauguration, having spent most of the transition time on selecting the Cabinet, was their biggest mistake of the first term. Erskine Bowles, who accepted the chief of staff position, was closer to being a peer to Clinton than Leon Panetta, the man he was replacing. (Bowles was one of Clinton's favorite golfing pals, and a confidant.) Bowles set out to run the White House on a more business-like basis—a daunting and perhaps elusive goal.

The President's rude treatment of Harold Ickes, his former deputy chief of staff, whom he failed to tell personally that he wouldn't be chief of staff and that Bowles had insisted on choosing his own deputies—who would not include the temperamental Ickes—was typical of Clinton's treatment of people he had once been close to. He simply couldn't face them with unpleasant news. Ickes had been told by Panetta in early October (when the President and his advisers were in Chautauqua, New York, preparing for the first Presidential debate) that he wouldn't be chief of staff.

Through both circumstances and intent, Clinton ended up with a much more centrist White House staff than he had gathered for his first term.

Clinton's second term began in a curious state of ennui. Fatigue and the downer ending of the campaign were part of it—as was the sense that the Clintons were likely in for a rocky second term. When the President entered the room for his first Cabinet meeting after the election, no one rose to applaud. Clinton's aides had difficulty getting him to focus on the substance of the second term. The Clinton people went through the Inaugural festivities in a subdued mood. Someone in the inner circle said, "It was going through the motions."

The events surrounding the House of Representatives' decisions about the ethics charges against Newt Gingrich were disturbing—marked as they were by the Republican leaders' strong-arming and contempt for process. The atmosphere was one of lawlessness. The leaders took the adolescent-at-best position that David Bonior, the Democratic whip, who had pursued the Gingrich case with more intensity than anyone else, "isn't going to tell us what to do." That Bonior's dedication was called unseemly by the Republicans was odd, given Gingrich's own very personal crusade against former House Speaker Jim Wright, in 1989, which forced Wright to resign from the House.

In insisting that the House vote on Gingrich as Speaker on January 7th, the day the new Congress convened, before it knew what the Ethics Committee had found, and then consigning independent counsel James Cole's presentation of the case against Gingrich—a strong one, it turned out—to the Friday afternoon of the Inaugural weekend, and holding the vote on the Ethics Committee's findings on the day after the Inauguration, the Republicans showed their contempt for the regular order. But the House can't function without an understanding that the two parties will follow the regular order, observe limits. The Republicans misrepresented the facts of the case, and labeled the main issue in contention—whether Gingrich had violated the tax laws by knowingly using charitable institutions to fund his college course, which was part of his long-term effort to build a political movement—as having to do with an "arcane" tax law. But anybody who deals in these matters knows what the law says: it's illegal to use charitable contributions for partisan political activity. The other issue was whether Gingrich had deliberately misled the committee.

In his presentation to the committee, Cole said that the Ethics subcommittee that studied the case found that Gingrich was using tax-exempt organizations for "partisan political goals," and that he had provided the committee with information that was "inaccurate, incomplete, and unreliable." Cole also charged that Gingrich's behavior was part of a pattern of "disregard and lack of respect for the standards of conduct that applied to his activities." The committee itself dealt not with the substance of the charitable foundation issue but of an ancillary one of whether Gingrich had sought legal counsel before setting up his course. The tax issue was referred to the I.R.S. Gingrich's blaming his lawyer for the false material wasn't credible, and the committee said that Gingrich "should have known" that he had submitted false information to the committee. (Before plea-bargain negotiations with Gingrich, the committee had said that Gingrich "knew" the material was false.)

Even Nancy Johnson, the Ethics Committee chair (who had been a longtime fan of Gingrich's), contributed to the wreckage, undermining the counsel and the committee itself by saying on television after the committee's work was done that as regards using tax-exempt organizations for political purposes, in effect, everybody does it. ("If that's a crime, then there are a lot of groups in town that are in trouble.")

If in fact, as was widely speculated, Representative Jim McDermott, Democrat of Washington, leaked to the press an intercepted phone conversation (on a cell phone) of Gingrich and others on how to handle the committee's actions—which Cole believed violated an agreement between Gingrich and the committee—it may have been unwise (and perhaps illegal), but it was also beside the point of the Gingrich case itself. The Republicans successfully exploited much of Washington's inability to think about two things at the same time and blew the McDermott matter up into the proportions of the Gingrich matter, and threw the Democrats on the defensive.

Gingrich's willingness to plea-bargain with the committee showed that he knew that his situation was serious, and he didn't want to have a prolonged public process of deciding his fate. In return, the committee agreed to weasel on its findings in several respects. The fine of $300,000 leveled against Gingrich by the committee was a way of raising his punishment above the level of a reprimand—but stopping short of a censure, which could cost him the Speakership. As a result of the bargaining with Gingrich, the committee characterized the fine as a "cost assessment" to reimburse the committee for its prolonged investigation—which was another way of distorting the truth.

Though they kept him in the Speakership, a number of Republicans were nervous about doing so—aware that Gingrich lacks discipline, as he showed in his complaining at town meetings in his district just after the House's vote on the committee's report that it was all the fault of the "liberal media" and the Democrats.

Quietly, some House Republicans began to prepare, in case a vacancy in the Speakership arose. Perhaps something else would arise regarding Gingrich; perhaps he would continue to be an embarrassment. Among them was Majority Leader Dick Armey, whose television appearances took on a new aspect of reasonableness, and who tried to cultivate moderate House Republicans—who had preferred Gingrich because he listened to them and tried to help. (And Armey went on a diet.) Many Democrats actually hoped Gingrich would remain Speaker, continuing to be a liability. Otherwise, they surely would have made more of the fact that Gingrich was second in the line of succession for the Presidency.

Whether Gingrich paid the $300,000 fine out of his own savings or his campaign kitty developed as a touchy matter for the Republicans. Many of them felt that if he paid it with campaign funds the public would be unforgiving. Even John Boehner, heretofore one of his strongest supporters, said publicly that Gingrich should pay out of his own pocket. The major voice against Gingrich's paying the funds himself was said to be that of his wife, Marianne—who had also been against his dropping his $4.5 million book deal just before he took office as Speaker.

Gingrich was determined to stay on, but his base of support was increasingly shaky. A prominent Republican said, "Especially those who have been most supportive of Newt—Bill Paxon, John Boehner—feel that they can't give him any more, that they can't take any more hits. And there are more possible hits out there. The willingness in the Republican Conference to protect him is pretty well exhausted." (Paxon lost some credit among his colleagues for assuring them, before the Ethics Committee reported, that Gingrich's offense was no more serious than "jaywalking." But now Paxon, too, was maneuvering for Gingrich's job). About thirty-five to forty Republicans were tempted to vote against Gingrich the first time around (only nine either voted against him or voted "present"). A number of Republicans aren't eager to go through another election with Gingrich as a liability. Regicide by the Republicans remained a possibility. A Republican strategist, not inimical to Gingrich, said to me in early February, "It could happen any minute."

After the election, Mrs. Clinton became more openly active, was striving to find a new niche. Before the election, she had made a run at taking back the domestic policy portfolio, over which she had effectively had control at the beginning of the first term—but others in the White House didn't think this was a particularly good idea. Then, both the President and she tried out in public that she would take charge of implementation of the welfare bill, seeing how it was working and reporting back—which would have been a perfectly good use of her talents and access to the President. But the idea went over badly with the public, which suspected her of wanting to become, again, co-President (and people in the White House didn't think that was a great idea, either). During the transition, she was heavily involved in decisions about appointments. She has a representative in a high position on the Domestic Policy Council staff. She found roles in such things as studying the disastrous state of the

District of Columbia, and she urged her husband hard, and successfully, to take more of an interest in the matter; and the fairly new
idea of helping needy people who want to start a truly small business through "micro-investments"—that normally banks won't
bother with. She went public more, meeting, after a long hiatus,
with the press, and even going on the *Rosie O'Donnell* show. She
knew that the year held peril for her—and her husband.

Clinton's Inaugural address was better than many of the reviews
said. It wasn't a great speech—Clinton falls short of greatness in
several respects—but he is intelligent enough and tried hard to
reach for large thoughts. Yet that very night, the sight of Mrs.
Clinton pouring out bitterness (and dropping her *g*'s) in talking to
the Arkansas Inaugural ball, was disheartening. At the annual prayer
breakfast on February 6th, both Clintons whined about their treatment by political opponents and the press. They had also done so in
Australia (the President comparing himself to Richard Jewell,
wrongly accused of the Olympics bombing). And this was what they
said *publicly*. Their self-absorption is breathtaking.
    Clinton's State of the Union address was one of his better
speeches. It was more disciplined—and he seemed more assured—
than usual. The emphasis on education represented a fortuitous
coincidence between what is popular and what had been a Clinton
interest all along. He was clearly hoping that the subject would
define his Presidency. Clinton's speech was rhetorically bold but the
details were cautious. His proposals on education, like his vow to
extend health care to needy children who aren't covered (as well as
to the unemployed), faded on closer inspection, but at least Clinton
got the emphasis on education, and the idea of national educational
standards (albeit voluntary on the part of the states) out there. In an
echo of his earlier political strategy, he said that Medicare and
Medicaid and education and the environment could be protected
while balancing the budget and giving the middle class certain tax
cuts. There was little for the poor or the inner cities. And he didn't
address the long-term problems for the entitlement programs. (Also,

his budget employed some traditional gimmicks in getting to balance in 2002.) He proposed restoring funds for welfare, including for legal immigrants and food stamps, but Republicans and even liberal Democrats said they didn't want to "reopen" the bill.

Clinton's aides insist that Clinton doesn't see the "vital center" as a safe refuge but as a place where coalitions can be formed to accomplish things. But the President started so near to the center on many issues that he didn't, in the view of some advisers, leave himself much room for maneuver. Democrats on Capitol Hill began right away giving signals that they might not support him on some issues. At a briefing at the White House before the State of the Union speech, his aides were at pains to make journalists understand that, as one aide put it, "The President has seized the initiative."

By the time Clinton gave his State of the Union address, the Republicans were still sorting out how to respond to him. They remained under the dual imperatives—work with him and try to ruin him. But they knew that they daren't appear too negative, that it was in their political interest to make legislative deals with him. The bipartisan talk at the beginning of any Congress, or Presidential term, is usually blather, and was this time, too. But the Republicans were anxious not to look as negative as they did in 1995, and therefore didn't pronounce the President's budget "dead on arrival." They were positioning—stating their differences with Clinton, while at the same time planning to deal. With Gingrich distracted and unable to lead, Trent Lott took charge of setting direction. Lott wanted to deal with the President on the budget, just as he had through their mutual friend Morris in 1995 and some of 1996 (on other issues as well).

In January, Ralph Reed announced an agenda, "The Samaritan Project," that included reaching out more to minorities and people in the inner cities, and more emphasis on economic issues—the political salience of which Reed had understood for some time. He wanted to be part of the movement among some Republicans to

264 • WHATEVER IT TAKES

find non-governmental answers to poverty and urban renewal—
and attract some attention, and, he told me, "move the ball a
little more." He knew that he would get votes in Congress on his
social issues, abortion, a "religious freedom" amendment to the
Constitution. So he decided, he said, "to put more things on the
agenda." He said, "The purpose is to make it clear we are not a
Republican organization"—this was by now a sensitive matter for
Reed—"but a Christian organization"; though, he added, it was
closer to the Republican Party because of its pro-life issue. This was
also a step toward improving the Christian Coalition's image—
something Reed had already been working on—as a bunch of
Southern white bigots. (Reed openly played a big role in the election of Jim Nicholson, a conservative Coloradan, as the new
chairman of the Republican National Committee.)

David Rehr, of the beer wholesalers, encouraged by the 1996 election, which he feels did achieve realignment, will now work to
increase the congressional margins favoring beer wholesalers and
small business in general. "I always knew the 1996 election would
be the historic one, the hardest one," he said. "We'll have to keep
working at it, and it will be increasingly easier. Now we can make
the gains we didn't make in '96." Emboldened by the new situation,
Rehr and the Beer Wholesalers will try to "roll back" the tax
increase on beer enacted in 1991—the last of the specific tax
increases in that bill that hasn't been repealed or scaled back.
(Those on jewelry, furs, pleasure boats, and small aircraft, also
enacted that year, were since removed and the tax increase on cars
was reduced.) Rehr said, "We've moved off of defense. We have to
worry less about Congress raising the beer tax and can concern ourselves with trying to eliminate it."

Peter Torkildsen and Randy Tate have announced that they are
going to run for the House again.

Marc Nuttle was working with members of the House leadership—
not Gingrich, because of his distracted state—on coming up with a

new "economic model," or theme, that the country would understand. He was also getting ready to launch a new survey to determine how the public views the economy. In early February, the N.F.I.B. had a three-day retreat at the Wintergreen resort in Virginia to discuss what to do to maintain the conservative majority in Congress and how to make it grow—looking at this through the year 2004.

Tanya Metaksa survived an attempted putsch against "the moderate" N.R.A. executive vice president Wayne LaPierre by the more conservative members of its board in early February—her job might have been involved. (Grover Norquist appeared in a taped video for the board meeting praising Metaksa for being "central" to the 1994 and 1996 elections.) Now she was planning for a sure battle when the Brady law "sunsets" in 1998, and is to be replaced by the instant check the N.R.A. favors. Metaksa was certain that there would be an effort to keep the existing five-day waiting period in effect. She would continue her efforts to defund the National Center for Injury Prevention and Control, and was looking toward a congressional inquiry into why the I.R.S. was auditing the N.R.A. and other conservative groups, and on guard against any campaign finance reform proposals that might impinge on "our members' freedom of speech." And she was looking ahead to making more gains in the midterm elections in 1998. "We'll keep on going," Metaksa said.

Grover Norquist is busy building up his Americans for Tax Reform, through fundraising, and is putting together some of the ancillary institutions he works through, such as the Islamic Institute. He's focusing more than before on gubernatorial and state legislative races, because "they'll be the building block for redistricting for 2002." In the House itself, to further the realignment, Norquist says, "the focus is going to be on those votes that will highlight the differences between Republicans and Democrats, to reestablish the wedge issues for House and Senate races.

"Dick Morris correctly had Clinton step across the line—on crime and other social issues Clinton was on our side of the line. But other Democrats weren't. They didn't triangulate. They were the left angle of the triangle. We'll have votes on the Balanced Budget Amendment, school choice, taxes, and tort reform—which is about the trial lawyers. We'll make the U.N. an issue. The Democrats like the U.N. the way they like gun control—because it's mooshy. But the country hates it."

Norquist continued, "All this bipartisan stuff is nice, but we need to be tough enough to get some of their senior Democrats to retire. That could set off a run on retirements, like we had in the Senate last time. Gephardt asked the Democrats to stay on one more term, said they could retake the House—but they didn't.

"And we don't give the Democrats the money they want, and we'll take the cuts Clinton is offering. Because every time you nick the budget, somewhere a Democratic precinct worker loses his job. So for the next two years the target is to squeeze the budget and smile, squeeze and smile."

And then Norquist came to the other part of the Republican strategy: "At the same time, through the hearings, do our job of oversight and raise before the country Bill Clinton's campaign financing and the question of whether in some of the agencies—the I.R.S., the F.B.I.—the government has been illegally politicized." ("All my friends are being audited," Norquist said, naming among others the N.R.A., the Heritage Foundation, the *National Review*.)

"If that happens, coupled with the Starr investigation, the 1998 election could look like 1974 [the post-Watergate election]—a discredited and corrupt party gets repudiated at the polls. We can't count on that, but we should be prepared for it."

The money scandals surrounding Clinton's reelection campaign continued to broaden and deepen as he began his second term. The story could no longer be limited by the Clinton people to the eagerness and excesses of John Huang, at the D.N.C., in his efforts to raise funds from the Asian-American community, of which he had an expansive view. (For what it's worth, Dole and the House Republicans won most of the votes among Asian-Americans. Grover

Norquist remarked, "They got the money, we got the votes." But Dole got a lower percentage of Asian-American voters than Bush had, partly because of the White House's elaborate "outreach" program, and partly because of the Republicans' image as anti-immigration—of which Norquist had warned.) It became clear that the scale, intensity, and brazenness of the Clinton campaign's effort to raise money was without precedent (even though the Republicans raised more money).

Though Clinton had tried to pass the whole business off to the Democratic National Committee (which he called "the other campaign" and "not mine"), the *Wall Street Journal* pointed out in a groundbreaking piece in early February that the now-famous White House coffees originated not with the D.N.C., but with the Clinton-Gore campaign. Since Clinton was the draw at the coffees—and since he approved them—it doesn't much matter where they originated. (But Clinton's attempt to mislead does.) In any event, it was widely known that the D.N.C. effort was part of the White House campaign machinery, under Ickes's command. (The *Journal* also said that Huang began to raise funds while he was still at the Commerce Department, which would be illegal.) Other questions arose about what Huang—who reportedly had a security clearance after he left the Commerce Department—was actually doing while he was there, and whether he was involved in getting information about policy toward China, in which the Lippo Group, which did business there, had a great interest. Several threads of the story ran toward China.

It's against the law for fundraising to be conducted on federal property—though there were technical legal points about whether this included the private rooms of the residence, or of what constituted "fundraising," the ethical point was the same. Clinton is known to revere the White House, has steeped himself in its history, and eagerly gives guests tours—which makes his willingness to dishonor it for money all the more curious. (He was said by a close aide to regret that.)

More unsavory characters who shouldn't have been in the President's presence came to light as guests for coffee with the chief executive. So did bankers, who got an unusual opportunity to meet with their regulators, along with the President. The apparent—if they're telling the truth, which can't be known now—breakdown in security, and failure to brief the President and his top aides as to who was coming to visit him, is astonishing. It's very unusual that the President isn't carefully informed about people with whom he is about to meet. (The N.S.C. staff warned against some, but was generally overruled. That Tony Lake said that he knew little or nothing of this increased concerns about his ability to run the C.I.A., and he was forced to withdraw.) Stories of people who did get government assistance of some sort after sipping with the President began to be published. So did the proximity in time between the coffees and the donations. D.N.C. officials said of course that people weren't to be told that for a certain donation they could drink coffee with, dine with, the President—but they were.

The relationship of Webster Hubbell and the Riadys attracted more attention, especially after Bruce Lindsey, the President's confidant, admitted that he had known earlier than the White House had said of Hubbell's being retained (for at least $100,000) by the Riadys' Lippo Group after he resigned from the Justice Department in 1994. (Other Clinton friends also sent work Hubbell's way.) Clinton himself wasn't quite categorical on this subject—one has to listen to him (and his wife) carefully—when he said, in his first post-election press conference, on January 28th, "To the best of my recollection, I didn't know anything about his having that job until I read about it in the press."

Clinton surprised a lot of people by trotting out at the press conference the old passive "mistakes were made" construction for the fundraising scandals; the phrase had become something of a joke after both Ronald Reagan and George Bush had used it to brush off the Iran-Contra scandal.

As Clinton's second term got underway, the office of the independent counsel, Kenneth Starr, let it be known that he was nearing decisions on whether to prosecute the President and the First Lady. Republicans on Capitol Hill were getting ready for investigations into the campaign finance and other scandals. The President announced unilateral reforms in gathering campaign contributions but they were peripheral. The politicians dithered over taking steps to clean up the system, although the most obvious step to prevent a repetition of the most recent scandal was quite simple: shut down soft money. That would put the Presidential fundraising system back to where it was when the Watergate reforms were enacted and before the soft-money loophole effectively killed them. It would sharply reduce the sale (or price) of access packages by the congressional campaign committees. The definition of "issue advocacy" should be redrawn so that it's no longer the large loophole it was in 1996, making the election laws a sham and forcing groups into fictitious separations of one activity from another. But even if these things were done, the system by which candidates for Congress have to spend a great deal of time chasing contributions, and hand out rewards (even if it's only preferred access) to big donors, would still be in place. The most effective way of dealing with that would be to put the congressional system under the same rules as the Presidential system: strictly limited donations and public financing—and lowering the cost of buying ads. (Broadcasting, a very lucrative business, could afford to give some free air time. Even without public financing, the costs should be lowered.) It is often said that the public wouldn't accept public financing of congressional campaigns, but that assumes that the public couldn't be led. Less radical proposals are floating about, which would help, but a lot of politicians have a vested interest in the status quo. The question was whether the money scandals of 1996 might embarrass them into changing the system.

As the campaign finance scandals kept growing, the Vice President was drawn in more deeply.

Clinton's standing in the polls was high (ratings in the 60s); the Republicans continued, despite their victory, to search for how to deal with him, and to try to figure out their agenda; the struggle over realignment continued (both parties were recruiting candidates for

the House and raising money for 1998); the investigating committees on Capitol Hill were gearing up; and the independent counsel
was making decisions. The mood at the White House was one of
apprehension and also aggressiveness. The President's deliberately
active schedule of making proposals and taking trips to promote his
program had an unannounced purpose. The impetus, one aide said,
referring to the impact on the White House of the campaign finance
scandals, was "There is a sense that the only way to counter this stuff
is to keep moving ahead in the policy area, that if we stop we die."

In a conversation in his office, White House press secretary
Mike McCurry said to me in early February, "It's a huge roll of the
dice right now. We could either descend into the worst nastiness
imaginable in the next six months or have a highly productive
period. We could have both, but I don't think that's going to
happen."

AUTHOR'S NOTE

THIS BOOK IS BASED on interviews with a wide range of figures: the central characters and others quoted by name, as well as those who, because they were in sensitive staff or advisory positions, had to remain anonymous some of the time. As always, I checked facts and hypotheses with a number of people.

All quotations are from direct sources. All thoughts or views attributed to anyone came from someone with direct knowledge. As always, I had to consider why someone was telling me something and put what I was told through several filters.

ACKNOWLEDGMENTS

ANY BOOK OF JOURNALISM depends for its material on people who are willing to take the time to talk. In that respect, I was most fortunate in doing the research and reporting for this book. Some unusually interesting people were most generous with their time. In fact, one of the joys of my chosen profession comes from meeting such people and understanding how they think. Another is the discoveries one makes along the way—which also depends on people who are willing to answer questions and help one sort things out. To be a journalist is to be given a license to learn. Writing a book may be (is) arduous, but I have to confess that I also had a most interesting time—and a lot of fun—gathering the material for this book. To those who helped, grateful thanks.

There were also some wonderful individuals who helped me put this book together. First among equals is Elizabeth Terry, my assistant, who brought to the task her exceptional mind, willingness to roll with it when the crunches came, and her delightful company. My marvelous alumnae club was always willing to backstop, read proofs, cheer us on. They include Christine Myers, Kathy Glover, Melissa Price, and Amy Brennan. Leslie Sewell and Jim Jaffe were, as always, there when I needed them, and provided wise advice as well as moral support. Such support was also provided by Michael Beschloss, who always gives good advice and knows how to be a friend. John Bennet was heroic, as good a friend as he is editor, which is saying a great deal. Tom Oliphant was always at the other end of the phone when we needed a fact, a judgment, and humorous encouragement. Ana Romero helped in all sorts of ways.

I'm also grateful to Wendy Wolf at Viking for her enthusiasm for this book from the outset, to Barbara Grossman, publisher of Viking, for backing this book with verve, to Patti Kelly and Gene Taft for their smart ideas and steady efforts, and to Michael Hardart for helping to move the book along. My agent, Sterling Lord, was empathetic and wise, always understanding what I was trying to do and encouraging.

My husband, David Webster, was an integral and essential part of this project, as he is of my life.

INDEX

able. She demonstrates conclusively the devastating effect of the revelations late in the election of the Clinton team's abuse of the campaign spending laws, and she provides important insights into what campaign finance reform must look like in order to fix a broken system.

Elizabeth Drew brings to this book her renowned and widely respected grasp of day-to-day events, public and private, and the deeper themes at play. Whether she's covering the local reelection efforts of a freshman Republican in Seattle or describing the earliest faltering steps of the second Clinton administration, she draws on sources that cover the full spectrum of political colors. *Whatever It Takes* offers an unparalleled view of the struggle for political supremacy that will determine America's course in the next century.

ELIZABETH DREW is the author of nine previous books on national politics, including *On the Edge: The Clinton Presidency* and *Showdown*. She is a former Washington correspondent for *The New Yorker* and appears regularly as a television commentator. She lives in Washington, D.C.